A man out of balance with
his wife is imbalanced.

# CREATED TO

# NEED

## A HELP MEET

A MARRIAGE GUIDE FOR MEN

Created to NEED a Help Meet
Copyright © 2011 by Michael Pearl

ISBN: 978-1-61644-036-7

First printing: January 2012 - 10,000
Second printing: February 2012 - 15,000

Visit www.NoGreaterJoy.org for information on this and other products
produced by No Greater Joy Ministries.

Requests for information should be addressed to:
No Greater Joy Ministries Inc., 1000 Pearl Road, Pleasantville, TN 37033 USA.

All scripture quotations are taken from the King James Holy Bible.

Cover design: Shoshanna Easling, Lynne Hopwood
Layout: Lynne Hopwood
Cover photo: iStockphoto.com


Printed in the United States of America

**The wise man King Solomon concluded:**

"TWO ARE BETTER THAN ONE;
because they have a good reward for their
labour. For if they fall, the one will lift up
his fellow: but woe to him that is alone when
he falleth; for he hath not another to help him
up. Again, if two lie together, then they have
heat: but how can one be warm alone?"
(Ecc. 4:9-11)

"WHOSO FINDETH A WIFE
findeth a good thing, and obtaineth
favour of the LORD."
(Proverbs 18:22)

# ACKNOWLEDGEMENTS

I dedicate this book to the hundreds of thousands of ladies who read *Created to Be His Help Meet* and unilaterally decided to assume the full burden of making your marriages heavenly. You allowed your husbands to dump on you while you developed a Christ-like spirit. Many of you stood alone and forgave wrongs and carried the burden for two. You are my heroines and my inspiration. As I read the thousands of letters and heard the glowing testimonies, you made me ashamed that you stood alone while the men sucked up the benefit of an obedient help meet. Then when I asked for suggestions for the content of a book addressed to men, you wrote almost more than I could read. But all the letters did get read and they formed the basis of my developing ideas. So I acknowledge you as my coworkers in this long overdue project that I trust will lighten your load and make you the recipients of great blessing.

I would acknowledge my wife, but that would be like acknowledging my self. We are so one that when either of us does something, it is the product of both. She was, of course, indispensable. Her wisdom is extraordinary and her judgment most holy. I leaned on her wisdom heavily.

# INTRODUCTION

When I first decided to write *Created to NEED a Help Meet*, I asked my happy wife what one thing I had done correctly and should pass along to other husbands. Her answer was immediate and straight to the point: "You let me be your help meet. You pulled me alongside you in everything you did. You stretched me. Participation made me grow as a person—made my life rich and rewarding and caused me to be a better mama."

You say, "What is your qualification to teach us to be good husbands?"

I've made one of the happiest, most cheerful, thankful, joyful ladies on this earth who thinks I'm the grandest thing in all the world. That gives me the confidence to believe I have something to offer.

But my most enlightening marriage material comes from the many letters and emails I have received from husbands and wives over the past 17 years. The daily stream of correspondence reveals common patterns that either lead to ruin or that heal and grow a marriage into something heavenly. It can almost be viewed as a science: the laws of sowing and reaping are extremely reliable. A marriage grows till it soars or it deteriorates till it's damned. In your correspondence, you have shown me a thousand times that a marriage can be saved and blossom into something beautiful.

In addition, I have been a student of the words of God for the past fifty-four years, spending hours searching out every subject, and the husband and wife relationship has always been of particular interest to me. Through my experience and that of others I have found that God is the best marriage counselor on earth, and beyond it as well. After all, he who imagined and conceived of marriage, with all its complexities, will best know how to make the most of it.

The theme of this book is unique, having never been the subject of any book preceding it. Sir, even though you think you are quite autonomous and complete in yourself, you were created to need a help meet. Marriage is God's laboratory for the perfecting of the human race. It is a recapitulation of the entire human experience, distilling the conflict and triumph of the ages down to a very personal, individualized experience—a test of all that makes us human. In marriage each of us has the opportunity to grow and develop into something much higher and nobler than the self-seeking ends native to one person alone.

Marriage is both the mount of temptation—where we have the opportunity to feed our self-centered natures—and the pinnacle of a paradise restored, where we become heirs together of the grace of life and develop the nature of a savior and a priest. Marriage is heaven's boot camp, the terminal of our future destiny, the place where we grow small and inward or become large with mercy and sacrifice.

In contrast to my introduction, this book is not philosophical. It is so practical you will squirm with embarrassment and hope your wife doesn't read that line.

## The Three Kinds of Men

The two halves of this book are so different, they could have been written as two separate books. In the first half we examine all the ways in which we men need a help meet. In the second half we look at the three kinds of men, as presented in my wife's book, *Created to Be His Help Meet*. But my approach is much more masculine and in your face. You will discover that by nature you come to marriage, as well as life, with certain strengths and weaknesses. You will come to know yourself, and you will learn to temper your natural excesses and strengthen your natural weaknesses. Most of all, you will learn the part your wife plays in this maturing process. You will learn how to make her your most suitable helper.

Mr. Pearl,

A funny thing happened on my way to send you my comments about my husband for your new book! I woke up in the middle of the night and could not sleep, so I got up to take the opportunity to write all I had to say. This was my big moment!

As I sat down and began writing every complaint that came mind about my husband and men in general, the conviction of the Holy Spirit came upon me and the Lord turned the whole thing around. I began sobbing and wailing before the Lord as I was brought into repentance and He had me write 30 specific items I needed to repent to my husband for. I was transformed, literally, from a woman looking forward to unloading a truckload of scathing comments about my husband, to a sinner broken and contrite before my God.

This was humbling, painful, cleansing, and refreshing at the same time! I wrote the whole letter of repentance to my husband, getting up a new creature in Christ and going back to bed. I gave my husband the letter the next morning and we have never been the same since.

It was the start of a brand new marriage with a brand new life! I am now becoming the help meet I was created to be and my husband is changing too! After repenting and having to take such a long, hard look at my own sin, I no longer look at my husband the way I used to. I see him as another child of God who is "working out his own salvation with fear and trembling," rather than the lazy bum who won't get off the couch and do anything (he's not like that, but that's how I viewed him!)

Just wanted you to know how the Lord used your plans for a new book to change our lives!

A Happy Wife

# CONTENTS

**Whoso findeth a wife
findeth a good thing,
and obtaineth favour
of the LORD.**
Proverbs 18:22

Chapter 1

# ANTICIPATION

## My First Love

It was a mile and a half walk down a hot tar and gravel road to the
country church where I would attend Vacation Bible School. I was
nine years old, and I discovered love that day. I don't remember her
name. I can't even remember what she looked like, but I do remember
her pink dress and the little red hearts on her starched petticoats as she
so gracefully walked on the opposite side of the road, not speaking or
taking notice of my presence. It had taken me about a half mile to catch
up to her, and then I had slowed to her pace, maintaining my position on
the other side of the road as we walked the last mile. I never spoke. She
never looked at me, but I studied her profile and her dainty little walk.
It was the most amazing and wonderful thing I had ever seen. I was
in love. I wanted one. But it was all too scary to this skinny, bug-eyed
boy. The thought of even speaking to this splendid apparition made me
tremble with a feeling of helplessness.

Later that same summer, my mother took me along to visit a family
that lived about a quarter mile down the road. I remember entering the
strange house and seeing Sharon. Her name I can remember. She had the
most dazzling red curls hanging all the way down her back, and her nose
and cheeks were covered with beautiful freckles. She too was nine years
old, and I fell in love again. She shyly stood in the background watching
the exchange between the ladies, and I fumbled uncomfortably, feeling
the intimacy of just being in the same house with this beautiful creature.
I remember Sharon's name because we would grow up in the same
community and ride the old yellow bus to school.

In the coming years many of those beautiful and intriguing creatures
caught my eye and stole my heart. Some I spoke to. Most I just looked
upon from across the room. I never declared my affection to any, for
such a commitment seemed too deep and out of control for me to
manage. I knew it was an adult thing to do, something I must defer until
I was old enough.

## Puberty

But then I went through puberty. That was like entering a cool tunnel and coming out of the other end in the middle of a fire. I gave my life to Jesus Christ at about the same time, and I had been well brought up and taught the Word of God, so I was quite clear on moral boundaries. But the fire burned and the only thing I wanted more than God was to have one of those lovelies they called the opposite sex. After a while I began to wonder if maybe the devil—rather than God—hadn't created sex. SEX with the big X in it, like "Danger. Don't touch." It seemed like such a consuming indulgence.

I started fasting and praying, studying my Bible, and walking down the road with my blinders on. I found all TV programs to be designed to create lust. Every billboard with a woman on it was a doorway to hell. The Sears and Roebuck catalogue was pornography. Many of the women at church were seductive whores. Cleavage was an attempt to damn me. Tight dresses were designed to make me wet my pants. It was enough to make a monk or a whoremonger out of a fourteen-year-old. The world was on fire and I was trying to keep from burning.

## Middle Teens

I was a normal youth, with one exception: I resisted my urges and made a commitment to walk in holiness. Many of my friends and peers succumbed to their bodily passions and I observed the result of their folly. I studied the Bible and asked God to deliver me from my lust. I can't tell you I stopped lusting while in my middle teens, but it was never voluntary. Lust was my enemy.

In my diligence to walk in holiness, I wrestled with my worldview. Why were we created thus? What is our purpose? Is there an avenue to victory? The Word of God enlightened me and I came to understand that God had a great plan for the human race and that love, sex, and marriage were at the center of it. By the time I got to be sixteen I had learned to manage my sexual impulses and maintain equilibrium from one hour to the next. It never ceased to be a battle, but I began to see that I was like the three Hebrew children in the fiery furnace: there was fire all around, trying to consume me, but I could walk in it without getting burnt. I saw the challenge as part of the training and the victory as preparation for a glorious tomorrow. By the time I got into my late teens I knew I could, and always would, have the victory over my flesh. I awoke every morning to a battle, and sometimes I got slapped around by my own flesh, but the devil lost the war. Thanks to the sanctifying power of the Holy Spirit, when I married at 25 I was still a virgin and had never viewed pornography.

For about seventeen years, since I first viewed the delightful girl in the pink dress, I had anticipated the day when I would finally get one of those beautiful, female creatures for myself. I knew that on that day my life would begin. I had no idea what to expect, but I was ready for the experience, or so I thought.

## Honeymoon

My immediate goal in marriage was to make up for all those sexually frustrated years—the sooner the better. A friend of mine that married two years before I did had bragged that he was able to "know" his bride five times on their wedding night. He was a puny fellow, so I had no doubt I would beat his brag, but the truth is, three times was all I could muster, and just barely. I quickly realized a single man's concept of marriage was a bit different from the real thing. After all, it was midnight before we got to our room, and we were up at six, headed to the Gulf Coast, where we would honeymoon for a few days in a cottage on the beach.

It was a long day's drive. We arrived at the cottage well after dark. We had brought all the gear for fishing and crabbing, as well as the groceries for her to prepare our meals. That way we could save a lot of money and be able to stay longer in the cabin. We dug all the gear out of the station wagon and placed it in the cabin. Deb fixed us a big supper, after which I tried to break my record. One time and I was asleep. I woke in the middle of the night and remembered that crabs sometimes run along the beach, so I woke Deb and excitedly said, "Let's go crabbing."

My new Mrs. complained about me not giving her enough time to find her tennis shoes. They were still packed somewhere and I was raring to go. Anyway, I had seen her going barefoot many times. As we scurried along the beach she complained about not having a flashlight. I was using it up ahead to scout the way and to chase crabs. I heard her say something about shells hurting her feet. For the next hour or two I ran along the seashore and she dragged along behind, carrying my crab sack. I put out some of those little round traps with bait in them and we eventually got about six or eight of the little pinching critters—not enough for a meal.

That was my first time to ever go crabbing and I was having a ball. What more could a fellow ask for? A cottage on the beach, a hot bride, plenty of crabs . . . this was living! We made it back to the cottage, where we grabbed a couple hours of sleep before I woke hungry and had to make love to a woman half asleep. She was willing but not very active.

Afterward she got up and fixed us a fine breakfast. Great cook. Her mother taught her well. She wanted to go back to sleep but I talked her into going back out for more crabs. By mid-afternoon we had a sack full of crabs and headed back to the cottage. Wow, was I tired. I told her I would just take a little nap while she prepared supper. I don't know how long I slept, but I awoke to her screeching and jumping about, and crabs crawling all over the cabin. The silly girl had left the sack open when she was trying to get the first crab in the huge boiling kettle. I sat up in bed and offered some constructive advice and she had a personality change right there in front of me, and us not yet married 48 hours. Who could have imagined a female could carry on in such a crazy manner? I tried to calm her down, but she just stomped off leaving the french fries turning black in the hot smoking oil and the crabs crawling. I yelled at her retreating form, "I don't need to hunt crabs; I married one!" Somehow that one remark has hung around our marriage like a ticked-off ghost. It seemed appropriate at the time.

To her credit, she did come back and finish cooking. After we ate I was ready for some more sex, but she just wanted to sleep. I had read in a marriage book how women always have excuses like being sleepy, having a headache, etc. I felt a great sense of satisfaction when I was so completely able to change her mind; it wasn't that difficult. She is wired right. It made me sleepy, so I dozed off again. I was just dropping off when I heard the crash. It came from the bathroom. She looked dead lying there all twisted up in a weird position, half in and half out of the shower. The curtain and rod lay flung out on the floor around her and water was spraying everywhere. It was one scary moment—my new bride dead on our honeymoon. I quickly turned off the water and bent to cradle her in my arms. I gently shook her while examining her injured forehead, which was quickly swelling and turning blue. "What's wrong, honey? Are you sick?"

After she opened her eyes it took her a minute to focus and then her expression changed. It was a mixture of pity and anger, although her voice was like a deep sigh as she whispered, "You really don't know, do you?" Man, it sounded like she was accusing me or something! Since she was hurt I let her have her say and, boy, she laid it on.

> **"You really don't know, do you?" Man, it sounded like she was accusing me or something!**

She sat up, pulling herself away from me, turning where she could look me square in the face. The gist of what she said was something along these lines: "In the last 48 hours I haven't slept more than two hours undisturbed. My feet have 20 or more tiny holes in them because you wouldn't let me take an extra five minutes to unpack my tennis shoes. My shoulder is sore from trying to carry 30 pounds of crabs for hours. [They didn't weigh that much.] My hand is burned from trying to stuff a fighting crab into a kettle of boiling water, which seems very much like torturing the poor thing, AND, all the while you lay in a state of repose. Due to lack of sleep and sun, my eyes feel like they are full of sand. I have had little to eat. I am a female, for crying out loud. I just want to sleep without you pawing on me. Besides, I have body parts I didn't even know existed until now and they are killing me . . . so what's wrong with me??? I'm the weaker vessel, remember? It's in the Bible, chapter 1 verse 1 . . . or somewhere."

Strange creatures, these females. My brother never acted like that when we traveled together holding evangelistic services. "Well, she will get adjusted," I thought. I won't even tell you about the next day, when we went deep-sea fishing and she got seasick. This was just three days into the marriage. I would have to chase her down that hot gravel road a long way before it dawned on me that I was the one that needed to make most of the adjustments.

## Grudging Admission

Okay, I am the first one to admit I did not start out the perfect husband (actually the second one to admit it), and haven't gotten there yet, but

I have experienced the reality that two imperfect spouses can have a perfect marriage. She even agrees. She really does; she says so publicly.

For ten years now my wife has been telling me I should pass on some of this hard-earned wisdom to you. But I keep telling her that after all these years I still don't understand women. I have come to know one woman, inside and out, all the way, but I would hate to start over again married to your wife. It took me about two years to get mine conditioned to tolerate my selfishness, and another ten years before I understood her needs. I think we have arrived at a perfect marriage. It seems perfect to me. I cannot imagine anything better. We are not only lovers; we are best buddies and trusted friends.

For many years now Deb and I have taught and counseled hundreds of men and women on how to make their marriage grow into something precious. We have seen beautiful fruit in the lives of so many. So with Deb looking over my shoulder and offering suggestions, I sit down before my keyboard and commit to paper some of the most important things we have come to know about how to have a heavenly marriage.

Now, in my old age, I know I have experienced heaven's best. Her old, graying, straight hair stirs me far more than did the long red curls on the freckle-faced girl. My heart beats faster and the love is far deeper than anything I imagined when running down that hot tar road to catch up to the pink-dress pretty with the red-hearts petticoat. I still experience the wonder and mystery of a love that transcends all other relationships and passions. Together we came to a quiet place, a noisy place, a beautiful place, and there we merge into one, experiencing what God intended when he made the first bride and brought her to the first groom, saying, "And the two shall be one flesh. Be fruitful and multiply." We can't bear fruit anymore, but we still practice, and with 19 grandkids and counting we are still multiplying.

This book is written to help you create your own perfect marriage, something every person should experience this side of heaven.

Chapter 2

# CREATED TO NEED A HELP MEET

## I Needed Her

The reason I chose Deb to be my bride was because I had developed a need for her. Not sexual at first. I had possessed a sexual need for thirteen years and knew many girls I felt could satisfy that hunger.

Before I met Deb she was already involved in winning guys to faith in Christ. In time she became one of about 40 men and women that worked together in a ministry of sharing the gospel with Marines and Navy men and women. Over a four-year period I found myself increasingly relying upon her as a friend in the ministry. We became buddies. I liked her. She made me laugh. She challenged me. She was good looking, but I knew other girls that were strikingly beautiful. I chose her because my life evolved to where I needed her. Not just her body, but *her*—her spirit, her mind, her courage, her wisdom. We were not romantically involved during those years. There was just this basic need that she alone came to meet, and I realized that if I could have her all to myself I would be fulfilled as a person. I didn't know it at the time, but I was created to need a help meet, and everything about her seemed to meet my need. She made me whole.

**Adam needed sex, but that is a small need compared to the need to have a soul mate.**

## Adam and His Helper

Just as I did, the first man Adam discovered his need for a woman. God created Adam alone, without Eve or any other human creature, and then gave him the job of naming all the animals. Observing the animals relating to one another in pairs and groups, Adam searched for his counterpart but found none. The author of Genesis observes, " . . . but for Adam there was not found an help meet for him." Genesis 2:20 "Not found" indicates he looked for his helper but found none among the animals. It was in Adam's nature to need his yet uncreated counterpart.

God said, "It is not good that the man should be alone . . . " because Adam had just discovered a fundamental fact of his nature—he was, in fact, created to need someone. So the Creator said, "I will make him an help meet for him." Genesis 2:18

Adam needed sex, but that is a small need compared to the need to have a soul mate. Sex is less than 90 minutes out of a week. That leaves 9,990 minutes for companionship. Less than 1% of our time involves sex. Good sex is great, but marriage is built on much more.

## What Is a Help Meet?

It is not *helpmeet*, as in one word; it is two words, a verb (help) used as a noun and a modifier (meet). When *helper* is modified with the word *meet*, it speaks of a particular kind of helper—one that is designed to fit the needs of the one being helped—a suitable helper. As two pieces of a puzzle *meet* in exact profile, so man and woman meet the natures of the other.

We must do a brief Bible study on the word *meet* so you will more readily understand its Biblical usage. Read these few examples and note the context. We examine these passages only for the purpose of defining the word *meet*.

> **Exodus 8:25-26** And Pharaoh called for Moses and for Aaron, and said, Go ye, sacrifice to your God in the land. And Moses said, It is not **meet** so to do . . .
>
> > To sacrifice as Pharaoh suggested was not proper or suitable to the purpose.

> **Deuteronomy 3:18** And I commanded you at that time, saying, The LORD your God hath given you this land to possess it: ye shall pass over armed before your brethren the children of Israel, all that are **meet** for the war.
>
> > He speaks of those who were prepared or suited to war—trained soldiers able to accomplish their assignments.

> **Matthew 3:8** Bring forth therefore fruits **meet** for repentance . . .
>
> > Jesus said true repentance comes with corresponding works.

**Matthew 15:26** But he answered and said, It is not **meet** to take the children's bread, and to cast it to dogs.

Not proper or fitting.

**Luke 15:32** It was **meet** that we should make merry, and be glad: for this thy brother was dead, and is alive again; and was lost, and is found.

Making merry was appropriate for the circumstance.

**Colossians 1:12** Giving thanks unto the Father, which hath made us **meet** to be partakers of the inheritance of the saints in light . . .

The work of redemption renders us suitable to inherit heaven.

**2 Timothy 2:21** If a man therefore purge himself from these, he shall be a vessel unto honour, sanctified, and **meet** for the master's use, and prepared unto every good work.

A sanctified believer is suitable to be used by the master since he is prepared to that end.

**2 Peter 1:13** Yea, I think it **meet**, as long as I am in this tabernacle, to stir you up by putting you in remembrance . . .

It was appropriate to do so.

Having gained an understanding of the word *meet*, consider the passage again.

**Genesis 2:18** And the LORD God said, It is not good that the man should be alone; I will make him an **help meet** for him.

Adam was missing something, so God prepared a helper that would **meet** his needs. A right hand glove is made to *meet* a right hand. It is not *meet* for a left hand. Eve was a perfect right hand fit for the right man Adam. She was created to be his right hand wo–man.

Read the passage pausing after the word *help*, and then read the last three words together: *meet for him*. "I will make him an *help—meet for him*." She was a helper meet for him. Got it? That's easy, and we didn't even need the Greek or Hebrew!

## Man Is Male and Female

Notice how God speaks of himself in the plural: "And God said, Let **us** make man in **our** image, after **our** likeness . . . " Genesis 1:26 The one God exists in a plural fellowship, so mankind created in that image must reflect that plurality.

> **God would create persons in his own image, but one person was not adequate to portray his image.**

The text says, " . . . in the image of God created he him; **male and female** created he them . . . and called their name Adam." Genesis 1:27; 5:2

God would create persons in his own image, but one person was not adequate to portray his image. He divided his attributes, putting half in the man and half in the woman. The text is clear: it is the man and the woman together that reflect the image of God. The Apostle Paul observes, "Nevertheless neither is the man without the woman, neither the woman without the man, in the Lord. For as the woman *is* of the man, even so *is* the man also by the woman; but all things of God." 1 Corinthians 11:11-12

The subject God would paint was too panoramic for one canvas, so he painted half of the picture on one canvas and the rest of it on the other, intending to display them side by side ("they two shall be one").

The subject on which God would write was too expansive to put into one book so he made it a two-volume set ("and called their name Adam").

This is a point you must fully appreciate, for it is the underlying principle for the entire book. So let me approach it from a more literal perspective. "Male and female created he them; and blessed them, and called **their name Adam**, in the day when they were created." Genesis 5:1-2 Adam was "male and female." The human race is split into two parts, one part male and one female. Together they are *Adam*— God's creation.

Looking at it another way, God created a single man with no capacity to reproduce, for he had no womb. So the human race was completed with the addition of the womb-man (wo-man).

## God's Program

It is as if God created "MAN Version 1.0" and then released him into the garden for beta testing. MAN worked beautifully but was not created as a stand-alone program: he seemed to lack a certain something that made his function complete. God then created a patch, calling it WO-MAN, and released it to support the original program. When downloaded together you have heavenly software capable of communicating with God, becoming "heirs together of the grace of life." MAN will function alone without the upgrade, but don't expect him to integrate well into society. He is a bit (pun intended) imbalanced and unpredictable. I know that's corny but my wife thinks it's cute.

## 1+1=1

Adam the man was created completely in the image of God and in God's likeness. Genesis 1:26 His nature is after God's nature (mind, will, and emotions) and his body is fashioned in God's likeness (to see, hear, touch, taste, smell—in short, to interact with the universe in physical awareness). But just as the Heavenly Father is supported by the Son, and the Son is supported by the Holy Spirit, and the three equal one God, 1 John 5:7 so Adam is designed in God's image to be supported and completed by another—woman. When man and woman and God are joined together, God's image is complete in a trinity of one.

God's goal is always to make ONE composed of cooperative and interdependent parts. John 17:11, 21-23; Galatians 3:28; Ephesians 1:10, 2:13-18, 4:3-6; Romans 12:4-5; 1 Corinthians 10:17; 12:11-20 In holy matrimony man—male and female—reach the highest expression of the divine image. Therefore "Whoso findeth a wife findeth a good thing, and obtaineth favour of the LORD." Proverbs 18:22 You, Sir, were not created to stand alone. You are insufficient to the task. You were made to be one of two parts functioning as a whole.

## Two Are Better Than One

The job God designed for humanity was too demanding and complex to be met by one soul and body, so he created a complementary pair, tailoring each to specific tasks, equipping each to possess the skills and temperament necessary to perform their respective duties for the good of both and the benefit of the family.

**Dedicate your life to elevating your woman to a place of maturity and fulfillment and you will save your own life and experience heaven's best.**

Man is not to live unto himself. Romans 14:7 He is designed to be a social creature, to care, to assist, to nurture, to protect, to love to the point of sacrifice. In that flowing-out process man expands to be something bigger than his original created state. To build for self is selfishness; to build for another is humanity beyond itself.

You, Sir, were created to be part of a union of two. Only in embracing your nature as a member of a duo will you discover your purpose in life. Utilizing your other half for selfish purposes is not what God intended. Your wife is not there just to scratch your itch. That is not the path to fulfillment. This is a spiritual, intellectual, and emotional journey of two souls becoming one. Neglect that fact of nature and you will die an old, loveless, lonely loser. Dedicate your life to elevating your woman to a place of maturity and fulfillment and you will save your own life and experience heaven's best.

## You Need One

If you are a man alone, you have a need. Like me before I married, you are not complete. You will always be looking, wanting, hoping until you become one with your helper. Likewise, if you are married but do not function as one with your wife, you are still alone. The aloneness is worse than it was when you were single and still had great expectation of fulfillment, for your empty relationship now mocks you like a thirsty man who spent his last dollar to buy a well only to discover that the water is too bitter to drink.

Remember, God himself observed Adam and said, "It is not good that the man should be alone." It is not good for a man to try to make it through life without one of those female helpers designed to meet men's needs. Man was created so that his soul needs the companionship of a woman. Many wives don't know how to supply their husband's needs, and many husbands won't let their wives perform their essential function as helper. Or maybe at one time your wife was a good help meet, but something caused her to change toward you. Once again she will become that wonderful helper when your life and your speech demonstrate that you need her.

Chapter 3

# MARRIAGE MADE ON EARTH

## I Married the Wrong Woman!

Mr. Pearl,

I was not a Christian when I got married. My wife and I were drunk at the time and I think she married me because I had enough money to keep her supplied in drugs. After five years of miserable marriage we both became Christians and we now have three children. We have attended counseling and read several books but we are still on the verge of divorce. I know I did not get God's choice. How could I? Satan was controlling my life. The fact is I just do not love her. I thought I did once, but if you only knew her, you wouldn't like her either. By staying together we are just hurting each other and the children. I have told her I do not want to have any more children because it would be crime to bring them into this relationship. Is it too late for me? Is the woman I should have married still out there waiting for me or did she marry the wrong man also? How do I get out of this mess?

Hurting

I have heard it many times. It is the number one cop-out of husbands divorcing their wives to make another try at finding a better match. Let me be clear. There is only one time in Scripture that God created one particular woman for one particular man and that was Eve, and she was essentially cloned from one of his ribs. God does not micromanage our lives, making us fulfill predetermined destinies. There is not a parallel world somewhere, an ideal one that is God's will for us, and then this present one where we must somehow discover and do all that is foreordained. Like it or not, "time and chance happeneth to them all." Ecclesiastes 9:11 The concept that God created a single match for each person is romantic, superstitious, wishful thinking. Marriages are "made in heaven" when God recognizes the earthly union of an opposite sex couple becoming one flesh.

However, miracles are a suspension of natural laws, and it is not beyond the scope to suppose that from time to time God has taken special note of one of his servants and cultivated a particular mate for him, and then supernaturally led them to intersecting paths so as to establish a foreordained union. I do not doubt it to be so in exceptional cases. Just as God appointed John the Baptist, even before his conception, and filled him with the Holy Ghost from his mother's womb to make of him a vessel to announce the coming Christ, so God has prepared and led some couples to form a marriage union, but most of us are not special and have no preordained calling to serve God in a unique and historical manner. Certainly he will lead us and guide us to make wise choices in all things, including choosing a wife, but most of us are not foreordained from eternity to marry one particular person.

Furthermore, when God does perform that special marriage miracle, preparing two people for each other, that in no way means they are going to jump right into a perfect marriage. God could bring two people together because he knows the wife needs sanctifying in the worst sort of way, so God prepares a man for her that has sufficient patience and grace to sanctify his wife. When Jesus chose his prophets or apostles, he didn't choose perfect men. When God chose David to be king, he chose a flawed man who would make some poor decisions resulting in the death of many in Israel. A truly perfect marriage can only occur when two perfect people come together or when two imperfect people spend many years integrating their souls into one.

What is so special about you, or what great work have you accomplished that God should provide you with a perfect woman? Would she still be perfect after having to endure you day after day? Maybe she was a wonderful woman when you married her, but she was just not mature enough to tolerate your inconsistencies and insensitivity. Have you ever seen a man buy a new tool, abuse it until it malfunctions, and then blame the manufacturer and try to trade it in for a new one?

## Don't Skip This Paragraph

As a point of clarification, God designed the nature of women to be help meets, not a particular help meet to a particular man; in other words, the nature of the woman is that of a helper suited to the needs of the generic man. Every woman is by nature equipped to be a help meet to any man. No matter the circumstances that brought you together as man and wife, she is equipped in every way to be your helper. You must discover the path to maturity for the both of you. That, my friend, is God's will for you.

## What's Wrong With My Helper?

Few men actually "marry the right lady" and live happily ever after. Two sinners decide to sign a contract that binds them in a partnership for the rest of their lives. They will live in the same house, share everything, and be in each other's faces for better or for worse until death separates them, and they are not allowed to kill each other. Such an arrangement seems doomed from the start. It sounds more like a recipe for psychosis and bipolar disorder.

**The hardest thing you will ever do in your walk with Christ is to bring your marriage into the blessed state of holy and delightful matrimony.**

You married a sinner. She may have been a dedicated Christian, but she was not even half sanctified. You assumed the responsibility for somebody's daughter. I can hear her father driving home from the wedding saying, "Well, she's his problem now." You might have thought you were getting a brand new car that was guaranteed to never need repair, but the one you bought was actually in recall. She came off the Eve assembly line—Chinese made. And, considering that you are not a trained mechanic, but rather a self-absorbed, fleshly, fallen creature, making this thing work is going to demand more than you supposed.

When you got married you signed on to the most colossal undertaking imaginable. The hardest thing you will ever do in your walk with Christ is to bring your marriage into the blessed state of holy and delightful matrimony. It can be done. I am a witness to many successes, but none took place automatically. It takes heart effort. This book will help you succeed.

## Of Conflict and Triumph

If a man could marry and immediately move with his bride into the Garden of Eden, a perfect place devoid of the curse, without death or disease, their marriage would be no easier than it is now, for all marital problems are rooted in the self-seeking of two people. In fact, I do believe that

> **We are placed on this earth to grow beyond our origins. There are some things God wants that he cannot create out of nothingness, like love, mercy, patience, grace, sacrifice, honor, and glory.**

God intended marriage to be a mini cosmos of human development. It is the perfect context for the sanctification of a fallen race. It replicates the world at large, having all the elements of temptation and trial. It is a personal character building package designed to try, prove, and perfect the content of our souls. If a man succeeds in marriage he has succeeded in life. That is why God designed marriage to be "until death do us part," for to bail out of a troubled marriage is to bail out of your sanctification program.

## Why?

We are placed on this earth to grow beyond our origins. There are some things God wants that he cannot create out of nothingness, like love, mercy, patience, grace, sacrifice, honor, and glory. Those things are only achieved in an environment where character is tested, a battlefield of good and evil choices, selfishness or service, where the end is a product of free will, and choices have eternal consequences. Marriage is the boot camp of life where men and women discover their strengths and weaknesses, and have opportunity to adjust their characters. If a man cannot succeed in marriage, he is not qualified to hold any position of authority in the church. "For if a man know not how to rule his own house, how shall he take care of the church of God?" 1 Timothy 3:5

Marriage is the second big challenge of life. Maintaining your virtue was the first. Marriage is like a three-legged sack race. You cannot win by leaving your partner and crossing the finish line alone. When she falls you must stop and recover your partner before you can proceed. You only win if you learn to cooperate and work together, running in rhythm, feeling your partner's every step and holding her more tightly when she is prone to stumble. Your strength becomes her strength and both of you become a crutch to lean on as you keep your eyes on the prize and the glory set before you. There are many winners. All you must do is cross the finish line together still smiling and on your feet with your leg in the same sack. You can't win by getting in the sack with someone else.

Like dancing, the male must take the lead, but he is likewise responsible to keep his partner in step with him. A dancer who blames his partner will never gain the favor of those watching. And a dance team or three-legged sack racers are never better than the weakest member, so it falls to the stronger to encourage the weaker. "Likewise, ye husbands, dwell with them according to knowledge, giving honour unto the wife, as unto the **weaker vessel,** and as being heirs together of the grace of life; that your prayers be not hindered." 1 Peter 3:7

Yes, marriages are made on earth, one act of kindness and goodwill at a time. Like expensive wine it takes years to mellow a marriage and it is worth every day of it, more so as the years pile up. The direction you are headed now is the place you will be when you are 66 years old, as I am now. If you are headed the wrong way, turn it around now or get used to sitting in the middle of the playground alone with an empty sack and no dance partner or aged wine.

**Yes, marriages are made on earth, one act of kindness and goodwill at a time.**

**Again, if two lie together,
then they have heat: but how
can one be warm alone?**
Ecclesiastes 4:11

Chapter 4

# HOW DO I NEED THEE?
# LET ME COUNT THE WAYS

A man needs his woman with his entire being—body, soul, and spirit. Every man knows his body needs his wife, but many do not know that their souls and spirits also have a deep need that only she can meet. Many men know by her complaints that they are not meeting their wife's needs. What they do not know is that the need they are most neglecting is the wife's need to be needed. Your wife needs you to need her in body, soul, and spirit, and she will never be content until you allow her to meet your needs. This is not something she can turn off. God created her with a female nature that finds fulfillment in being your suitable helper. Likewise, you will never truly cherish her until you welcome her to minister to your soul and spirit.

Men who complain of their wife's lack of sexual response are ignorant of the realities that women who are not allowed to meet the needs of their husband's soul feel used when they are called upon to meet the needs of his body. It is not that women don't like sex; they just want the sex to be an expression of something deeper than animal hunger. A cherished woman is a sexy woman.

## Companionship

I need my wife's companionship. Everybody needs a friend, someone to share experiences, to ride along in the truck, maybe in conversation, maybe in silence, but just being there to fill up the empty spot inside and out. I have had many friends with whom I shared experiences. There have been fishing and hunting buddies, guys who like to work on cars and tractors, or another woodworker who loves table saws, shapers, and planers like I do. Other friends like to discuss the Bible, and some enjoy a good laugh, but there is only one person in the world of whom I can say,

"This is my very best friend," and that person is my wife. I would rather spend time with her than anyone I know. I never tire of her presence.

There are some places I go where my wife would rather I take someone else. She doesn't want to get up at four in the morning and head to the lake to fish in the hot sun all day. But she does like to go for a short fishing trip and a picnic once or twice a year.

It is all about how you make her feel. If she is jealous of your friends, it is an indication that you are not allowing her to be your number one companion. When a wife knows that you enjoy her companionship, she is much more willing to allow you to go do those man things without her. But if she ever gets the feeling that you are choosing other friends because you like them better, then be certain you are failing to meet a need in her, and you are failing to allow one of your own needs to be met. Another man cannot truly meet your companionship needs. If you think he can, it demonstrates that you are a man only partially fulfilled.

## I Need Her Fellowship

Aren't companionship and fellowship the same thing? Not at all. I have fellowship with people who are not my companions. I don't spend time with them, but when we do occasionally meet we have good fellowship. Likewise, I have had men as companions with whom I had no fellowship. We shared a common experience, hunting or working, but I did not touch their souls nor they mine. There was no communion of spirit between us. I knew nothing of them, and may not have cared to.

The word *fellowship* implies communing and communicating. It involves a transparent sharing of one's spirit. "For what man knoweth the things of a man, save the spirit of man which is in him?" 1 Corinthians 2:11 I spoke of needing our wives body, soul, and spirit. It is in the human spirit that fellowship takes place. Fellowship occurs as we walk in the light of honesty and truth. There is no fellowship walking in darkness. "But if we walk in the light, as he is in the light, we have fellowship one with another . . . " 1 John 1:7 Unless both parties are walking in the light of truth they will not care to be open and transparent with one another. A man with secret sins cannot fellowship with his wife. Likewise, if a husband or wife is critical they will not be open in fellowship. True fellowship draws strength and encouragement from the one with whom we commune. There is acceptance and lack of criticism in fellowship. It refreshes the spirit and encourages the soul.

A man who shuts himself off from communing with his wife is hiding his soul, either because she hurts him when he opens up or because he is concealing the darkness inside his soul, for "men loved darkness rather than light, because their deeds were evil." John 3:19

**We need the fellowship of our wife because it has a sanctifying effect.**

" . . . neither cometh to the light, lest his deeds should be reproved." John 3:20 A guilty man's shame is compounded in the presence of light. "But all things that are reproved are made manifest by the light: for whatsoever doth make manifest is light." Ephesians 5:13 The light of fellowship manifests the state of our heart.

We need the fellowship of our wife because it has a sanctifying effect. She becomes a constant mirror of our soul. Every time we look upon her with openness we are forced to come into the light "that our deeds may be made manifest." John 3:21 Fellowship with our wife guarantees that we will never be able to walk in darkness without it being known. A man who learns to walk in darkness will always have the curtain drawn on his soul and will be as shallow as a shadow on a sunless day. His wife will never feel she has his heart. She will sense his distance. It is a place of safety for us guys to have a wife with whom we fellowship.

You need her fellowship, but she needs yours just as much. A man who does not have the fellowship of his wife will experience a great lack, but a woman who does not have the fellowship of her husband may become emotionally unstable. Many women base their self-worth on the companionship and fellowship of their husbands. Your wife was created to give herself in fellowship just as you were created to receive it. Let her become your source of fellowship.

## I Need Her Comfort

We tough guys don't like to admit that we need comforting. And I can admit it only as a matter of principle. Now understand, if tomorrow my wife says, "Do you need some comfort?" I will say, "Who, me? Why should I need comfort?" A wife can soothe the troubled soul of a man like good news. Her touch, quiet smile, reassuring words, and positive outlook can give rest to the weary. A man without the fellowship of his wife will have no place to dump his burdens. There would be more war and personal duels if we didn't have our women to comfort us.

I realize that many of my readers are thinking, "Yeah, my wife just makes me angry. She doesn't comfort me at all." That is my point. You have failed to bring your wife to the place where she can provide that comfort your spirit needs. You would see a tremendous change in her if you could communicate that you desire her fellowship. Where there is distrust and hurt, one act or word on your part is not going to purge her of so many negative feelings, but many acts of patience and kindness will eventually open her soul to you. It is your responsibility to sanctify and cleanse your wife with your words. Ephesians 5:26

A woman by nature needs to be the source of comfort to her children and her husband. If she is denied this role she will be significantly unfulfilled as a woman. She is comforted in comforting. Let her be the woman God created her to be.

## I Need Her as a Confidant

There are private things all of us need to discuss from time to time. I know that when I am confused or uncertain, I need to air my thoughts in the presence of someone who will not jump to a conclusion for me and will not immediately judge the right or wrong of my preliminary conclusions. A wife that is a good listener is invaluable because she is so handy, always there when thoughts run through our head. Most of what we say or propose never goes beyond words. Plans and ideas die with the speaking of them. To vocalize an idea is to build an imaginary model of it. Sometimes it doesn't look as good spoken as it did in the imagination.

Brainstorming is a corporate technique for coming up with new ideas. It also works between a husband and wife. Everyone throws out wild ideas, the first things that come into their heads. Ideas fall like rain, most of them running off like unwanted water, but occasionally an idea sparks the interest of the brainstormers and it is put on the table for further examination. All creative people need a confidant, someone who will not laugh or ridicule or run to the press or the neighbors. Wives are hungry to share their husband's personal thoughts about work, worship, goals for the future, raising kids, and all manner of wandering thoughts.

If your wife has proven to be an untrustworthy confidant, it indicates that she is hurt and is crying out for respect and recognition. If she is quick to ridicule or judge or makes you feel foolish, it is because she is in an attack mode, retaliating for previous hurts and her belief that you do not have goodwill toward her. If you have not depended on her as your help meet, and she has futilely knocked on your door a thousand times, saying, "Here I am; let me help," and you have turned her away, it indicates that she is deeply unfulfilled and feels that the hurt you have caused her is intentional. So she hurts back. It is time to absorb the blows and embrace her when she is exhausted. Begin confiding in her "here a little and there a little" and she will mellow out like a hound dog by the fireplace.

## I Need Her Intimacy

Even the toughest, most independent man needs intimacy. I know, for I have never met a man more independent and self-sufficient in deportment than I. We were created to love and be loved and to care deeply. We began life cradled in Mother's belly and then spent our first year cradled in her arms. Several more years passed with us continually fleeing back to the lap of Mother and Father and anybody else that would give us a hug and a word of approval.

I can still remember when I was a child taking an afternoon nap with my mother. We lived in a one-room house and had no air conditioner or fan. The bed sat next to the window and my mother would lie down beside me and tickle my ear or twirl my hair. It never failed to put me to sleep. For a long time I thought she was sleeping as well, but I eventually learned that she got up and went back to work while I slept, happy and secure. Men do not grow out of the need for intimacy.

Mister, you need something more than sex, and your wife needs you to seek intimacy that is not initially sexual in nature. Many men are irritable because they do not experience enough intimacy with their wives. When opportunity arises, lie down on the couch and put your head in her lap. Let her twirl your hair or tickle your ear. Lie on the bed and scratch her back and she yours. Talk quietly and fellowship. Some of you guys that think you married a cold turkey will stoke the fire and awaken the beast with a half hour of intimacy. Women who are cherished will give until they pass out. You need her just as she needs you.

If getting close results in getting hurt, start ministering to her needs. When you meet her needs she will meet yours, but you must first be willing for it to be a one-sided relationship. At first you will do all the sacrificing and make her the beneficiary of your blessing. In time it will balance out until you are both trying to outdo the other in giving and blessing. That is when it gets real good.

## I Need Her to Balance Me Emotionally

Again, we guys don't like to admit that we are emotional beings. It is quite obvious that the gals are 90% emotion and 10% adulterated reason. We fellows pride ourselves on being logical and objective. But keep in mind that anger is an emotion. Irritability and grouchiness are emotions. Men are just as emotional as women; we just have a male pride that will not let us publicly express weakness or vulnerability. I am not suggesting that there is anything wrong with us men, for I don't intend to get publicly vulnerable either. I build strong walls and protect them against mushy intrusion. But men can be just as imbalanced emotionally as can women. It is just that our imbalance must be masculine while the girls' imbalance is feminine. So be it. I don't want any men friends that act like girls. I have known a few—very few. I knew them a short time—not short enough.

Men without women can grow cold, hard, and unyielding. As we adjust to the presence of a woman in our life, the hard edges of our psyche are rounded off. A woman draws us out of our hardness and makes us care deeply. We need those female creatures to be just what God made them to be. The balanced nature of God is expressed in the combination of male and female emotions.

## I Need Her to Encourage Me

I have never in my life admitted to, or even recognized, a state of discouragement—until five years later. To me it seems weak that a man should be discouraged, but we read of prophets like Elijah and kings like Saul becoming discouraged. Even John the Baptist grew discouraged after being locked in the dungeon for months. Peter and all the apostles were discouraged after the crucifixion. A good woman with whom we have intimacy and fellowship can keep us from getting discouraged. A wife must believe in her man if he is going to maintain courage when he fails. She can be our "bridge over troubled water" to ease our minds if we cultivate her in the good times. We need a helper to keep us from losing our vision. The wife will recognize discouragement long before anyone else does and long before we will admit it, so we need her all the more.

If your wife has not been an encouragement to you, don't blame her; ask yourself why she does not have faith in you. People whom we encourage tend to reciprocate in kind. Let me tell you a little secret: a wife has more faith in a man who includes her in the decision making process. When she is shut out, she feels at the mercy of a fallible man who doesn't have her best interest at heart. It is as scary for her as it would be for you if your life were inexorably tied to the fate of another. But when she is part of the decision making process she will appreciate the complexity of the problem and will be assured that the two of you have explored all the options and are making the best decision considering the circumstances. She will become encouraging when she can believe in your decisions. After all, if she has a say in the decision then she shares the blame when things don't work out so well. And about half of life doesn't work out well. So why take all the responsibility?

> **A wife has more faith in a man who includes her in the decision making process.**

You will need encouragement from time to time and God gave you that gift in the person of your wife. You were created to need an encourager. She's it.

## I Need Her to Challenge Me

Sometimes we men can drag our butts. We can get stale and indifferent, or we lose sight of the noble goal. If left to ourselves we could just drift into territory that makes it hard for us to recover. We can get, as the country mamas say, "wrong-headed," which is wrong hearted, wrong attitude, wrong battle fought with the wrong people—just plain wrong. Let's face it, when we take a survey of the people we know and the population in general, we are forced to admit that most men are wrong a good portion of the time. We need an early warning system, and they call it WIFE.

Now, a wife can be just as wrong-headed as her husband. She can lead him in the wrong direction like Job's wife, who actually tried to discourage him. But just because the little woman can be wrong doesn't change the fact that she can be right sometimes as well, and we still need a helper to challenge us. The beauty of it is that two very different natures (male and female) provide a broader perspective on the same issue. So it is quite common for the woman to see more clearly in those areas where the man is limited, the reverse also being true. Where the woman's nature prevents her from seeing clearly, the man is more likely to be constitutionally endowed with the mental and emotional tools to make wise decisions. If a man shuts his wife out of the process, he is denying himself the benefit of her more informed insights in areas where he is deficient. Likewise, if a man leaves the decision making to his domineering wife, it may bring him temporary peace, but he can be certain that she is not innately equipped to make the correct decisions in many cases.

> **It is terribly counterproductive for the duo to be untrusting of each other.**

It is terribly counterproductive for the duo to be untrusting of each other. The solution is for the man and woman to learn to see things from the other's perspective before jumping to conclusions. My wife and I sometimes "argue" (in the classical sense of point and counterpoint) our perspectives until we have aired our views and understand each other. It is rare that we do not come to a consensus. When we fail to agree, I— the man, head of the household—reluctantly do what I think is best. If I make the wrong decision after hearing her out, she is compassionate with my error, knowing my attitude was not haughty, and it should result in me being more humble. I am not sure it has ever actually worked out that way, but it should.

I hear some of you Independent Baptists saying, "The man is the head of the home and the woman is supposed to obey." How long have you been preaching that? How is it working out for you? Yeah, God told her to submit to you, but he never told you to dominate her or disregard her, nor does her obeying you make your decisions right. If you want more than a relationship based on law, it is time to act as if it is your responsibility to earn the right to lead.

Remember I am talking to men and would never say these things in the presence of the women. We should never let on that we could be wrong and ought to listen more and demand less. We do have our pride. Let her read *Created to Be His Help Meet* and she will obey even when she knows you are wrong and your decisions hurt the family. Thank God for godly women.

The answer is for you and your wife to grow into maturity together. If the family is dysfunctional it is time to take her hand and start confiding in one another. If you plan on driving the old truck on vacation next year, you had better start working on it now. Likewise, knowing you are going to need to be challenged and kept on the straight and narrow, start working on that woman so she becomes an able early warning system.

## "Let's Go," She Said

I remember my wife performing admirably in this regard. When I was much younger and the children were small, I contracted encephalitis and was hospitalized for 11 days. I had no memory of the first nine days. They didn't know if I would live or die. One-third of the people who contract the disease die; one-third are brain damaged, and one-third escape unharmed. We thought I was in the latter third—unharmed, but my wife soon discovered that I had lost much of my short-term memory. It was a shock to me when I went out to buy some hardware for our kitchen cabinets and came home to show Deb. She looked troubled and picked up another sack containing hardware and said, "You already bought hinges and door knobs two days ago." It was unbelievable that I could not remember.

At the time I was making kitchen cabinets for a living. I would head out to install a set and forget where I was going. I got scared to leave the house. I felt confused and uncertain and lost my confidence. I felt normal until I got into a stressful situation or someone called my attention to something I had forgotten. I began to fall behind in my business and was unable to get out and do the necessary sales.

One day my wife said, "Let's go." She rode with me through new subdivisions and we stopped at houses under construction. She sent me inside to talk to the homeowners or builders. Our first trip out netted two jobs. She had to continue challenging me to keep me going, but after several years I seemed to return to normal. She tells me I was grouchy during that time and seemed to resent anyone thinking that there was anything wrong with me. I still have trouble remembering names. I sometimes forget the names of people I have known for years. If she hadn't challenged me with an offer to help, I might have shrunk into depression (but I doubt it).

I am a minister of the gospel and often speak publicly. In my earlier ministry there were times Deb challenged me in regard to the appropriateness of something I said in a sermon, or in a public setting—still does every once in a while. At first I resented her challenging me, for it felt like rejection, criticism, condemnation. I will admit—but just this once—there were times her challenges just made me more stubborn. I didn't care about the issue; I just wanted her to think I was the best, number one, Mr. Infallible. I would have been happier if she had been just an ignoramus who had no discernment and couldn't see my errors. So what if I hurt someone else through lack of sensitivity or over-zealousness, my wife should be loyal to me regardless. Why did she have to be so smart?

**And you must garner enough humility to recognize that you do indeed need a help meet to challenge you to greater things.**

When husbands and wives don't have goodwill toward one another, a wife's challenges will be met with resistance, for he thinks she is judging him or "trying to be boss." You must bring your wife to the place where she has the wisdom and grace to challenge you without pushing. And you must garner enough humility to recognize that you do indeed need a help meet to challenge you to greater things.

When a husband has a bad attitude that may cause him to lose his job or make a fool of himself at church, his wife is his first line of defense. He needs her to be wise and sensitive. If she runs in too fast with too much, he might just bite her like a dog being pulled out of a fight. If he is already in a fighting mood, she shouldn't appear to be taking the side of his enemies. Diplomacy is called for and a carefully crafted question is in order. "Honey, if you do confront the preacher, how do you think everyone else will respond?" "Honey, I know your boss is sometimes rude, but if you say something to him and lose your job, where can you find employment in this economy?"

You may tell me that your wife is more likely to say, "Don't be so stupid. You have no marketable skills, and if you lose this job I am going to take the kids and live with my mother until you find another one." If that is your situation, then you have a bigger job cut out for you at home than you do at work. You need to bond with your wife, let her know she is cherished, fellowship with her; walk in the light, and then be ready to allow her to second-guess your attitudes. It is amazing that when a wife knows her husband is going to consider her critique, she grows more tactful in her approach. But if he has proven to be a stubborn fool, she will treat him with scorn.

When a woman finds her soul refreshed by her husband, she will not speak to him in a way that might cause her to lose the blessedness of that fellowship. When he values her and she values him, they stop hurting one another and treat each other with respect and tolerance. You need someone on the front line to challenge you. Wives are real handy. They just need to know they are valued for their perspective.

> **When a woman finds her soul refreshed by her husband, she will not speak to him in a way that might cause her to lose the blessedness of that fellowship.**

## I Need Her to Keep Me Civilized

Men are basically uncivilized animals. Ask any man who has been in a war zone for a year. Most won't talk about it, but they know. Ask someone who has been in a state penitentiary for ten years. The presence of women in the house, especially one whom we value, has a most amazing civilizing effect upon men. They keep us from being too crude. They cause us to build houses and decorate them, to cut the grass and clean up after ourselves. If the world had no females, men would live in the most basic shelters. They would not maintain regular employment and would be lawless. We institute law as a means of protecting our wives and children.

God placed a nesting instinct in women, something that is missing in men. Because of the women in their lives, men eat their vegetables instead of all meat. The women cause us to put a napkin in our laps and use another to clean around our mouths. We learn to say "May I" and "Pardon me." In a world of all men there would be no napkins, probably no table, and no one would apologize for burping or farting.

The few times my wife was away for a week visiting our grandkids, I forgot to take a shower and went to bed dirty. I have found myself going three days without bathing. But as soon as I know she is coming home I clean my body and the house. What would I be without her? A man who doesn't bathe has no right to make love to his woman. A shower is an absolute prerequisite. To approach her unclean is insulting and degrading. It shows a lack of respect. Women are much more responsive if you are like Kentucky Fried Chicken—"finger lickin good." On the other hand, if your wife likes a little odor and grit, pay me no mind.

Obviously God put the civil side of his nature in the female gender. We need our wives to help us be civil and to establish social order. She is given to us as a help meet to manage this side of our existence. I said all that to make one statement: A man's home may be his castle, but she is lord of the manor. Bend to your wife's wishes when it comes to the house. My wife owns the house and the kitchen. She tells me what to do and what not to do in the house, and I obey her. She can't make me wash dishes, but she can tell me where I can put my feet and where I can take my shoes off and where I can drop a dirty towel. Don't contend with your wife over the home. It is her nest. Our job is just to gather the sticks, build the nest, bring home the food, and get her pregnant so she can fill it up with little bundles of joy. We men need this direction and structure supplied by our wives. It is their created nature and we should honor that.

## I Need Her Morality and Conscience

It is well known that the women are the moral anchors of any society. When the ladies become depraved, families perish and society disintegrates. Men are less introspective and better able to ignore their consciences than are women. Wives and mothers are created with a nesting and nurturing instinct that is not dependent upon religious beliefs. They feel secure in a moral environment, sensing the necessity of a structure and an ordered society based on values that protect them and their children.

Excuse the base comparison, but as men are predators in the human kingdom, women are the prey. Feeling their vulnerability, women support a society based on the rule of law. We regularly read of a gang of men raping a woman, but not the other way around. A man may walk off and leave his children, but a woman of sound mind will walk three thousand miles to tend to her offspring—substance abusers excepted.

Some depraved women will view pornography, but most men will become addicted to it to the point of abandoning all nobility. Women never start or conduct wars, but men grow bored unless their generation settles some dispute with a river of blood.

Mister, you need your wife's conscience. She is the smoke and fire detectors waiting silently in the home . . . well, maybe not so silently, but she is there to sound the alarm when her conscience is pricked by your careless moral meanderings. So don't take the batteries out.

Men will hide their sin from their wives while boldly displaying it before others. Why? Because she is a resident judge who will not let us lie to ourselves. A good woman, like a clean mirror, will cause a man to see his shame. Some men are angry with their wives for that very reason. Rather than accept the judgment of their wife's conscience, they rail at the messenger. If a man is ever successful in corrupting his wife to the point of causing her to join him in depravity, he will go to hell faster than a drunk in a Ferrari.

Two problems can arise from the reality of a man's wife being his moral stabilizer. The first is that she becomes immoral and can no longer fulfill her role. The second is that she becomes haughty and judgmental, denigrating her less-than-righteous husband. Certainly the second is to be preferred but will cause a man to stay on the golf course or put in extra hours at work.

I have known many men who have just enough Bible teaching to know that God commands their wives to submit and honor them, but not enough grace to seek to be worthy of that position. It is the lowest form of hypocrisy to be immoral and expect your wife to draw the curtain on her conscience and honor you as if you were honorable. Stupid jerk. Such a man becomes the predator demanding the prey be silent while eaten, and all in the name of God. Woe, woe, woe unto that man.

"Render therefore to all their dues . . . honour to whom honour." Romans 13:7 A good wife will interpret that passage to mean that she should honor her husband because of his God-appointed office, just as we honor a police officer or judge irrespective of his character. But a righteous man will interpret that passage to mean that he should come to be worthy of the honor. Don't expect your wife to pretend you are honorable when you are not. Many men don't want their wives to be moral help meets; they want them to be covers for their immorality.

If God gave us what we deserve, we would all be in hell. If wives gave us what we deserve, we would be chained to the doghouse, eat leftovers, and have to potty in the yard. God's mercy and free gift of righteousness motivate us to walk in conformity to his most undeserved favor and grace. Likewise when a good woman honors her dog-of-a-husband, he should have the humility to seek to be worthy of her most undeserved grace.

> **A warning to wives:** That's right, I am aware that some of you nosy wives are reading this book while your husbands are at work so you can "help" them remember it—or hold them to it. My warning to you is that just as husbands are prone to read *Created to Be His Help Meet* and demand that their wives obey them—a most inappropriate response—wives may read my scathing exhortation to their husbands and decide not to honor the dog until he can do his tricks properly—again a most inappropriate response. One of you must do his/her duty before God regardless of what the other is doing if this marriage stands a chance of getting any better. A husband can make a marriage half good if he loves and cherishes his wife no matter her response, and a wife can make her marriage half good by honoring her dishonorable husband. A marriage that goes completely bad is one where both parties hold out until the other fulfills his or her duty. That is no marriage at all. It's a war where everybody loses.

I remember a lesson my daddy taught me when I was learning to drive. I asked him, "What do I do if the other guy keeps his lights on bright even after I flash him a warning? Should I just put mine on bright and teach him a lesson?" He answered, "One blind driver is enough; no need for two blind fools."

## I Need to Be Her Protector

You were created to protect your wife. Just as women are created to nurture, men are created to protect. There is a need met in a man when his woman looks to him for protection. And there is a need met in the woman when she sees her husband's readiness to protect her. There have been innumerable fights and acts of manslaughter over men defending the honor of their wives, mothers, or sisters. It gets to be a matter of pride. "Nobody says that about my mother." Pow!

It is very unlikely you will ever need to defend your wife against violent attack, but the instinct to protect is expressed in other ways. The custom of a man walking on the sidewalk next to the road dates back to an era in Europe when people threw their slop water and waste out of the upper floor windows. There were awnings that provided cover for the one walking close to the building. Likewise, passing wagons or horses might splash the one waking on the street side, so men protected their ladies by having them walk inside. The customs of men opening doors and helping women mount horses are derived from the man's need to protect his woman.

**Men mature when given family responsibilities.**

Women feel vulnerable in a man's world, like a rabbit in a field of foxes. Women who depend on their husbands' ability to provide food and shelter feel at risk when their husbands do not demonstrate an ability to provide. And men mature when given family responsibilities, or they should.

A good husband will not want his wife out at night in compromising or risky situations, like shopping alone. A man with a good and honest heart will not want his wife dressing immodestly, knowing that other men will lust after her.

Some men are too smothering in their protection, becoming possessive in a way that leaves the woman feeling controlled, the opposite of being protected. Other men are careless and indifferent, leaving the wife feeling he doesn't care much what happens to her. There is a balance. The wife needs to know he will die for her but will not enslave her.

Men, we need to protect our wives, but we cannot take away their humanity in the name of keeping them safe. It is all about the feelings we communicate. Do we make the lady in our life feel cherished and safe, or do we make her feel used and controlled? If you are in doubt, ask her. In fulfilling your needs, don't deprive her of fulfilling hers.

## I Need Her Sensitivity

I need her compassion, mercy, and grace. The nature of man is found in the husband/wife combination. God created Adam "male and female." Genesis 1:27 It is as if one body and soul could not contain and express the fullness of God so the Creator divided his attributes, grouping similar traits, putting them in the two genders. If we were to make a long list of human traits and read them before an audience, asking them to respond "male" or "female," I suspect we would see 90% agreement.

Give it try. Put an M (male) or F (female) after each one.

- Sensitive
- Merciful
- Courageous
- Logical
- Intuitive
- Just
- Compassionate
- Forgiving
- Hasty
- Full of Grace
- Tender
- Cautious
- Imaginative
- Analytical
- Creative
- Aggressive
- Kind
- Gentle
- Meek

- Full of Faith
- Discreet
- Honoring
- Nurturing

My wife and I went through the above list and had about a 90% agreement. Where we disagreed we did agree that they could go either way, depending on the character of the person. For instance, creativity can be found in either gender, as can faith. But there would be nearly 100% agreement that sensitivity is more the domain of the woman whereas justice is more of a masculine trait. "Nevertheless neither is the man without the woman, neither the woman without the man, in the Lord." 1 Corinthians 11:11

Sir, you are not complete without the full input of your wife. Your wife is more than your sex toy; she is the other half of your humanity. A man out of balance with his wife is imbalanced. You need a help meet, a helper suited to your nature. God made her to assist you—not just to hold the other end of the board while you nail it up, but to balance you in temperament and human traits. If you despair of bringing her along, when you leave her behind you leave yourself behind. God wisely designed man and woman so as to maximize human development, elevating it to a state higher than the original creation. You must flow with God's program or fail altogether.

> **Your wife is more than your sex toy; she is the other half of your humanity.**

I know in my own experience that my wife has fulfilled me as a person. She hasn't changed me that much, but she continues to help me by supplying that which I lack. In the process of trusting her I grow in faith and humility. I am still not as sensitive as she is, but she provides the impetus for me to recognize the moment when sensitivity is called for, enabling me to do what needs to be done even when I do not feel it. Wow! That is "heirs together of the grace of life." 1 Peter 3:7

I am prone to deal with situations based on cold, hard logic and justice.

"You sow it, you reap it."

"Here are the facts, like it or lump it."

"This makes sense to me; if it doesn't make sense to you then you are either ignorant or contrary."

I can hurt people's feelings. I can be most insensitive, not out of a feeling of maliciousness or uncaring. I just cannot fathom why anyone else would be upset by my "cutting to the chase, telling it like it is." As a man I have trouble walking a mile in another man's shoes, but you would think my wife shared shoes with every suffering and insecure person. She seems to know ahead of time how others will feel in any given circumstance. She "feels their pain." God put his sensitiveness in the female gender, but he gave her to Adam and told him to become one flesh with the little lady, depending upon her as his helper.

> **A woman doesn't expect you to always concede to her views, but she deserves the respect of being heard and understood.**

In most cases women are the first to show mercy and offer grace. The only time the female creatures are unmerciful and ungracious is where there is feminine competition. Pussycats will fight if they think the other is trying to horn in on their old tom, and they will show no mercy in a verbal battle. Otherwise women are full of mercy and pleasant goodwill toward the failings of others.

Don't shut your wife out when she has feelings about situations. That doesn't mean you will always succumb to her suggestions any more than she will always appreciate your logic and justice when it is called for, but always pause and patiently consider her perspective. If you think she is one-sided, which she can be, then explain your position and have a good back-and-forth discussion.

A woman doesn't expect you to always concede to her views, but she deserves the respect of being heard and understood. If she knows you understand her and that you care what she thinks, she can relinquish her will to yours and trust your wisdom. As time goes by and decisions come out of this duo brainstorming, it will be clear to both of you where your strong points are. If developing circumstances prove a wife correct, the humble man will learn to trust her instincts more and more. Likewise when a man's logic and rationality prove themselves in the outcome, the wife will learn to see things from his perspective and trust him more. In time they will sense when to yield to the other and all decisions will be by consensus. Wow again! That's beautiful and it works wonderfully, but it takes time and practice. Get off your high horse and boost your wife up there with you. She will be riding behind, but let her whisper in your ear. You still have the reins, but remember, if you take a wrong turn, she takes it also, so she deserves your esteem.

## I Need Her Counsel and Judgment

Headstrong, independent men sometimes forget that in the "multitude of counsellors there is safety." Proverbs 24:6 "For none of us liveth to himself, and no man dieth to himself." Romans 14:7

Mister, you need counsel. Having done many stupid things, I don't trust Michael Pearl like I did when I was young and knew everything. I have gotten dumber with the years. I am known to say "I don't know" more often than I did just after graduating from college.

But I will admit that early in our marriage I didn't want my wife's advice. At the time I felt that she was minimizing me in her criticism, so it angered Boss Hogg when she "got out of her place" and took the lead. At least, that is the way I interpreted her suggestions. I will tell you the truth: I don't know what happened first. Maybe she gained wisdom in the way she offered input or maybe I became less sensitive to suggestions. But the end result is that we grew and matured to the point where I trust her judgments and she trusts mine, and we both know we can be wrong and therefore are open to considering other possibilities. We can challenge one another without feeling put down. It is a fact of human nature that all of us listen with concern and introspection to those whom we respect, and we dismiss with derision those whom we think are unworthy to challenge us. Poor wives.

The bottom line is that insecurity and fear make us angry with perceived criticism. The smallest man has the biggest anger.

Wives can irritate us more than anyone else because it is so important to a man to look good in his wife's eyes. We are still like kids trying to impress that one girl, and it is disturbing if she thinks we are less than perfect. We all want to be praised and approved, and we get so little of it from work or friends, so we expect the little wife to provide all the positive affirmation necessary to keep up our self-image.

Am I saying all this? I hope my wife doesn't read it. I feel vulnerable being this honest. Now don't expect me to get in a circle, hold hands, say I am sorry, and sing kum-bah-ya. A man still has his dignity, you know. I don't mind making changes, but I am not going to admit that I was wrong until five years have passed. It is much easier to say "I WAS wrong" than to say "I AM wrong." My suggestion is that you hurry and make some changes before you have to admit that you ARE an immature, selfish, and insecure jerk. It worked for me. Then when you get old, you can be humble too.

I will set you on the road to recovery with one good suggestion. Ask your wife for advice and counsel. Welcome her judgments even if you feel she is attacking you. Pretend to be humble and thoughtful. Be patient and ask her to expound further on her concerns. Pause and look enlightened. Nod in appreciation for her wisdom and then modify your actions in some measure based on her suggestion. If unfolding events prove her wrong, be kind and gentle, not gloating or mentioning what is obvious. On the other hand, if her counsel and judgment prove to be right, praise her for it and thank her for saving you from error. You will make a new woman out of her. She will get ten years younger and smile like a kid opening birthday presents. But I warn you, she will get addicted to being happy. She will want to have sex more often and will initiate contact. If you are not up to it, you might want to continue with your "know it all" attitude so she can maintain her coldness as she continues to be your unhappy critic.

When I write an article or book, I submit it to my wife for editing. If she thinks there is a part that is not appropriate or could be said a different way, or that a point needs a little different slant, I discuss it with her until I see her point of view. There are times that she catches a skewed perspective or bad attitude coming through my writings. (For my reader I would like to soften that "bad attitude" thing, for it might lead you to have a lower estimation of me, but today I will admit to it just to make a point. Consider it rhetorical.) I have come to trust her goodwill toward me and to accept the fact that she likes me even when I am bad—sort of like a mother. She doesn't expect me to be perfect. She does like to see me honest and open to her wisdom. I would be stupid not to take advantage of her sanctified perspective. I would never have developed my ministry to where it is today without my wife. She is the sheath in which the knife rests and the stone that keeps it sharp.

Think about it. One day, maybe soon, I am going to appear before the Judgment Seat of Christ to be rewarded or to lose reward according to the things done in this body, whether they be good or bad. 2 Corinthians 5:10; 1 Corinthians 3:8; Matthew 10:42 At that day I am sure I will wish I could go back and have a do-over in regard to many things. Right now, before I stand before Christ embarrassed, my wife is enabling me to have that do-over, to correct areas where I am ignorant or insensitive to the Holy Spirit. She is sanctified in some areas that I am not and can see things I cannot see. She is not just editing my writings; she is editing my life so that the end product is better than I. I was created to need her counsel and judgment.

> **Think about it. One day, maybe soon, I am going to appear before the Judgment Seat of Christ to be rewarded or to lose reward according to the things done in this body, whether they be good or bad.**

In my defense, it works both ways. I edit her writings and her life as well. Like any woman, she can get her feathers up and claw the blood out of a timid soul that still needs a little understanding. You should have seen her book *Created to Be His Help Meet* before I softened the edges. She has an occasional blind spot. Because I trust her judgments and censorship, she trusts mine, and we are heirs together of the grace of life, sanctifying one another so as to reduce our embarrassment at the Judgment Seat of Christ. My favorite dying song is "I want to stroll over heaven with you some glad day." Heaven will be much sweeter with my best friend by my side.

## I Need Her to Support My Vision

Every man has a vision, and visions are tenuous and iffy by nature. A man with a vision hopes to surmount difficult circumstances, doing what others think impossible. A vision will waver like a mirage, sometimes promising cool water and other times looking like shifting sand. Most men lose hope of fulfilling their dreams and settle for a TV series. If you have a vision, you need a helper suited to that vision. It is not necessary for her to believe in it as you do, but she must believe in you. A man can keep his own vision alive if his wife runs his supply line and praises his endeavors. Most of us aim for more than we will ever accomplish, but in aiming we accomplish much more than our high school teachers ever dreamed. It is not the end that makes a man successful; it is all the many joyous days of trying. A help meet who supports our vision will make life a journey worth the effort, and we will be remembered for our humanity if not our accomplishments.

> **It is not the end that makes a man successful; it is all the many joyous days of trying.**

If your wife denigrates your vision, it indicates she is not being fulfilled as a person. Tend to her needs and she will get so contented she will tell you that you sing well, you are talented, smarter than everyone else, and should be promoted to work at the cash register instead of cooking the french fries.

You need your woman to support your vision. If you have no vision, I suspect you are not in good standing with your help meet. An encouraging woman makes a man think he is taller, stronger, and smarter than he is. And coupled with her wisdom he will be smarter. You cannot leave her sitting at the kitchen table griping and be successful at life without her. You may be manager at work, but that has nothing to do with life more abundant. If you will devote your energies to building her as a person, you will have more time and energy to pursue your dreams.

## I Need Her to Cover Me in Prayer

It is essential that "husbands, dwell with them according to knowledge, giving honour unto the wife, as unto the weaker vessel, and as being heirs together of the grace of life; **that your prayers be not hindered**." 1 Peter 3:7

Life requires a great deal of grace from God, but a particular grace for one unique purpose, and it is accessed only by means of two keys. The wife gets one key and the husband gets the other. They must go into heaven's bank together and insert the two keys at the same time if either of them is going to access the grace of life. If, according to the passage, a husband fails to "give honour" unto his wife, "the weaker vessel," then their prayers are hindered. Husbands who are ignorant of their wife's needs and fail to relate to them as weaker vessels, not dwelling "with them according to knowledge" will fail to "obtain mercy, and find grace to help in time of need." Hebrews 4:16

> **The wife gets one key and the husband gets the other.**

Mister, this may be the most important warning in this book. By not relating to your wife with knowledge of her status as the weaker vessel—the vessel being her body—your prayer line to heaven is cut, as is hers. That means the person closest to you in the world will not be able to pray for you, and as such you will not be a recipient of the grace you will need to deal with the issues of life.

**1 Timothy 2:8** I will therefore that men pray every where, lifting up holy hands, without wrath and doubting.

**James 5:16** Confess your faults one to another, and pray one for another, that ye may be healed. The effectual fervent prayer of a righteous man availeth much.

**Colossians 1:9** For this cause we also, since the day we heard it, do not cease to pray for you, and to desire that ye might be filled with the knowledge of his will in all wisdom and spiritual understanding;

## I Need My Wife to Meet My Erotic Desires

I am not a sex therapist and don't want to be. So I am not going to say all that needs to be said, not here and not in response to any letters you write. But we are going to view the subject through a window of light and hope. Read the Scripture below very carefully.

**Hebrews 13:4** Marriage is honourable in all, and the bed undefiled: but whoremongers and adulterers God will judge.

**Proverbs 5:19** Let her be as the loving hind and pleasant roe; let her breasts satisfy thee at all times; and be thou ravished always with her love.

**Song of Solomon 2:4-6** He brought me to the banqueting house, and his banner over me was love. Stay me with flagons, comfort me with apples: for I am sick of love. His left hand is under my head, and his right hand doth embrace me.

**Song of Solomon 4:10-11** How fair is thy love, my sister, my spouse! how much better is thy love than wine! and the smell of thine ointments than all spices! Thy lips, O my spouse, drop as the honeycomb: honey and milk are under thy tongue; and the smell of thy garments is like the smell of Lebanon.

**Song of Solomon 8:7** Many waters cannot quench love, neither can the floods drown it: if a man would give all the substance of his house for love, it would utterly be contemned.

**1 Corinthians 7:3-5** Let the husband render unto the wife due benevolence: and likewise also the wife unto the husband. The wife hath not power of her own body, but the husband: and likewise also the husband hath not power of his own body, but the wife. Defraud ye not one the other, except it be with consent for a time, that ye may give yourselves to fasting and prayer; and come together again, that Satan tempt you not for your incontinency.

## Associations

Through the years, in the process of hearing testimonies and counseling with many families, it has become clear that the reason most wives are frigid in sex is because of the guilt and shame they brought into the marriage. Our first experiences of anything stupendous, and especially sex, create an association that remains with us the rest of our lives. When the first sexual experiences occur in a context of shame and guilt, thereafter sex is associated with shame. The sensitive nature of women leaves them more subject to the restraints of guilt. If you, Sir, had sex with your wife before you were married, her present coldness is probably related to the residue of guilt.

Speaking of sneaking around to have sex, Solomon mused, "Stolen waters are sweet, and bread eaten in secret is pleasant." <sup>Proverbs 9:17</sup> A woman may be hot before marriage, eating stolen bread in secret and finding it quite stimulating, but once sexual desires are satiated in marriage, the guilt and shame that was shouted down by youth and passion begins to assert itself. Eroticism is overridden by shame and the wife does what she should have done before marriage; she freezes up sexually and crosses her arms in front of her body, shutting out the source of her guilt.

Years ago, I heard from a man that his wife couldn't get sexually aroused unless he took her parking. That was a term used for driving to some out-of-the-way place and "necking, smooching" or having sex. Her experiences before marriage had defined the terms of arousal and she couldn't shake them.

Most recently, a woman wrote and said that she met her husband online and they communicated through the digital media, finally meeting in person and eventually getting married. After several weeks of glorious sex, they cooled down, he especially. But they made a discovery one day when they were texting between home and work. Now he goes into one room and she in another and they text back and forth until they both get aroused. I am laughing again. I don't think I can stop. The world is crazier every day.

I get my wife aroused by walking in the room uttering a couple grunts. She gets me aroused by . . . well I don't know; I have been perpetually aroused for the past 40 years and one week. We have been married 40 years today as I write this. The additional week occurred just before marriage. I took the admonition seriously, "If they cannot contain, let them marry; it is better to marry than to burn [with lust]." 1 Corinthians 7:9 When Deb and I married we were both virgins and the only association either of us have with sex is the memories we have made together. I thank God for that. But I know some of you are not so blessed. Yet there is a way to undo the screwy associations that suffocate your sex life.

## Romance

There is another cause for a woman's lack of enthusiasm for sex. The "weaker vessel" is more sensitive by nature and cannot easily separate erotic pleasure from romantic feelings. A man needs no association to become aroused and seek fulfillment. But most women view sex as the fulfillment of deep feelings of love, protection, and commitment. You may marry a virgin and she freezes up on you like dry ice if you fail to draw her close to you emotionally.

Or you may marry a girl pure in body and mind, but you have a history of being a pervert, either through pornography or former immorality. The innocent-of-heart girl comes to marriage expecting gentle love, but she immediately encounters the raw and twisted passion of a man who sees his wife as an extension of his masturbation or as a whore to give him pleasure. She is shocked and feels soiled. Her first experiences of sex, though in marriage, are nonetheless dirty, soiled, and sordid. She calls you an animal and crawls into a fetal position emotionally, disillusioned with the frightening world of salacious lust. You didn't come to marriage caring about her; you just cared about legitimizing your own erotic self-stimulation.

**The Bible calls copulation "knowing."**

When two inexperienced people come together in marriage, they slowly discover the variety of eroticism at a pace that keeps their relationship expanding and advancing into something more complex and richer in experience. The Bible calls copulation "knowing." "Adam **knew** his **wife Eve and she brought forth a son.**" The innocent couple comes to *know* more and more of each other at a pace that is not jarring or shocking. When the sexually experienced man brings his highly tuned passions into the bedroom of a naive virgin, he looks like a nasty old man and can scare her into withdrawal.

## The Two-Minute Pop

One final situation of which I am familiar that causes marriages to fizzle is a husband who is just hasty and insensitive to his wife's needs. He is too quick on the trigger and doesn't take aim. He takes the first shot and the hunting trip is over before she knows it has started. She is left sitting like a kid who missed her ride to the party. I have known many innocent and naive young men who came to marriage with no expectations except that which nature suggests, and they have no idea that women are not emotionally and physically furnished like men. Take time to court your wife, to woo her, to give her relaxed pleasure, and she will climb the mountain with you, maybe beat you to the top and want to go again, and again.

## Cleaning Up My Act

The cure for all of the above is pretty much the same, with some additional spiritual actions that need to be taken by those who come to marriage with a whoremonger's mind. The man of corrupt mind and heart must repent before God and his wife. If they fornicated before marriage, they must both repent and confess their sin to each other and to God.

We talked about the power of associations. When a girl sneaks around and has sex with her boyfriend before marriage, lying to parents and concealing it from friends, the girl in particular comes to view her husband as a man with no self-discipline and capable of dishonesty in the pursuit of pleasure. She knows he is not a man of honor or integrity. He is not ruled by principle but by passion. Her view is that he will say anything or do anything to get what he wants. When they have a little falling out and his pleasure is deferred for a few days, and he stops knocking on her door, she gets suspicious, wondering where he is depositing his semen. Suspicion and distrust can spiral downward into an abyss of anger and resentment.

The man whose heart and mind are corrupted with pornography and former immorality must develop a pure mind. A wife will know when you are pure in heart and she will respond with her body. Reclaiming your virtue is not easy but I have seen it done a thousand times. I spoke a series of nine messages called *Sin No More*. It reveals God's method of walking after the spirit and ceasing to sin. If your flesh is still tangled in the snares of the devil, you should get the series and listen to it carefully. Many have been set free. You can be as well.

## Innocent Ignorance

I have a friend who came to marriage in a state of integrity. Both he and his wife were virgins in good standing with God. After they had been married for about two years the man sought counsel on his wife's lack of fulfillment. She was willing but did not enjoy it and had never had a climax. He was mystified. All his friends testified of hot wives. Some of them may have been doing some "Christian" lying but it didn't make that man feel any better. My daughter and son-in-law plied him with questions, discovering that he was not aware of his wife's needs. He was hasty and abrupt. They encouraged him to take time throughout the day to woo her with romantic gestures and to spend time blessing her with back scratches, leg rubs, massages, or anything that made her feel cherished. They then suggested a few techniques for slowly stimulating her in a romantic way. I will not go into any details. Others have written on the subject, I am sure. It took them about six months to transition into full passionate erotic sex that he now says must be the best on earth. She chases him down if he doesn't show any interest for a couple days. Whatever her hang-ups might have been, his patience and perseverance on her behalf brought her out of the frigid waters of indifference into the warm sunshine of summer love.

> **A man is never satisfied with sex until he is a master at pleasing his wife.**

Your wife was created to fulfill your sexual needs, and one of your sexual needs is for her to need you. A man is never satisfied with sex until he is a master at pleasing his wife. There is more to copulation than getting relief. It is a restoring and healing emotional experience that brings two souls into a union that is a perfect type of our spiritual union with God. We will discuss that point later.

If your wife is not fulfilling you, know that you are not fulfilling her either. If you think of yourself as the man of the house, then man up and take the steps necessary to bring her to a plane of erotic excellence.

## She Needs You to Need Her

Just as you were created to **need** a help meet, your wife was created **to be** a help meet. It is all by divine design. Have you forgotten to take her along with you as you fulfill your divine purpose? Most men, even husbands, think they can make it alone, that they can be successful in their life purpose without having to drag their wife along with them. They are wrong. She was created to be your right hand man—wo-man. She needs the key position in your life. Anything less will leave her defeated or rebellious. She will either get sickly or go out into the world seeking to discover personal fulfillment. Both are nasty choices. Until you arrange your life in a way that convinces her she is indispensable to your success, your relationship will remain less than fulfilling. You need her and she is waiting for you to show her the way. It is her nature to be your helper. Don't think she will be fulfilled doing other things.

You did not marry a trained, ready-for-the-job helper. Her nature is suited to your needs, but she comes to you untrained. She is a prodigy waiting for instruction. If you feel she is unequipped to help you, then take the time and exercise the patience necessary to equip her. The goal is not the efficiency of producing a product; it is the union of two souls in the work of life.

---

**Until you arrange your life in a way that convinces her she is indispensable to your success, your relationship will remain less than fulfilling.**

---

And God said, Let us make man in our
image, after our likeness: So God created
man in his own image, in the image
of God created he him.
Genesis 1:26-27

Chapter 5

# IN HIS IMAGE

## Not All Husbands Are Created Equal

Upon examination we find that not all husbands are created equal. They range from hen-pecked pushovers to monarchal slave drivers, from comfortable, laid-back, couch-crouching family men to radical, ready-to-revamp-everything-from-government-to-the-garage go-getters. All make different demands of their help meets. Likewise wives are different in their strengths and weaknesses.

**Imbalance is the bane of marital bliss.**

Therefore, there is no single answer suitable to all. One man's cure is another man's curse. Water is great for a brush fire but terrible when applied to gasoline. A domineering husband needs to mellow, and a mellow husband needs to command. One wife needs her husband to encourage her to seek outside interests, and another wife needs her husband to tell her to stay at home. Imbalance is the bane of marital bliss.

In rare cases, husbands and wives are paired in a combination that is complementary. For example, a girl who lacks confidence and decision-making ability marries a man who is by nature decisive but lacks a measure of confidence. He would not do well married to a highly confident and aggressive woman; it could diminish his confidence even further. On the other hand, being married to a woman who depends upon him will cause him to rise to the occasion and grow as a person; and under his patient guidance, she will gain confidence and learn to be more independent without intimidating him in his leadership capacity.

A natural balance is rare. As positive and negative poles have a magnetism that forms a strong bond, in contrast most marriages are composed of two poles that repel one another, competing for the same space. Starting a marriage with a natural balance is either a freak of nature or a miracle. Most of us must learn to yield and respond in ways that are not natural to us.

The faults of husbands are great and varied, on opposite extremes and all in between. But a near-faultless single man, when married, may discover faults he never imagined, for in marriage one becomes responsible for

> **In marriage one becomes responsible for another's temperament, weaknesses, and strengths.**

another's temperament, weaknesses, and strengths. A natural human trait—not bad in itself—may be harmful in one marriage while it is a strength in another.

Therefore, a call back to center to one errant husband will be interpreted by another as affirmation of his folly. One man's answer is another man's license. Medicine for one can be another man's narcotic. Some men are addicted to dictatorial rule while others cowardly submit to a brass-willed woman. The dictator needs to become a servant-husband while the servant-husband needs to dictate his will to his willful wife. What are your strengths and weaknesses and how do they affect your relationship to your wife? Have you placed your otherwise positive strengths under the tempering restraints of wisdom?

Observing men, it is readily apparent that they come in basically three different natures. A few men are very commanding by nature. Others are visionary and creative, expressing themselves as artists, inventors, religious leaders, and social reformers. But the majority of men are steady, wanting neither to take a commanding lead nor to shake up the status quo. We call these three types: **Command Man, Visionary,** and **Steady Man**. The way you relate to life and to your wife will reflect one of these three natures. We are going to look at those differences in men and women and explore the best approaches to achieving marital harmony and maturity.

## Alike Yet Different

God did not create men alike. "For who maketh thee to differ from another?" [1 Corinthians 4:7] God didn't create all butterflies the same color or shape. He didn't create just one kind of fruit—one size, one nutritional content, or one flavor. Not all cats are kitties, and not all snakes have rattles. Likewise God created men in different colors, shapes, sizes, and with different capacities—emotionally, intellectually, and physically. Everyone is aware of the various natures of different breeds of dogs. Some men are beagles, some are dobermans, and some border collies. God loves variety—contrast even.

Some men are proud of their distinctive natural qualities, while others feel less gifted. Acknowledging the differences in men and their tendency to compare themselves, God says, "For who maketh thee to differ from another? and what hast thou that thou didst not receive? now if thou didst receive it, why dost thou glory, as if thou hadst not received it?" [1 Corinthians 4:7] Again, we read, "For we dare not make ourselves of the number, or compare ourselves with some that commend themselves: but they measuring themselves by themselves, and comparing themselves among themselves, are not wise." [2 Corinthians 10:12] It is clear, God notes that men are indeed created different. So we ask, wherein is this difference and how does it relate to our role as husbands? That is the theme of this section, and we must go back to the beginning of our Bible to find the answer.

## Made in His Image

> **Genesis 1:26-27** And God said, Let us make man in our image, after our likeness: So God created man in his own image, in the image of God created he him; [1]

Since we are in the image of God, we can best understand ourselves by understanding the nature of God. God is "one Lord," yet revealed to us in three distinct persons: Father, Son, and Holy Spirit.

> **1 John 5:7** For there are **three** that bear record in heaven, the Father, the Word, and the Holy Ghost: and these three are one.

In our search to discover the nature of the image we bear, we note differences in the three persons of the godhead—in whose image we are created. Each person of the godhead retains the entire image of the one God, but they clearly manifest themselves in different capacities. Their attributes are one and the same, but their ministries differ.

---

[1] Some say the divine image was lost in the fall. Not so, for 1777 years after the fall God said, "Whoso sheddeth man's blood, by man shall his blood be shed: **for in the image of God made he man**." [Genesis 9:6] Murder is a crime because it is terminating something that bears the image of God. Likewise the Apostle Paul said, "For a man indeed ought not to cover his head, forasmuch as **he is the image and glory of God** . . . " [1 Corinthians 11:7] That settles it; fallen sinners retain the image of God even though it is defaced by sin.

Notice in the passage above, God speaks of himself in the plural—"Let **us** make man in **our** image . . . " The three persons of the godhead share the identical image, yet manifest that image in three distinctly different ways. Therefore since man is created in God's *image* and *likeness*, each man will reflect one aspect of God's image more than the other. That is why men can be so dissimilar. One will more markedly express the image of the Father, while another will be like the Son, and a third will be in expression like the Holy Spirit.

The Heavenly Father is King and Lord, the commander in chief, top of the hierarchy. "And when all things shall be subdued unto him, then shall the Son also himself be subject unto him that put all things under him, that God may be all in all." 1 Corinthians 15:28 The Son subject to the Father? That puts the Father at the top, King over all. Those men created in the image of the Father will be equipped to rule and command. They will distinguish themselves as ready to take charge and make things happen.

The Lord Jesus Christ, who gave his life for the sheep and ever lives to make intercession for us based on his shed blood, is the Priest of God. Those created in the image of the second person of the godhead will be priestly in nature—steady and faithful servants.

The third person of the godhead is the Holy Spirit, the conscience of God calling men to repentance and convicting them of sin. Men created in the image of the Holy Spirit are prophet-like in nature—visionaries.

So which person of the godhead do we resemble? Is it the priestly Jesus? Or is it the kingly Father, or maybe the prophet Holy Spirit?

## Observation

All of creation comes in threes. There are three dimensions and three primary colors from which all other colors are derived. The atom is three parts, and the proton and neutron are constructed of three quarks each. The earth is composed of crust, mantle, and core. Plants require nitrogen, phosphorous, and potash. There are three kinds of flesh— mammal, bird, and fish. The body is bone, blood, and tissue, with three layers of skin and three joints in our fingers. There are three parts to the eye and the digestive system. There are three heavens. The family unit is man, woman, and child. We are body, soul, and spirit. The soul is intellect, volition, and sensibility. The evidence is endless wherever you look—sea, land, or air. So we would expect to find three types of men created in the image of God, just as the Scriptures imply. As you look at the evidence I am confident you will agree. And you will laugh with amazement at seeing yourself as a reflection of one of these three types.

- Were you created in the image of God the Father? Are you a natural born leader? Do you rise to the top in business and social settings? Are you a take-charge guy? In this book I will refer to your type as **Mr. Command Man**.

- Is your likeness that of Jesus? If so, you are the priestly type that enjoys helping people—faithful and steady, compassionate and understanding. The one word that best describes you is steady, so I will refer to you as **Mr. Steady**.

- Are you created in the image of the Holy Spirit? Then you are a man of judgment and action, not content with the way things are and ready to change them for the better. You are prone to come up with wild ideas and seek sweeping changes. You are the prophet type and are recognized in society as a visionary, so we will call you **Mr. Visionary**.

The reason we generally do not call the three types Father, Son, and Holy Spirit or King, Priest, and Prophet is because fallen humanity is too far removed from its source to be worthy of those higher designations. Though man still exists in the image of God, that image is terribly marred by sin. The three types of men can manifest good or evil. Therefore men are better defined in amoral terms reflecting the outward expressions of their image—**Command Men, Steady Men,** and **Visionaries**. That fits the good, the bad, and the ugly.

| Father | King | Command Man | Steps out front to lead |
| Son | Priest | Steady Man | Dependable, compassionate, servant |
| Holy Spirit | Prophet | Visionary Man | Radical, man of judgment and vision |

As we explore the profound variance found in men, considering the strengths and weaknesses of each, it will enable you to understand your wife's responses, thus allowing you to better steer her into her role as your helper. Each image has amazing strengths and weaknesses. Gaining wisdom and knowledge in this area will help you develop your gifts and avoid your weaknesses. It will help you understand your wife's reactions and cause you to curb your inclination to extremes.

When you know your natural strengths and weaknesses you will not demand of yourself something different from your capabilities. All problems are solvable, but the solutions are different for different types of men. So we are going to help you know yourself as God created you. This will be fun.

We have spoken of the three types of men as if a man is exclusively one or the other. A few men do manifest one type to the exclusion of the other two, but most men are predominantly one type with a little of one other mixed in. I have never met a man that completely expresses the well-rounded image of God. Can't pinpoint what image you are? You will, but first we must consider the nature of the little lady in our life.

## Female Natures

It seems God did not create women as he did men, strongly fixed in one dominant type. You will remember that Eve was created differently from Adam. Adam was taken from the dust of the earth and God breathed life into him. Eve was taken from Adam's side, bone of his bone, flesh of his flesh. It is as if the ladies are T-cells, meant to grown into conformity to their husband's nature—not to be identical, but to complement with contrast. In that sense they are not as limited as are we. But women who are not married, or those who have not grown into their roles as their husband's help meets, will also manifest one of the three images in a significant way. As such, they are imbalanced. Likewise, a girl who waits until she is in her late twenties or older to get married is more likely to have trouble conforming to her husband's type because she has been independent so long, growing in her own direction.

> **The woman's nature is designed to adapt and diversify for the sake of the relationship.**
> **It is your job to make her long to fulfill her position.**

The woman's nature is that of assistant to an autonomous man. She is designed to adapt and diversify for the sake of the relationship. A helper doesn't set the agenda; she follows. Learning to give her life to help another succeed does not come naturally. It is a growing process that is not always frictionless.

It is your job to make her long to fulfill her position. It is her job to do her duty even if it doesn't seem to be personally fulfilling. This book is for you, to help you steer her into becoming your most suitable help meet. Earthly marriage is a picture of the great mystery of Christ and his bride, the church. Therefore it is of eternal significance that you bring your marriage into conformity to its heavenly pattern.

> **It is of eternal significance that you bring your marriage into conformity to its heavenly pattern.**

## Encouragement

Marriage can be glorious. Mine is and has been for many years. I know of only two couples married for over ten years who claim to never have had a fight. They commenced marriage wise in personal relationships and with knowledge of how to make a marriage work, and, from observation, I think their natural strengths and weaknesses complemented each other while not creating conflict. The vast majority of my readers cannot testify to a frictionless marriage, but, I assure you, a beautiful marriage is attainable for those of you who are now at the end of your rope with the last grip unraveling in your hand. I have seen countless married couples, even those who have already divorced and lost all hope, find the path back to repentance and restoration. And now, many years later, they testify of experiencing an uninterrupted joyous marriage.

Most couples simply lack knowledge of how to relate to and understand each other. God tells us in Hosea 4:6, "My people are destroyed for lack of knowledge." It is also true that marriages are destroyed for lack of knowledge. God says, "Wisdom is the principal thing; therefore get wisdom: and with all thy getting get understanding." Proverbs 4:7 We have a wonderful promise from God, "If any of you lack wisdom, let him ask of God, that giveth to all men liberally . . . " James 1:5 So "Seek, and ye shall find." Luke 11:9

---

**But if any provide not for his own,
and specially for those of his own
house, he hath denied the faith,
and is worse than an infidel.**
1 Timothy 5:8

---

Chapter 6

# MR. VISIONARY

## <u>Visionary</u>, Steady, Command

God the Holy Spirit is a prophet. He comes into the world with the mission of rectifying wrongs and moving men to repentance. "And when he is come, he will reprove the world of sin, and of righteousness, and of judgment:" <sup>John 16:8</sup> Some men are created in the image of the Holy Spirit, but that image is marred by the reign of sin. "They are all gone out of the way, they are together become unprofitable; there is none that doeth good, no, not one. Their throat is an open sepulchre; with their tongues they have used deceit; the poison of asps is under their lips:" <sup>Romans 3:12-13</sup> Yet there is one recognizable trait that remains whether they be sinners or saints: it is the visionary aspect of the third person of the godhead—the disposition to right the wrongs, seeing the world as a place that needs changing, howbeit wisely or unwisely.

Some men are shakers and changers, dreamers and makers, sometimes breakers, but always weighing the status quo against their vision of a better way. You will know you are a Visionary if you get the entire family upset about peripheral issues like, should a Christian celebrate Christmas, should we use state marriage licenses, or should a Christian opt out of the Social Security system? You are radical in your political views. You think of yourself as part of the sane minority. You have a lot of ambition and big dreams of accomplishing great things, of making a much needed impact on our stumbling world. Maybe you are a street preacher, or a motorcycle designer, or buy antique furniture and resell it. You could be an inventor or want to be. You are not content with anything that comes packaged.

A true Visionary will have tunnel vision, tenaciously focusing on single issues. Visionaries will easily pick up and relocate without any idea of what they are going to do for a living at their new location. They are often the church splitters and the ones who demand doctrinal purity and proper dress and conduct. Like a prophet, they call people to task for their inconsistencies. Mothers-in-law are troubled by Visionary sons-in-law.

## Strengths of a Visionary

Artists, musicians, writers, and most actors are Visionaries. To communicate ideas, pain, love, justice, and truth is paramount for a man with a vision. He is the "voice crying in the wilderness" striving to change the way humanity is behaving or thinking. He loves confrontation and hates the status quo. "Why leave it the way it is when you can change it?"

**Visionaries are the men who keep the rest of the world from getting stagnant, dull, or complacent.**

Today, all over our nation, the Visionaries are prominent on both sides of the political spectrum. They are found clustered in what is called "the extreme right" and "the extreme left." They stir up people to join a rally or to march, or gather by the thousands in Washington. Their enthusiasm and firm belief are the conscience of any movement. They are the men who keep the rest of the world from getting stagnant, dull, or complacent. Most good salesmen are Visionaries, because they will press in close and personal, making the customer believe he really needs this purchase. Visionaries are not as effective at managing banks or investment firms. They are too impulsive. They make much better attorneys, architects, spokesmen for disenfranchised minorities, abortion opponents, or robot designers.

Though Visionaries can be obnoxious in their tunnel vision and fanatical zeal, they have saved us from mediocrity. They have seen the toil of men and women and turned to innovation, creating a better way. They are the Galileos, the Benjamin Franklins, the Thomas Edisons, and the Alexander Graham Bells. They designed the ships that Steady Men built and then launched into the unknown to discover and chart continents beyond. They were the wildcatters who speculated on oil and spent their mother's last dime to bore a well. They looked at the moon and had a vision of going there. They built telegraphs and railroads and the space shuttle. They splice genes and seek to cure diseases. They are responsible for every revolution, peaceful or violent, that has occurred since Nimrod built the Tower of Babel.

The Visionary will quit a job in Silicon Valley and move to rural Montana to raise sheep. He will drag his family from one project to the next, sometimes as unstable as a pickup truck on a wet street with five pounds of air in the back tires. No one understands him and he doesn't understand himself, but he is on a mission and he will figure out what it is when he gets there. Expect great things from the Visionary, for he expects them of himself.

A woman married to a Visionary is going to have an exciting ride. His passion spills over into their relationship. There will never be a dull moment, although there will be plenty of questionable days. His drive exceeds the Steady Man and the Command Man. Every large business hires Visionaries to open up new markets and come up with original ideas. On the upper end, some of them are paid just to think. Their ideas are worth millions . . . billions.

## A Visionary's Weakness

All three types have their strengths and weaknesses. A strength in one area implies a weakness in others. And the strength itself can be a weakness when it assumes a disproportional role. An undisciplined Visionary can become so focused on a peripheral issue that he lacks practicality and accomplishes nothing toward his goal. Only humility and wisdom can check the excesses of a strength. A man may have a strength that serves him well as a single man on a mission, but finds that it is destructive in a marriage if it is not modulated by wisdom.

Rarely, if ever, do we see a man that is a balance of all three types. A realistic goal is for one to temper his strengths while strengthening his weaknesses. The Visionary who lacks humility is especially obnoxious, for he gets pushy with his agenda to change something. If he is a religious person he will paint issues with moral imperatives—contending that, "It is the right thing to do." If he is a leftist-leaning liberal he will likewise represent his agenda as a moral necessity, seeking to change laws, willing to take away the freedom of others just to force his worldview on society. If he is a Christian, he can get very pushy in his interpretations of things like dress, music, which version is the Bible, eschatology, or any number of doctrines. Not all pushing or contending is bad, but most Visionaries end up with more vision than wise discretion. They don't know when to lay it down—how to do all things with moderation. Because of their tenacious, narrow focus they sometimes end up accomplishing what everyone agreed was impossible, but too often they are just impossible.

To complicate matters, Visionaries are prone to be spiritually minded. They are the ones who are ready to proclaim themselves prophets and demand the church follow them out of Egypt. Like Satan's first temptation in the Garden of Eden, Visionaries can be guilty of adding to what God said by their zealous interpretations. They are the ones who want to keep the Jewish feast days, observe dietary laws, say "Yahweh" instead of God or Jehovah, or baptize in Jesus' name instead of Father, Son, and Holy Ghost. They become obnoxious proponents of some obscure doctrine.

Visionaries give extra weight to the issue that consumes them at the moment, and they are not able to rest until they have effected change. They are known to butt into other people's business and try to turn a conversation to controversial issues, knowing they have the solution. They can get heated in a debate and overly excited in their enthusiasm to convict the world of its error.

## Will Mr. Guilty Please Stand Up

Most Fundamental Independent Baptists are Visionaries. For that reason they get more evangelism done than all the other churches put together. They will knock on your door while everybody else is "concerned for you." But they have the most obnoxious pastors this side of Balaam and his ass. The wives of Independent Baptists have to be tougher than John the Baptist when King Herod dropped by his out-door evangelistic meeting, for they are surrounded by Visionaries who pump each other up and say "Amen" even when watching a football game.

> **And why beholdest thou the mote that is in thy brother's eye, but considerest not the beam that is in thine own eye?**

A few Visionaries get so busy judging the other guy for something like not going out on the street to preach that they fail to notice they are not even providing for their families. Simply stated, all Mr. Visionaries need to consider Matthew 7:3-5, "And why beholdest thou the mote that is in thy brother's eye, but considerest not the beam that is in thine own eye? Or how wilt thou say to thy brother, Let me pull out the mote out of thine eye; and, behold, a beam is in thine own eye? Thou hypocrite, first cast out the beam out of thine own eye; and then shalt thou see clearly to cast out the mote out of thy brother's eye."

If Visionaries are not wise, they might criticize good Steady Men who are doing what God called them to do. They might speak disparagingly of their Mr. Command preacher who is honoring God but just not zealous about something they deem paramount. Moderation is something every Visionary needs to practice. "Let your moderation be known unto all men." Philippians 4:5 If you will allow your help meet to speak her mind she can be a moderating influence on your tendency to volatile action, enabling you to see the bigger picture. If you are wise you will trust your judgments less and consider hers more.

> **A radical Visionary can be saved from dead ends and useless eruptions by his wise help meet's simple words of caution.**

From what I have said it may seem that Mr. Visionary is a radical danger to the world. Not so. Visionary types are critical members of society. They are the vision and catalyst for positive growth. I am confident that without Visionaries the Americas would still be undiscovered, walking would be our only means of transportation, and our caves would lack paintings. I know, for I am about one part Visionary for every two parts Command Man, and, contrary to the media, I can assure you I am as normal as cherry blossoms and watermelon. It is the Visionary in me that drives me to write this book and the Command Man that makes me believe I should take a lead on important issues.

## The Visionary's Help Meet

A radical Visionary can be saved from dead ends and useless eruptions by his wise help meet's simple words of caution—that is, if he hasn't converted her to his radical worldview. Visionaries are prone to see the world in black and white and can become critical of everyone around them. Some wives are influenced by their negative attitude and lose the ability to see clearly. He cultivates her into an amen corner for his attitude and actions when what he really needs is a smoke detector that sounds an alarm when his direction is likely to start a conflagration that will burn the entire family. If a man gripes about the pastor, his boss, politics, the church, the Illuminati, or the Bilderberger long enough, he may encourage his wife to join him in his pessimism. Instead of controlling his fire, she fans it. An immature Visionary that believes in his own infallibility likes to smother his doubts with the blind affirmation of his wife. He wants his help meet to do all the meeting; he already knows what he must do, come hell or high water.

The loose cannon Visionary may chastise his wife if she shows any indication of thinking on her own, especially if her conclusions differ from his predisposed position. He is like a man awakened by a screaming smoke detector who gets up and turns it off so he can go back to sleep and continue his dream.

If you have identified yourself as a Visionary, you need a wife that feels free to express her concerns. And you should listen carefully. You can argue your point, but never diminish the value of her opinion or demean her for speaking up. If you break off fellowship when she expresses concern, you will intimidate her into blind acquiescence, leaving you with no early warning system. A wife who sits beside you in the front seat and hollers, "Cop!—Radar!" is an asset, but if you are so insecure as to speed up just because she warned you, you deserve the wreck that is coming, but she doesn't and neither do the kids.

## Helping a Visionary

Not all Visionaries are given to wild judgments of people, but many are. If you happen to be one of those and if your wife has been converted to your negative point of view and is now given to trashing people with her words, then, brother, you are a scuba diver with no depth meter or oxygen indicator. Don't despair. That is why we wrote the book—to help you help her help you.

The first step to recovery is to exercise wisdom in what you say and how you react. Express you're sorry at having been so negative and judgmental. Tell her that you know you have allowed your image type to lead you in an unhealthy direction. Then show compassion and tolerance of others. You need to model the attitude you want your wife to assume. She became what she is to please you. In time she will, at your example, turn loose of the pessimism that is now rooted in her soul. When you express concern for the inadequacies of your image type, letting her know that you have a blind spot that needs a sharp eye and a sensitive heart to guard your flank, she will want to be your helper in that area and will rise to the occasion, no longer railing her criticisms but tactfully cautioning you instead.

In the recesses of her conscience she has her doubts about your outlandish side; it is unpleasant and ugly, so she will be relieved that you have "seen the light." The first time she expresses caution and you heed her admonition she will be transformed with the pleasure of being a true help meet and not just a "Yes-Ma'am." She will learn to exercise restraint in her conversation concerning other people. She will become happier in the marriage, and you will be saved from grief. You need to continue by teaching, reminding, encouraging, and thanking your wife for being the kind of helper you need.

When your honey understands that what she says will really affect you, she will mold to your needs. It is in a woman's makeup to want to bless her man. Ask her to pray for you. She needs to know that when you start raving about something or somebody that she has a right, even an obligation, to suggest that you might not be seeing the whole picture. Any woman who sees her man is earnest will make an effort to curb her tongue and will work to develop discretion. Ask your wife for your sake to make Philippians 4:8 her life verse: "Finally, brethren, whatsoever things are true, whatsoever things are honest, whatsoever things are just, whatsoever things are pure, whatsoever things are lovely, whatsoever things are of good report; if there be any virtue, and if there be any praise, think on these things."

**Ask your wife for your sake to make Philippians 4:8 her life verse.**

Don't wait on your wife to respond perfectly before counting your marriage a success. Most likely, neither of you will ever be 100% perfect spouses. She will continue to have some faults and will occasionally say things in a way that could cause you offense. That is where grace and wisdom bridge the gap. Learn to be generous of spirit and patient in your reactions.

## Depressed Visionaries

Visionaries are much more likely to have mood swings and even depression than are the other two types of men, for they have high hopes and great expectations that are sometimes impossible to realize, and they judge themselves by the same standards they judge others. It is self-flagellation, punishment for failure. I ask, who made you responsible for righting all the wrongs and achieving great things? I am not telling you to be content with less than the realization of an impossible dream. I say dream on and give it all you've got; enjoy the trip, but don't take your failures personally. The man who climbs high falls back to earth more than the man who picks from the lower branches. Have fun aspiring to great things; just be sure to feed, clothe, and minister to your family along the way, and don't view yourself through the lens of your imagined greatness.

> **Don't view yourself through the lens of your imagined greatness.**

Having a wife with a positive and cheerful outlook is priceless. And an understanding of the peculiar propensities of your nature will enable you to laugh at the caricature you present. The bottom line is you need to bring your wife alongside in an emotionally supporting role. You need her to believe in you. Everyone finds satisfaction in being needed, but for your gal it is life. It gives her worth; it makes her feel truly loved, and her encouragement can keep you from experiencing the great mood swings that come from occasional failure.

If you don't have a productive relationship with your wife, then chances are you are just sitting around the house complaining while wanting to change the world in some way. Don't blame her! Remember, Visionaries have a tendency to blame others. Talk to her about how you can change the direction you are going. Then go somewhere together, even if you must stop short of the crest. It is all about traveling together, not just reaching the top.

## Letter from a Visionary's Wife

Dear Mrs. Pearl,

Thank you so much for writing your book, *Created to Be His Help Meet.* I have read it through twice and it still hurts! Something I have been greatly blessed by is your section on the different kinds of men. I had no idea, but it sure helped me understand my husband. He is 100% certified Visionary. He is an awesome man. He has a brilliant business idea at least once a day. I'm sure if we had the capital to invest we would be rich. But we don't. Basically we are broke, and my husband doesn't seem to care. I think he is discouraged. We are living in a beautiful house rent-free until we are able to pay our good friends who wanted to help us out since we have little ones. So far we have not paid them a dime.
I feel so guilty using their friendship that I can't stand to even look at them. We haven't paid our water bill in months, we use food stamps, and last winter we didn't have heat due to unpaid bills. My widowed mother has helped us out in the past, but I really feel guilty that she has to give her little mite for us. The car notes are overdue as well; so soon it will be gone.

My husband has his own shop. He always thinks that what he is doing will suddenly succeed, but months, years have passed and it is not happening. No one has shown interest in what he sells. I want him to be successful. I don't want to destroy his vision, but I am expecting another baby. I wonder if we will have electricity when it is born. We almost froze last winter. I would treasure any advice or encouragement you could offer.

Please pray for us,

Cathy


## Not-So-Dear Mr. Visionary,

You have one very great weakness, and you are permitting it to control you like substance addiction. If you allow your dreams to rule your common sense, while walking with your head in the clouds you will step on your family. Your despondence and discouragement are the results of making yourself a slave to your impulses to achieve success in areas that have proven unproductive.

Once when I was young, I asked an investor where I could best invest $40,000 I had on hand. He answered wisely, telling me to never invest money that I needed for the subsistence of my family or the upkeep of my lifestyle. "If you can't afford to lose it; don't invest it," he said.

You, Mr. Visionary, are investing time and energy on things that are a losing endeavor. They are not turning a profit. You are pouring your life and the souls of your wife and kids down the drain of a vain belief that what hasn't worked in a number of years will suddenly become a paying venture. Stop investing what you cannot afford to lose. Your first duty is not to fulfill your dreams, but to provide for your own house. If you have to work at an assembly line sorting screws and bolts to keep the family comfortable, then swallow your pride and shelve your vision until the family is secure. You can experiment with fulfilling your visions in the evenings and on weekends, but it is morally unacceptable to spend your wife's emotions on failed dreams. If you think she should just shut up and make the best of it, you, Sir, are a double-dog jerk.

## Your Guiding Verse

**1 Timothy 5:8** But if any provide not for his own, and specially for those of his own house, he hath denied the faith, and is worse than an infidel.

## Nothing But the TRUTH

No able bodied man should be living off the generosity of friends, welfare, parents, wife, or widowed mother-in-law. The only excuse is complete disablement. If you can't do anything else, cut grass, wash windows, or, perish the thought, get a job. But don't mooch, and don't put your wife in the position where her side of the family feels sorry for the kids and "voluntarily" helps out.

Any of the three types of men can be lazy or irresponsible, but the Visionary is most prone to dreaming and scheming without doing anything redeeming. And don't hide behind your image type. God made you this way so you could rise above the animal instinct to do as you

ought. You as a man have the power and
duty to act wisely and responsibly rather
than by pure instinct. Anyone can do what
he feels like doing, what his natural drives
dictate. A godly man does what he ought,
and what you ought is to provide for
your own family no matter how boring or
unfulfilling the job.

> **A godly man does what he ought, and what you ought is to provide for your own family no matter how boring or unfulfilling the job.**

"All work is pain," says a French philosopher. Maturity is learning to
endure the pain of work. Gainful employment can be painful in many
ways: physical exertion, enduring heat and cold, mental stress, or the most
painful of all, boring work—work that offers no personal satisfaction,
repetitive work, monotonous, mentally numbing, dumb work. It is worse
than a headache. So an immature, selfish man will forfeit his dignity and
idle himself before he will endure the pain of boring work. It feels good to
dream and imagine one's self to be above the menial labor of the masses,
to be destined to great success through some invention or brilliant idea
come to fruition. But a man with a family has a duty that must be fulfilled
regardless of his personal satisfaction. Hope of future achievement cannot
take the place of today's dignity and duty.

## Dummy Dumbed Down by the Devil

I heard a Visionary say, "I can't keep a job more than a few days; they
fire me for witnessing to everybody. I guess the devil just doesn't want
me working." My answer is, "Well, it is too bad the devil is winning;
where is your armor to resist his fiery darts?" He is living rent-free in a
friend's house. He likes to define his state as "suffering for Christ."

There are other men who cannot tolerate the moral corruption in the
work place, so they quit and then spend months idly looking for another
job while nursing the government and "trusting God" to meet their
needs. God has made it abundantly clear that a man who doesn't work
shouldn't be allowed to eat. A man of God honors what God says and
continues to work to support his own family. If you are taking any
sustenance from others without giving back equal or more, then you
are a user. And users are losers depending on others who are willing to
endure the pain of work.

Women were created as the weaker vessel to depend upon their husbands for daily sustenance. Don't expect a woman to understand and appreciate you if the family finds it difficult to keep food on the table and maintain a properly furnished home with functioning appliances and a loaded larder. Certainly don't expect a woman to respect you if you are forcing her to depend on someone else to provide her daily bread. My wife will tell her to respect you regardless, as she should, but I am telling you that if she does she is becoming a super-Christian while you are becoming a super-cad.

## Dawdling David

We receive hundreds of letters from wives whose husbands are living in sin due to their idleness. Otherwise good men are drawn away by their own lust when they "hang out" all day. Consider King David, a man after God's own heart, who "tarried" at home in a time when he should have been engaged in a battle with his men.

> **2 Samuel 11:1-3**
>
> 1 And it came to pass, after the year was expired, at the time when kings go forth to battle, that David sent Joab, and his servants with him, and all Israel; and they destroyed the children of Ammon, and besieged Rabbah. But **David tarried** still at Jerusalem.
>
> 2 And it came to pass in an **eveningtide, that David arose from off his bed,** and walked upon the roof of the king's house: and from the roof he saw a woman washing herself; and the woman was very beautiful to look upon.
>
> 3 And David sent and enquired after the woman. And one said, Is not this Bathsheba, the daughter of Eliam, the wife of Uriah the Hittite?

The text includes all the elements that led to David's sin. Note the salient points:

- It was the time when kings go forth to battle. David was neglecting his duty.
- But this king tarried still at Jerusalem. He intended to go, but just hadn't left yet.

- David is lying on his bed late in the day. Must have stayed up late.

- He rises up and idles himself on his roof patio—taking in the view.

- He turns on his wide-screen and views a beautiful woman taking a bath. That cured his boredom.

- He wants more of her so he enquires further.

The rest of the story is recorded in 2 Samuel 11, and it is reenacted every day by men whose first error is the same as David's. At the time when men should be out to work, they tarry at home and, rising up from their beds, view beautiful women and enquire further, leading to terrible sin that reflects back upon their children. God presided over the death of David's child in judgment on his sin.

**Idleness is the devil's workshop.**

"Idleness is the devil's workshop." Not a Bible quote, but it is a Bible truth. David was not idle all the time, just at that moment in his life. But it was enough to cause him to spend the rest of his life repenting of that one sin, and the price was paid over and over again in blood and degradation upon his family.

Many of the Psalms of David reflect his lifelong penitence.

### Psalm 51:1-3
1 Have mercy upon me, O God, according to thy lovingkindness: according unto the multitude of thy tender mercies blot out my transgressions.

2 Wash me throughly from mine iniquity, and cleanse me from my sin.

3 For I acknowledge my transgressions: and my sin is ever before me.

## Great Expectations

Idleness is not exclusive to Visionaries. Any man can become discouraged or lose his vision and idle himself at home. The Visionary is just more volatile and prone to mood swings. He has high hopes and expects great things of himself; and, let's face it, most Visionaries never do anything notable. The world does not provide that many opportunities. You must learn to enjoy little things like repairing the lawn mower or improving on the outdoor grill.

A Visionary, like all three types, must learn that life is not given to greatness; rather it is great when we live in fellowship with God and family and "rejoice in his labour; this is the gift of God." Ecclesiastes 5:19 We can take ourselves too seriously and miss the everyday goodness of wife and kids and trimming the hedges. I have a good bit of Visionary in me, and Deb can tell you that I have had many "brilliant" ideas over the years. In my imagination I have done notable things, but 99% of all my dreams are unfulfilled. I have said it a thousand times, "In another life I would . . . maybe in the Millennium I will . . . If I could live to be a thousand years old I would . . . ." We must not allow our pride to condemn us for falling short of glory goals. It is a full day's work just keeping food on the table and paying for the place where the table sits. Reach for the stars in your spare time, but don't neglect that which is within reach—your dear help meet and the kids that so need an honorable daddy investing his time in them like they were each worth a billion dollars.

## Your Motto

Provide for your family first, then pursue your dreams as time and money allow.

## Exhortation to Visionaries

✓ Don't let your drive drive her away. Demonstrate a soundness of judgment by first meeting the needs of the family, and then when you share your daring vision with her she will have the emotional energy to dream with you. You will then be emotionally free to actually do something out of the ordinary. Talk to others about how great she is to stand with you. A wife will put up with a great deal of nonsense if her man makes her feel secure and appreciated.

✓ If you are a Visionary, you probably enjoy talking about radical things. You often hash over ideas, plans, and dreams. There will be a thousand ideas for every project attempted, and most of those attempted will never be finished, and most of those that are completed will not matter to anyone but you. Solomon said, "I have seen all the works that are done under the sun; and, behold, all is vanity and vexation of spirit." Ecclesiastes 1:14

✓ If we spend our lives dreaming and scheming but fail to impart meaning to the life of that one special woman, our existence is a failure. Over time, a wise Visionary will become more practical. The world needs the Visionary Man, for he is the one who seeks out hypocrisy and injustice and slays the dragons. He calls himself and those around him to a higher standard. He knows how to do nearly everything, or thinks he does, and is ready to advise others. In time, if he maintains his integrity, he will be quite accomplished in many things.

✓ You are a man with a mission. As a Visionary you will be subjective, thinking about feelings, moods, and spiritual insights. You will spend your life looking through a telescope or microscope, and will be stunned that what you see is of little interest to others. Looking though your microscope, little things that others cannot see will look large to you, and small things so far away that no one else considers them will be large in your perspective. You will not be understood, and you will be blamed for your lack of practicality. You are not balanced. No man is. It is knowing yourself that enables you to be patient with others and cautious of yourself.

**It is knowing yourself that enables you to be patient with others and cautious of yourself.**

✓ You need to find balance. Sometimes that is only achieved by bumping into hard realities. The Old Testament prophets of God must surely have been the Visionary types. Remember Elijah, Jeremiah, and Ezekiel and all their trials? A wise man will know that he has a large hole in his thinking and needs his wife to help him keep his feet from rising too far above solid ground. He needs to have a very balanced, steady friend that is not afraid to laugh at his newest idea and then offer some commonsense suggestions. Every visionary needs to be open to the wisdom of a good friend, especially in regard to relationships, finances, or health.

✓ As a Visionary you will be the initiator, the point man, trailblazer, and a voice calling others to a mission. With your enthusiasm and faith you will start and keep the movement going until the Command Man gets there to organize the troops into practical action.

✓ As a Visionary you expect others to believe with the same fervency as you. When they don't understand or they resist your vision, you will be prone to push harder and may have a tendency to become bitter with blame. It is important that you keep a good attitude toward others and resist becoming unteachable. A bitter Visionary can be dangerous like a broken tool. You must keep your spirit free from criticism and judgment of others. Be content to pursue your vision alone if necessary. Respect the right of others to ignore you or to believe differently.

**Of the three types of men you most naturally kindle in a woman what she most needs—to be needed.**

✓ Teach your wife the passage found in I Peter 3:1-2 concerning a chaste conversation. Remind her to be positive in her conversation and outlook so as not to stir your ire. Ask her to help you by not speaking negatively of others. Stop her in the middle of her conversation if she encourages your criticism of others. Remind her of your tendencies to brood. Ask her to pray with and for you. When she sees you are serious, she will change her conversation.

✓ As a Visionary you will need your lady to be patient and filled with joy. A wise man will cultivate his wife so she stands ready with a smile and a cautioning word as is needed.

✓ As a Visionary you can be a leader. Similar to a Command Man, if you are making sense your passion will draw others to your cause, but because of your tunnel vision, your leadership will have a more narrow focus. A wise man will know both his strengths and weaknesses.

✓ Of the three types of men you most naturally kindle in a woman what she most needs—to be needed. This is why your woman will be glad to put up with your eccentric ways. She will know her input in your life is priceless. You need a friend, a buddy, someone to listen to your newest idea and to appreciate your heart. You, of all the images, most need a help meet.

## Mr. Visionary's Five Ls

- ✓ Listen
- ✓ Love
- ✓ Laugh
- ✓ Labor
- ✓ Leave

**Listen:** Be willing to stop your dreams long enough to hear your wife's concerns. At her urging, seek counsel from another man of wisdom—a Steady Man, but not another Visionary.

**Love:** Love her and appreciate her at home and publicly. She goes through a lot on your behalf, so she needs to know you truly recognize her sacrifice.

**Laugh:** Look back and laugh at some of your crazy ideas, dreams, and the schemes you once thought were so wonderful. When your sweetie hears you making light of your own past ideas she will breathe a sigh of relief, knowing you are maturing in your thinking.

**Labor:** Labor in gainful employment even when you feel like dreaming. Life is not just fulfilling your dreams; it is about doing your duty. You must conquer your weakness and drive yourself to do as the breadwinner ought.

**Leave:** Seriously consider moving far away from both sets of in-laws for the first year or two of your marriage, or at least until you and your honey are firmly made into one heart and mind. She doesn't need anyone pointing out how crazy your ideas are. She will see enough with her own eyes. If she doesn't have her parents or your parents reinforcing her fears, she will have a better chance of developing into a helpful mate.

## Added Benefits

Mr. Visionary is not boring. Few would read a blog written by Mr. Steady. Some might read one written by Mr. Command, but when Mr. Visionary has a blog everyone enjoys reading because it is certain to be bizarre. Use your strengths and gifts cautiously. It is easy to take notoriety as a statement of being right.

## Wish List from the Ladies

- ✓ "I wish he didn't misinterpret my motives. I mean him goodwill but he takes my suggestion as a personal insult."
- ✓ "I wish he would be more positive. His down-in-the-mouth attitude leaves the family defeated."
- ✓ "I wish he would be more consistent in what he tells me. He tells me it's okay to do something, then gets mad because something else was set aside when I did what he told me I could do."
- ✓ "I wish he would notice when I do something right. I try so hard to please him but he forgets to ever say, 'thank you'."
- ✓ "I wish he wouldn't stare at pretty girls. It makes me feel old and ugly."
- ✓ "I wish he was patient, more understanding, less critical."
- ✓ "I wish he could make me feel more valuable and important to him than his friends, relatives, and hobbies."
- ✓ "I wish he would be more considerate when I'm sick or hurting. He almost seems mad if I am sick because I can't be his servant."
- ✓ "I wish he would spank the kids instead of yelling at them."
- ✓ "I wish we could do fun things together."
- ✓ "I wish he would stop being angry at little things that happen."
- ✓ "I wish he would give me time to think before he thinks aloud for me. When he asks me for input, I would like for him to actually consider it."

**Let your moderation be known unto
all men. The Lord is at hand.**
Philippians 4:5

Chapter 7

# MR. STEADY

## Visionary, <u>Steady</u>, Command

God the Son is as steady as an eternal rock, caring, providing, and faithful in his ministry as priest. He created many men in his priestly image. They are the backbone of society, the middle ground that keeps the world moving on a steady course. They are not given to extremes. We are calling them **Steady Men**. Everyone feels comfortable with Mr. Steady. Down South he is called "a good ole' boy." Up North they call him a taxpayer—or, more accurately, hardhat worker, farmer, repairman, maintenance man, and the endless line of white collar workers filling the cubicles.

> **Steady Men are the backbone of society.**

The Steady Man doesn't jump up and change occupations in midlife, and he is not consumed with revolutionary ideas. He is constant and reliable, minding his own business, not taking any chances with his money. He is the one who begins accumulating savings and maintains a growing account all his life, or for forty years he works at the same place anticipating his retirement and medical benefits. He avoids controversy. He is not a tornado or hurricane like the Visionary; he is a constant tide, predictable. And like the tide, he is in the majority. He will build the factory and manage the assembly line that utilizes the robot that Mr. Visionary designed, and in the end he will know more about it than the guy that designed it, making practical suggestions that will improve the next generation of robots.

The Steady Man does not organize political movements. He does not make speeches at town hall meetings. He will not tackle a bank robber or attempt to rescue hostages unless led by a Command Man. He would never lead a revolution against the government or the church. He will quietly ignore hypocrisy in others. He will selflessly fight the wars that Mr. Visionary starts and Mr. Command leads. He builds the skyscrapers and the interstate highways, grows the wheat and corn, attends church, and peacefully raises his family. He is the one who buys the row house and lives at the same address for the rest of his life. His family may think he is an old fogy and boring, but he is greatly loved.

**The Steady Man is the one most likely to remain married to the same woman.**

Young women are generally not excited by the Steady Man, but as they grow older they come to appreciate the peace and safety he provides. For that reason the Steady Man is the one most likely to remain married to the same woman. Divorcees usually leave a radical Visionary or an overbearing Command Man looking for a Mr. Steady, but he is rarely available except where a foolish woman seeking excitement leaves him, looking for more romance. This man is content with the wife of his youth. But it is often the case that the wife of his youth is not so content with her Steady Man. She desires to see more spontaneity or spirituality or aggression, so she grows critical.

A Steady Man's progress will be marked by slow, steady growth. If a Steady Man is poor, he either accepts his poverty and learns to serve others with what little he has, or he faints with hopelessness and lives without vision; whereas a Visionary may wildly succeed and then lose everything on a venture, only to get up and fight another round. Or the Visionary may grow bitter and blame others for his failures, but the Steady Man keeps his own council and finds little occasion to blame others.

Down South, a good number of the Steady Men are named Bubba and everybody likes them. They will stop work and talk with you for an hour, never seeming rushed or anxious. If you interrupt a Visionary at work, you have to talk to his back side. He has "important things to do." If you interrupt a Command Man, he will put you to work after explaining exactly how the job is to be done.

## Steady Man Positives and Negatives

Being a Steady Man has its positives and negatives. On the positive side, you are a good husband. You would never put pressure on your wife or make unreasonable demands. You don't expect her to be your servant as may Mr. Command Man. And unlike Mr. Visionary, your wife never has to deal with emotional fires. You rarely make your wife feel hurried, pushed, pressured, or forced. The women married to Visionary Men look at you in wonder because you seem so stable. The wife of Command Man marvels at the free time your wife seems to have. You seem so balanced.

On the negative side, it is that very balance that some women find boring and unchallenging. Like a rock, there is less movement in the Steady Man. He is not as likely to seek glory and praise. He is not going to be out front. There is less mystery in him, less intrigue and drama. He is slow to change and slow to make decisions. His spirituality is revealed in practical ways rather than outward expressions. Not being a leader, he may appear to be less interested and involved than the Visionary and Command Man. A Steady Man, slow to make up his mind, may wait so long he misses the boat while others get a cabin with a view.

## Ocean Tides

Women, like the ocean, are given to tides, storms, change, and upheaval; they are unpredictable, their moods changing unexpectedly. Like the tides, it's the moon's gravitational pull that sets a female's monthly cycle, making her hormones go amok. When her hormones are off balance, your life will be also. It takes degrees in chemistry and several of the soft sciences to even claim to understand the ladies during that time, and anybody that claims to understand them is lying.

Early in our marriage it came to my attention that when my wife pitched a hissy fit it was during her monthly cycle. So, being the smart fellow I am, I simply used a little logic and explained to her that she was not really upset at me; it was just her hormones. That is when women really became a mystery to me. I thought she would be relieved to hear that I was not as bad as she was making me out to be, it was really just an uncontrollable physical fault in the female as a result of the fall—part of the curse, you know—punishment on the man for listening to his wife in the first place. Wow, she would go ballistic, denying that it had anything to do with her hormones. But it was clear to me, once a month she had a discharge and I was it. In my smooth logic I called her attention to the fact that the last three explosions were exactly one month apart on about the third day of her cycle. She just got more irate, telling me all my faults. It was then that I learned a woman has a lot better memory than a man. They can remember the smallest things, like when you failed to clean up after yourself 22 days ago, or when you said you were going to fix the door 19 days ago and never got around to it, or how insensitive your remark at church was two weeks ago. None of this stuff had bothered her until now, so it was clear that the devil took away her patience and left her with a critical spirit.

I eventually learned my lesson: keep her pregnant and hang in there until she goes through menopause, although I have heard menopause makes some women crazier than ever. But not mine; it only turned her into a sweat machine. Every time I get near her she breaks out in a sweat, but at least I know my presence makes her hot! At any rate, you younger men can keep a calendar of your wife's cycles and about two days before she starts, take her out to eat, fix something around the house, and apologize for anything you can think of.

> **Knowledge is key in a relationship. To truly "know" in the Biblical sense one must be completely open and honest in marriage, free to speak and dream without criticism.**

If my mature wisdom hasn't shed much light on this great mystery of the female, understand this: Females can only stand a certain amount of calm waters before they create a storm of their own. It would seem that the Steady Man's greatest error is providing days and days of calm, flat water. When you take a week to make a simple decision without ever so much as talking about what is going on in your mind, you will drive your lady crazy. The fact that a Steady Man doesn't talk about the weird guy at church and doesn't even seem to be disturbed that his crazy brother is leaving his wife, is mind-boggling to a Steady Man's wife. To her you often appear to have more in common with a rock than a live human.

## Drama, Drama

As a rule, women occasionally like to be stirred up. Visionaries and Command Men supply all the tension a woman can stand, but the Steady Man provides only dull stability. If you are the steady and cautious type, and your wife has a little of the impatient romantic in her, which most women do, then she may not see your value as clearly as do others. She may chafe at your cautiousness in taking authority. Women like to fill a vacuum, and they will fill it in a hurry. But hurry is not in the tool kit of a Steady Man. When you appear to drag your feet at making decisions, it will agitate her. A dominant woman sees her husband's lack of hasty judgment and calls her Steady husband "wishy-washy." His steadiness makes him the last to change, the last to react; he is seldom out front forming up the troops. The Steady Man is just too practical to understand his wife's aggressive need for excitement and immediate action. That is the great impasse.

Be assured, Mr. Steady, your wife will prod you to make up your mind and take a stand in church or business conflicts. She will whine that you seem to let people use you. Most of the time she will wish you would boldly tell her what to do so she would not have to carry all the burden of decision-making. This pushing and pulling wears her out. These wives equate their husband's wise caution and lack of open passion as being unspiritual. Good Brother, you are in trouble, and it doesn't just come on the full moon.

To compound your problems, you may be married to the type woman my wife calls a "Go-to Gal." Other people have been known to refer to them as bossy. Steady Men seem to be drawn to dominant women. I think in courtship Mr. Steady is not aggressive, so when some beautiful babe continually tries to get his attention, he is awed. Mr. Visionary would rebuke her. Mr. Command wouldn't even like her, for he is attracted to gentle, quiet girls that possess a natural desire to serve; whereas Mr. Steady enjoys her aggressive interest in him. But that is courtship and this book is dealing with marriage, so what happens after you say *I do*? She is still the aggressor, and you are still the guy that finds it interesting to just watch her in action, but now that she has won her man she has no challenges, and is not as ready to settle down as are you. Trouble is brewing.

In a tug-of-war between husband and wife, the Command Man commands his wife to drop her end of the rope and join him. The Visionary hooks his end of the rope to a tractor, and Mr. Steady just ties the rope to his butt and sits on it. Some women would much rather argue with a Command Man or pull against a tractor than to pull against a seemingly indifferent stationary object.

## The Making of a Shrew

I feel sorry for Go-to wives married to Steady Men. They are like kids visiting the zoo strapped into a stroller. Consider this: When a woman is married to a bossy, dominant Command Man, people marvel that she is willing to serve him without complaint, so she comes out looking like a wonderful woman of great patience and sacrifice. A woman married to the impulsive Visionary who puts the family through hardships will stir amazement in everyone. "How can she tolerate his peculiar ideas with such peace and joy?" She comes out being a real saint, maybe even a martyr. But if the wife of a kind, gentle man grows anxious in demanding action, she appears overbearing and bossy. He will always appear to be the underdog and she the dog. A Command Man would channel her energies and ideas to his own end. A Visionary would give her a cause along with the headache he imparts. But the Steady Man leaves her on idle until she could scream, "Get up and do something!"

> **Your wife needs a vision, a purpose; she needs to be employing her gifts and talents helping you become successful.**

When you help her, adore her, protect her, and provide for all her needs, she still seems to be unhappy and unthankful. How can you please that kind of woman? She is well aware that others think she is a shrew, and it makes her worse. Wives don't do well under condemnation. No one does. Poor lady; it is better to be treated badly by her man than have half the church thinking she is a bossy brat.

Disappointment and unthankfulness can make a woman wearier than any amount of labor. Her trials are conceived in discontentment over what she perceives to be your shortcomings. This is why many disgruntled wives married to Mr. Steadies fall victim to "hormonal imbalances," physical illnesses, or emotional problems. Is your lady sickly? I have seen many sick women get happy and then get healthy when their Mr. Steady gave them a challenging job.

## Wrong Response

As a Steady/Priestly Man, your natural response to your lady's unhappiness is exactly the opposite of what she needs. You will be confused at your wife's unhappiness and try to serve her more, which may further diminish her respect for your masculinity. Your weakness is giving over when what she really needs is for you to make some simple decisions—now, not tomorrow—and stick with them regardless of who pushes you. But you must pick your battles and make sure you are in the right, that you are not acting selfishly or with malice. She should be able to eventually see that you were wise and correct in the stand you took. As a woman hates a vacuum, she loves just authority. Justice without authority is weakness, and authority without justice is tyranny, but just authority is peace and security for a woman.

Welcome to being a husband and trying to understand the female nature. It would be easier to fix a recently discovered World War I land mine. But be assured, she is just as confused trying to understand what makes you tick as you are about what alarms her.

The lady who lies by your side each night doesn't know what goes on in your mind. She wants to see, hear, feel, and know what you are thinking; she wants to be your suitable helper, not just your wife. As Mr. Steady, you don't go around with your ideas scrolling across your forehead. For a woman, just knowing how you think and feel is sooooo romantic. Your lady hungers to share your dreams and to know what you are feeling. She would be much more patient with your reluctance to make a decision if she just knew you were carefully weighing the issues.

Unless you step up and take charge, you are providing a context for your wife to look and act like a shrew. You are placing more temptation on her than she is able—or willing—to bear. It is your job to sanctify and cleanse your wife of all impurities. If you become the man she needs, she will become the woman you want.

## Healing

Dear Mike,

I am writing in response to your request for info for your new book. The most amazing thing happened in our marriage a few years ago, when, after almost 20 years of being married, my husband gave me the gift of time alone with him in prayer on a consistent basis. This began revolutionizing our relationship. Now we say things in prayer that have never come easily between us. We pray about tough issues, past hurts, hopes, dreams, etc. We were able to cover subjects that we hadn't been able to approach for various reasons . . . mostly over-sensitivity and/or defensiveness on one or both parts. This time together became a refuge, and I looked forward to being able to bring up important events, problems with the kids, conflicts within; I finally was getting to know him. It is the best gift he has ever given me. He told me that he battled within himself to do it because getting started was so uncomfortable for him. We have both reaped incredible benefits because he took the incentive and made a decision to lead! All I want is to be a good help meet to this wonderful Mr. Steady. Now he looks forward to our time in prayer as much as I do.

Louise

## Knowledge Is Key

A man avoids intimacy of soul when he has something to hide, possibly the shame of ongoing evil in his soul, fear of being known for who he really is; or some men just lack confidence, feeling that if they are truly known they will be rejected. Others have been hurt by people they loved and have developed a defensive position of remaining beyond emotional reach so they cannot be hurt or rejected again. What people don't know, they can't throw back in your face. I don't like my wife to read my "to-do list" because I don't want her to remind me of what I need to do.

**Knowledge is key in a relationship.**

The Bible says, "Adam **knew** his wife and she conceived . . . " Copulation is identified with intimate knowledge. Men desire sex; wives desire intimacy—with exceptions. What is the difference? Many men and some women seek sex without intimacy, and they are never satisfied with the experience, only addicted to its pursuit.

**A great marriage is a sanctuary.**

Knowledge is key in a relationship. To truly "know" in the Biblical sense one must be completely open and honest in marriage, free to speak and dream without criticism. A great marriage is a sanctuary where you are never laughed at unless you make a dumb joke; you are never mocked or ridiculed, and old failures are never brought to mind. The two never use their intimate knowledge to hurt the other. It is a safe place, a garden of rest and peace, a refreshing drink of sweet juices, a place of healing and

safety. If you don't talk to your spouse—really talk from the
are depriving her of yourself, leaving her without knowledge

The Steady Man can make small talk all day with acquaintand
often has a hard time sharing his heart and soul with his woman. He has
close friends who he enjoys spending time with, discussing a variety
of things, but really opening up to his wife doesn't come naturally. The
poor, lonely lady never feels she knows her man or that he really knows
her. Emotionally, she hangs in limbo.

Communicating with his lady is easy for both Mr. Command and Mr.
Visionary—with exceptions of course. But you, Mr. Steady, are very
uncomfortable teaching or praying with your wife. If you want to be a
wise Mr. Steady with a good marriage, you will make an effort to teach
your wife even if it means simply reading a book with her or listening
to a preaching MP3 together. Memorizing Scripture together would
also be an easy way to study together. Praying together while lying in
bed at night will help a woman become more settled and secure. Once
you start certain habits it is not so hard to continue. It will mean a lot to
your honey.

## Understanding Your Roles

If Mr. Steady Turtle were to come out of
his shell, what could he do immediately
that would encourage his wife? First,
you need to address her concerns that
you are not spiritually minded and are
not open to her. I have read her concern
in a thousand letters.

**To be a whole person,
well rounded, sometimes
we must get out of our
comfort zones and act in
ways that are not natural
to our types.**

"He is not the spiritual leader. I just pray and pray that he will
step up and do what God has designed him to do as head of our
home. He won't even pray with the family at meals."

You can fix the problem. Lead the family in prayer at the table. At least
once a day, express your gratitude for God's blessings on your family,
either in family prayer or just an offhanded comment. Set aside a time
each day when you and your wife sit down together to read the Scriptures.

Announce that the two of you are going to review all the Scripture on the duties of husbands and wives. Write on a calendar the verses you will read each day. Go slow, "here a little, there a little." If you don't like to read then tell her to read aloud to you because you like the sound of her voice. Discuss the texts. She needs to know that you are aware of what God says about your duty, and she needs to know what God says about her responsibilities as a wife. Sharing your heart is what will change her actions.

Certain passages are key for a Mr. Steady and his help meet to read together. First Peter chapter 3 talks about a wife being in subjection. Titus 2 covers the man and his wife's positions before God. Ephesians 5 is often used in marriage counseling, as is Colossians chapter 3. These verses are not for you to use to lord over your wife, and I would not recommend Mr. Command or Mr. Visionary read these verses to their wives unless they just happened to be reading through that book of the Bible.

But if you, Mr. Steady, will open a dialogue with your wife she will relax, knowing that you are not asleep at the wheel. Then she can begin to trust your quiet spiritual leadership.

## Your Wife's Greatest Need

In good economic times the vast majority of letters our office receives are from women criticizing their laid-back, quiet, slow, unassuming, undemanding, hardworking husbands for their "carnal" habits. These women are not rebellious; they are just floundering in uselessness. In times past when people were less affluent, these women would be busy just trying to survive. Mr. Steady's wife would be hauling water, milking cows, growing a garden, and preserving thousands of pounds of food for the coming months. She would be a grand asset. Now these ladies married to Steady Men are just ornaments, and it is a boring, unrewarding job.

> **Your wife needs a vision, a purpose; she needs to be employing her gifts and talents helping you become successful.**

Your wife needs a vision, a purpose; she needs to be employing her gifts and talents helping you become successful. You, as a Steady/Priestly Man, need to help your wife be a thriving success. Let her know you would like her to show some initiative. If she grew up under a Command or Visionary father, the idea of accomplishing something apart from you might seem unfeminine. She might need more than just an encouraging word; she might need a clear directive. Would you like her to learn accounting, photography, natural medicine, or some other skill? What has she shown an interest in? Ask her to study Proverbs 31:10-31. Have her choose key words that describe a virtuous woman. Ask her to think about what she wants to learn and accomplish. She needs to be assured that you will not see her success as competition but as a complement to your goals. Tell her that you want her to use her natural skills, abilities, and drives to add to your life as a couple. Let her know that her achievements will be an honor to you. If she is uncomfortable with it, teach her how to handle money and invest it with an eye toward profit, how to pay bills, make appointments, and entertain guests with competence.

Don't just finance an idle hobby. Invest in her side business or venture with an eye toward financial returns. It is very important for her to succeed in something worthy and even bring in additional income as long as it doesn't hinder her family responsibilities. She needs to know her success is HER success.

Encourage her to adopt hobbies that involve your children so she can teach them to be busy and productive every day. At the end of the day, talk to her about what she has accomplished and rejoice in the value of having a worthy partner in the grace of life. All women will thrive under this opportunity, but few would reach it without their husband's strong encouragement. A Go-to Gal will think she is in heaven. No need for drama if she is fighting the winds of business or struggling to help someone. Every day will be glorious.

My wife has directed many Go-to wives into activities like helping stop abortions, and lately she has encouraged ladies to establish ministries to stop child sex slavery. This terrible plague is growing at alarming rates here in America. Every state in our union is guilty of entertaining this debauchery. Your wife could be making a difference in our society while growing as a person. Children are not the only ones that need a good self-image.

## Your Role as a Steady/Priestly Man

In the church, Steady/Priest-natured men are very important to stability because they are compassionate, steadfast, and loyal. Their lack of hastiness in making decisions puts the brakes on potential conflicts. They help bring balance when a headstrong Visionary gets out of line. Priestly/Steady Men are rarely rash or foolish, although (to their discredit) they will sometimes tolerate foolishness or error without dissent. A Visionary doesn't make as good an elder as does a Steady Man. The Visionary/Prophet types make better evangelistic preachers and reformers. The Command Man is more suited to eldership, although a plurality of elders should contain all three types with Steady Men predominant. The modern concept of pastor (though not Biblical) is best filled by a Command Man.

Usually Mr. Steady's children grow up to highly respect their gentle-speaking dad. If mother has been negative towards Dad, the adult children will strongly resent her. It is a man's responsibility to make sure this doesn't happen. Children need to grow up adoring their mother, lest they have emotional issues as adults. When you walk together as a team, your children will admire you as successful people. It is good soil for the seeds of little souls.

Women and men alike are drawn to a Command Man. Likewise people are often drawn and compelled by the volatile Visionary, finding him exciting and stimulating. But the Steady Man is taken for granted. He is like the pain you don't have and don't know you don't have it, whereas the Visionary is a chronic sensation—good or bad.

The Steady Man is seldom a campaigner. He is needed, but not flashy enough to win the spotlight. He will never brag on himself and is typically very poor at promoting himself and his skills. A Visionary will sell you a handmade hat before he attempts to make one. The Command Man will organize others to make the hats, but the Steady Man will take the job and undersell his product and forget to put his label on it.

The Steady Man employed by the Visionary or Command Man does not promote himself and does not do as well in management, not being comfortable telling others what to do. His employer may not know his value until he is no longer employed.

Many Steady Men become quite competent in their fields and rise to own a business. When they first employ others to work in their business, they find it difficult to command their employees—even more difficult to fire them. Even a good employee never knows if he is pleasing his boss. In time Steady Men mature and assume a more commanding role, but it is emotionally difficult for them at first.

Typically, Steady Men do not become as well known as Command or Visionary Men. They are not odd or standout men. They are not loud. They are neither irritating nor particularly magnificent. If they do rise to public notice, it will be because of a great achievement or because they are trusted for their very visible traits of honesty and steadiness. Yet they are so well liked that when they die a greater number of people attend their funerals.

## Mr. Steady's Most Damning Sin

Some Steady Men who lack a vision, and therefore lack motivation, will eat too much, sleep too much, and watch too many movies or play questionable video games when they should be with their families. Many Steady Men are known to cross out their humanity on their Xbox. Basically, they will take their ease more than they ought. Through video games and media of all kinds, the lounging Steady Man will open the door of his home to devils who then steal the souls of his children and erode his marriage until the family is more a type of hell than of heavenly love. The withdrawn Steady Man will sit on the sidelines condemning but doing nothing while socialists take over the country, the preacher dabbles in false doctrine, his wife develops a deep relationship with a dominant woman, and his kids spend time with their lascivious neighbors.

**Make sure you are a friend of God.**

If that characterization fits you in some measure, then it is understandable why your wife is pushy and demanding. She sees the family in danger of manslaughter and you sit like a frog on a log trying to decide whether you should jump or go back to sleep. You would rather keep your nice guy handle than suffer the emotional trauma of standing up for country, community, or even family.

God tells us whom he favors and why. Abraham was a man highly favored of God because he was active teaching and leading his children. "For I know him, that he will command his children and his household after him, and they shall keep the way of the LORD, to do justice and judgment; that the LORD may bring upon Abraham that which he hath spoken of him." Genesis 18:19

Abraham was called "A friend of God." As a Steady Man you have more friends than do the other two images, but make sure you are a friend of God.

To be a whole person, well rounded, sometimes we must get out of our comfort zones and act in ways that are not natural to our types. The Command Man must slow down and show a priestly side when it is called for. The Visionary must set aside his drive to do great things and work like a Steady Man. And the Steady Man must rouse himself to command his family and children and adopt a vision of something greater than peace through pacification. There will be many times in your life when you will need to make a splash, offending many, and throwing caution to the wind. To do nothing or to delay action is often the most damning of all sins.

## Your Guiding Verse

**Rev. 3:15-16** I know thy works, that thou art neither cold nor hot: I would thou wert cold or hot. So then because thou art lukewarm, and neither cold nor hot, I will spue thee out of my mouth.

## Dominant Mamas and Dawdling Daddies

We have received many letters from young ladies whose marriage plans have just been crushed by decisions made by their dominant mothers. The stories are the same over and over again. It's almost like there is a species of mother out there that is predestined to repeat this patterned response so as to fulfill some twisted dark destiny, and their Steady husbands dawdle away in dreamland. It is the stuff from which tragic love stories are written by old spinsters whose mothers destroyed their one chance at happiness while henpecked Father sat by quietly.

The events unfold like this: There is an easygoing Steady Man who doesn't say much and has always allowed his wife to take the lead in family matters, mostly because he wants to keep the peace instead of listening to her give him a piece of her mind. The daughter is a happy, obedient young lady with great hope for a glorious marriage. Into their lives comes a young man that is attracted to their daughter. Mother immediately likes him because not only is he highly moral and disciplined, having made preparation for his future, but he is exciting too. Not like her dull husband, he is commanding and has a vision of accomplishing great things. Mother would be proud to have him as a son-in-law, and Daddy goes along to get along, liking the fellow just fine and glad his daughter is going to get such a fine husband.

But when we get the letter from the young lady, stuff has hit the fan. After planning the wedding and going through several months of the families getting to know each other, Mother discovers that her exciting prospective son-in-law is not like her submissive husband; he is "self-willed." He acts like he is a king or a prophet. He is stubborn and opinionated. Mother characterizes him as "not kind" or "not teachable." The young man has recognized the mother-in-law's overbearing attitude and has taken charge. He may have made it clear that when they are married they are going to do things a certain way—regarding homeschooling, or where they live, or what church they go to, or any number of life choices. Mostly it is just his personality she doesn't like. He acts like he intends to be head of the family in ways this mother doesn't appreciate. So after failing to persuade him to make changes in his personal demeanor, she calls off or postpones the wedding. Postponing is more to her liking because she can use this time to "get the boy in line" by holding the bait in front of him.

But the boy is too much of a man to put up with the old biddy. The girl is brokenhearted and blames her Steady father for not taking a stand against her domineering mother. But he has his head down, making sure he doesn't catch any flack. His wife makes the bed and allows him to sleep in it, so he doesn't want to pull the rug out from under her. The young man, being a King (Command Man) or a Prophet (Visionary), is not at all wired to cater to a bossy woman, and he has too much pride to grovel. There are plenty of other fish in the pond, so he winds up his line and goes downstream to fish, careful to "not again make the same mistake" of getting involved with one of those "courtship" families where Mother presides over the court.

The most tragic letters are those we receive from girls in their thirties who have given up hope. They had one chance at marriage eight years earlier and Mother "didn't feel the leading of the Lord" in it. And Daddy is still sitting in the same chair, watching old *Gunsmoke* programs on Netflix. Hey, Mr. Steady, grow a pair and tell the lady when to cease and desist. She might even begin to find you exciting for a change.

Remember, your responsibility as a husband is to sanctify and cleanse your wife with your words, not support and condone with your silence. As a Priest your love is made known to your wife by nourishing and cherishing her, even as the Lord the church. She will know you love her by your willingness to lay aside your uneasiness in taking the lead on important issues. Love doesn't just allow; it leads in the right direction.

And now you have a disgruntled old maid to take care of until you die. Thanks, Mama, that was a real cool move. And Father can go back to watching Matt Dillon and Kitty; there are now two unhappy women in the house.

I know, I know, I have an attitude. After hearing from 500 old maids blaming their bossy mothers and laid back daddies, I've earned the right.

## Five Ts of a Steady Man

- ✓ Tell
- ✓ Take action
- ✓ Teach
- ✓ Talk
- ✓ Target

**Tell** her what is on your mind—every day, every night.

**Take** action even if you don't really care which way things go. Be aware of everything going on in the family and function as the manager.

**Teach** your wife to be productive and useful as your help meet.

**Talk** to her like you would if she were a very good friend and business partner. Explain your goals and how she is helping that dream come true. Talk to her about what you have already accomplished and what your goals are as a team.

**Target** key issues in your life. The dictionary meaning of the word *target* is "an object aimed at." The second meaning is "goal or objective toward which effort is directed." You need to incorporate both meanings in your life. Focus on a goal and go forward.

## Your Theme

Get out of your comfort zone and assume the headship of your family, for the lives of many people are affected by your actions or the lack thereof.

## Proffered Points to Ponder

- ✓ Of the three types, you, the Steady Man, are most liked by everyone.

- ✓ As a Steady/Priestly type, bringing comfort to those in need is easy. You seem to know what a person needs in times of great sorrow. Your still, quiet presence brings peace. That is one area the Command Man will back away from and surrender to another. There is nothing that makes him more uncomfortable.

- ✓ You are not a leader. You will not thrive if you are thrust into the position of a Command Man. So pursue those areas that are most consistent with your nature and give attention to commanding when it is called for. Outside the family you were not meant to lead, but to support. Don't let your wife push you into a commanding position. Know your strengths and strengthen your weaknesses, but don't choose a path contrary to your nature.

- ✓ As a Steady/Priestly Man your strongest trait is that you do not focus on the eternal picture, nor do you look through a microscope at the details, but you do respect both perspectives. You are the glue that makes both Visionary and Command Men able to function as a team. Without your balance there will be stress between them.

- ✓ You bring balance. If you will lead and direct your wife, as a couple you will bring balance to many people. Together you will be the key to any organization, church, or community. When it is needed you must step out of your comfort zone and rule your wife to keep her from becoming a problem for everyone else. You, Good Brother, must get off your comfortable recliner and get your house in order.

## Female Emotional Breakdowns

Mr. Pearl,

I have a few words to contribute to your men's book. I call it: **What Men Should Do and Not Do.**

As I am sure you have noticed, women are very emotional creatures. Sometimes crazy hormones or over-the-top emotions get the better of us. Now these instances should never happen, but we are human and sometimes they simply do (like after the birth of a child or the day before our periods are due to start). My desire for all married men is that they understand the following:

✓   She is just having a "moment" so, please, don't take her seriously.

✓   Perhaps just step out of the room for half an hour.

✓   Go buy her some chocolate and be sure to give her a hug.

✓   Then move on from the "moment" and let her move on too.

This is not a cop-out, only a plea for some occasional room to be emotional.

Hopeful Lady,

Amy

## Other Suggestions from the Ladies

✓   A man needs to understand when his wife is having an emotional fit. He needs to just pretend that she is acting completely as she should, and just hold her in his arms and tell her how much he loves her.

✓   I think all men should understand that a woman has times when she is not as emotionally equipped as other times. During such times she might yell or demand things that she normally would not. He should not take this occasion to tell her what is right or wrong but just give her time to get things together.

✓   Sometimes I feel real emotional and my husband just tries to calm me, which makes me feel worse. I wish he would just let me cry and yell and not get upset with me.

✓ When I am mad and on a frustrated rampage, when I cry, when I'm moody or ornery, just give me a hug.

✓ Don't tell me I must be on my period and will feel better later.

**Neither be ye called masters:
for one is your Master,
even Christ.
But he that is greatest among
you shall be your servant.
And whosoever shall exalt
himself shall be abased; and
he that shall humble himself
shall be exalted.**
Matthew 23:10-12

Chapter 8

# THE COMMAND MAN

## Visionary, Steady, <u>Command</u>

God the Father is King, ruler of the universe, commander of heaven's forces, the fullness of the godhead. He is dominant, sovereign, omnipotent God. Since God created man in his image, after his plural likeness, some men more naturally express the image of the Father. Those men that bear the image of the father are the dominant leaders among us. They have a way of rising to the top and organizing other men into a functioning group. For obvious reasons, we hesitate to call them kings, just as we hesitate to call the Visionaries among us prophets, or the Steady Men priests. Since there are benevolent kings and tyrannical dictators in this group, we chose to call them by the more generic name of Command Man. As we said before, that fits the good, the bad, and the ugly natured alike.

These Command Men are readily recognizable. They have what is called *gravitas* or *presence*. When they walk in the room and speak, everyone stops to listen. When they make a suggestion it sounds like a command. The history of invention and innovation is the trail left by the Visionary Men, those created in the image of the Holy Spirit, the prophet of the godhead. The history of medicine and orphanages and agricultural is the trail left by the Steady Men, the priestly men created in the image of God's Son, the priest of God, the compassionate healer and shepherd of lost sheep. But the history of war and the rise and fall of empires is the bloody trail of the Command Man, the king seeking a kingdom. Ship captains, presidents, kings, and czars are the roles filled by Command Men. To these men we owe our countries, our liberties or our enslavement, our victories and our defeats, our civilizations, and our local organizations. They were the Hitlers, the Moses, and the Maccabees. Patton and Rommel were quintessential Command Men, as was Stalin. The moral extremes expressed in the many Command Men reveals that the image of God is marred in all of us, some more than others.

Since our world needs only a few leaders, God seems to have limited the number of Command Men. There seem to be many Steady Men for every Command Man. They are marked by a lack of interest in small talk or insignificant, petty complaints. They are not as quick to blame others for their plight but ready to dismiss the inept. In the arena of conflicting ideas, Command Men are often able to see the full picture and encapsulate it to the satisfaction of both sides. People like clarity. For the average Joe, the Command Man seems wiser than normal. In a way he is. The Command Man doesn't focus on the minor points or the emotional side of an issue. His objectivity springs from his nature as an overseer. He considers the issues in light of all concerned.

> **In the arena of conflicting ideas, Command Men are often able to see the full picture and encapsulate it to the satisfaction of both sides.**

That is the nature of a commander. In war, it will not do to have a Steady Man in charge. He would sacrifice the mission and even the war to save his men. His compassion rules above his head. Nor would it do to have a Visionary in charge. If he felt like it was "a good day to die" and he could "stick it to the enemy," he would risk sacrificing everyone just to make a magnificent and glorious statement. But the Command Man considers the overall picture and weighs the cost against achieving the objective.

### Luke 14:31-32

31 Or what king, going to make war against another king, sitteth not down first, and consulteth whether he be able with ten thousand to meet him that cometh against him with twenty thousand?

32 Or else, while the other is yet a great way off, he sendeth an ambassage, and desireth conditions of peace.

And when the rank and file face the guns, it is the Steady Men who stand shoulder to shoulder and go into harm's way to protect their families and their nation. Visionaries start wars. Command Men lead them, and the Steady Men fight them. Remember, there are Command Men on both sides of any war. The Japanese fleet that bombed Pearl Harbor was led by Command Men. There is no virtue in our image itself, but in the use we make of it.

Command Men disproportionally fill the pulpits due to their tendency to push their way to the front, and because of the inclination of the public to mistake a commanding personality for spiritual power and authority. If the truth be told, it is rare to find a Command Man qualified to be a pastor, because he does not focus on the individual. The Steady/Priest Man is best equipped by nature to fill the Biblical role of pastor. The Visionaries will do well leading revival services or camp meetings, and they make great evangelists, but as pastors they are too radical to hold a congregation together. They change direction and try new ideas too often. Although they are effective at stirring the congregation out of its indifference or lethargy, you don't want to give them the reins altogether or they will run the horse till he drops. The Steady/Priestly Man will "weep with those that weep and rejoice with those that rejoice"—the perfect trait for a pastor. But Steady Men are not usually chosen to be pastors because they do not seek the position and they are not as dynamic as the other two types.

> **The Command Man is readily identifiable by his quickness to step forward and take the lead.**

## Where Mr. Command Leads, Others Follow

The Command Man is readily identifiable by his quickness to step forward and take the lead. The Steady Man may have a readiness to act but hesitates, feeling overwhelmed, too timid to take responsibility to step up front. Visionaries have a vision for achievement but sometimes fail to gain the confidence of others to join in their endeavor. The Steady Man waits to see which way the wind is blowing before he moves, and then he moves cautiously. In time of crisis, in business, in war, and in the church, when immediate, bold action is called for, someone has to be the head that wags the tail and synchronizes the feet. The Command Man doesn't think twice.

> **Being a Command Man carries with it the burden of being expected to make decisions that have profound consequences on the lives of others.**

He rallies the troops and tells the Visionary to develop a new weapon and then he organizes the Steady Men to build it. When the Command Man, in counsel with others, decides it is time to go forth to battle, he directs the Visionary to sound the charge and the vast number of Steady Men rise up to carry the burden and win the day.

Being a Command Man carries with it the burden of being expected to make decisions that have profound consequences on the lives of others. It is bearing the load emotionally, hoping that what you have decided is the correct course. It is making decisions without having the luxury of hindsight or second-guessing. It is spending your whole life encumbered with responsibility. Like it or not, you are the man in charge.

Amazingly, just as the Command Man is by nature a leader, most people are by nature followers, waiting to be directed to profitable ends. That is scary indeed. Very few people have enough confidence to strike out on their own; and they are not willing to accept the responsibility for making decisions that affect so many. The Command Man sees the big picture and feels compelled to act, and for that purpose God created king-like men. It is not an easy road, for James said, "My brethren, be not many masters, knowing that we shall receive the greater condemnation." James 3:1 The verse says don't seek to be a master of others, for those who rule will come under greater condemnation because of their expanded responsibilities. When they make a mistake it affects everyone under them. And a Command Man cannot take charge five times without being wrong at least once.

**The Command Man sees the big picture and feels compelled to act, and for that purpose God created king-like men.**

## Good Command Men Are Servants

In the early summer of 2011, Alabama was hit by many huge tornados. Within hours several family members and friends rushed down with supplies to help the victims. They all came back with the same observations. The victims stood around dazed and lacked clarity as to what needed to be done. Government organizations had not yet arrived—no FEMA, no Red Cross, no National Guard, not even local authority. There was a singular lack of leadership among the many local volunteers.

**A Command Man will take charge as a ministry to others, or he will take charge in pursuit of his own selfish ends.**

They were all good-hearted Steady Men wanting to serve, but no one knew where to start. No one was taking command. So one of the young men in our group took command. He started directing our group from Tennessee, male and female, as to the division of responsibility. The locals gravitated to the authority of the young man and asked him what they could do, as if he were wearing a uniform and had an unlimited supply of goods. He didn't. When relief workers came donating a truckload of food, someone of our group stepped forward and assumed control. They assembled a team to distribute the goods.

> **A righteous Mr. Command sees the bigger picture and strives to help the greatest number even if he must call upon his family to share the sacrifices.**

One of our older ladies came home laughing, saying people were coming to her asking what they could or could not do. She is a Go-to lady, so she fell right in place as boss in her area of food preparation and distribution.

Due to the overwhelming magnitude of complete destruction, the victims and even the volunteers could not decide what to do until someone organized them and began giving directions. Early in the recovery of the tragic event, leadership was more important than the goods pouring in from everywhere. The Command Man did not have a desire to rule or to be at the top. He desired to serve and understood his greatest service was to make use of the human resources available.

## The Servant or the Self-Seeking

A Command Man will take charge as a ministry to others, or he will take charge in pursuit of his own selfish ends. We know of one selfish Command Man that rushed to the scene of devastation seeking profit by taking advantage of the desperation of the victims. Things like wars, business deals, church disputes, and times of tragedy manifest the character of everyone, especially the Command Man. Is he benevolent or egotistical?

There will be times in a Command Man's life when he will ride the line, not exactly doing evil but not sacrificing either. He might strive to get ahead and selfishly take advantage of the vulnerability of others. These Command Men often don't see what they do as self-seeking. They think of themselves as strong, not conniving. "In whom the god of this world hath blinded the minds of them which believe not, lest the light of the glorious gospel of Christ, who is the image of God, should shine unto them. For we preach not ourselves, but Christ Jesus the Lord; and ourselves your servants for Jesus' sake." 2 Corinthians 4:4-5

---

**A Command Man doesn't hang around where he can't make a difference.**

---

A righteous Mr. Command sees the bigger picture and strives to help the greatest number even if he must call upon his family to share the sacrifices. If he is an honest man he will take financial loss in order to help lead those in need, but in the end he will usually come out on top. If he is not a man of integrity he will be selfish and use the resources of others to further his own interests. If a Command man is selfish toward his wife, he is more likely to be selfish toward others. Consequently, if he is selfish or pushy in business toward others, he is likely to become callous toward his wife and maybe even toward his children. Every man is indivisible, not one man at home and another at work. He is who he is in all areas of life and nothing escapes his benevolence or his selfishness, as may be.

A Command Man doesn't hang around where he can't make a difference. He is only comfortable when he is needed to change things in an obvious way. The hospital room, a weeping woman, or household projects are not part of his job description. He doesn't like committees unless they are functioning at his discretion. He won't share power, but he will delegate it when it serves his goals.

## The Command Man's Help Meet

If you are a Command Man, chances are you expect your wife to wait on you hand and foot. By choosing not to comply she may have broken you from your native expectation, but your need for a close subordinate remains. Kings need advisors and heads of state to carry out their wills. The Commanding/King type just assumes that those within his jurisdiction, especially his wife, are there to assist in his rule. What other purpose in life could they have . . . could SHE have?

Are you guilty as charged? I am, but I don't feel guilty about the drive, only the use I make of it sometimes. I am a Command Man first and a Visionary second, so it is one type I know well, both strengths and weaknesses. And you can expect my bias toward the Command Man type to come through in my writings. I can't help it; just ask my second in command—my wife. At 66 years of age I have made my share of mistakes, and I have also seen the constructive things a man can do if he uses his leadership powers to organize others in the pursuit of worthy goals. Working together we accomplish much more than the sum total of our individual endeavors. Without a strong leader, people don't rally or focus.

How does being a Command Man affect a marriage relationship? A Command Man does not want his wife involved in any project that prevents her from immediately attending to his interests. His endeavors are the most important thing going; everything else is a waste of time. He likes for his wife to stay busy

> **The Command Man can be the most principled and outwardly loyal to his woman of all three types.**

being productive, but when he calls he expects her to drop everything and come running to his side. He needs and wants a helper and will value her greatly, exalting her to a place of prominence, setting her beside him on the throne.

The Command Man can be the most principled and outwardly loyal to his woman of all three types. He will do everything he can to make her a queen in private and public, but he does so on his own terms. Don't expect him to conform to the customs and amenities that regulate others; he charts his own romantic course. But if his wife resists his authority and shuns his overtures, he of all the types is most likely to just move forward without her as if nothing is wrong. He will not come back to beg or apologize and make a third appeal. If he is a generally intolerant and immature person he can become very cruel to his unsubmissive wife.

Of the three types of men, it is the Command Man that is most likely to shut the door on his wife and leave her behind if she does not share his vision. A Command Man will often demand respect, honor, even homage, whether he deserves it or not. When his wife, who might have been raised by a kind, forgiving Steady father, doesn't chalk his line, he will often walk off and leave her before she has a chance to realize she is even close to losing her marriage. When a man quits, he is a quitter.

When a man shuts the door, he is not only shutting out his wife, he is shutting the door through which the blessings of God were to be delivered. He is relegating the rest of his life to second place or lower.

## The Command Man's Greatest Weakness

The Command Man's greatest weakness is confidence in his hormones—in his innate nature. He trusts his own judgments above others'. He is often accused of being proud, arrogant even. Of course, pride comes readily to the one in command. That is why the Apostle Paul warned that in selecting leaders to "rule" in the church, "Not a novice, lest being lifted up with pride he fall into the condemnation of the devil." 1 Timothy 3:6 A novice Command Man, one that has no history of humble leadership, is in danger of being carried away with pride. Being created with the nature to lead does not qualify one to lead any more than being born a man qualifies one to be a parent. The will to lead is not the same as the wisdom to lead. The ability to persuade others to follow does not mean one is going to lead them in the right direction. So the greatest weakness of a Command Man is his stubborn assumption of his own superiority.

**The will to lead is not the same as the wisdom to lead.**

This is expressed in marriage by his presumption that his wife should joyfully support him without questioning the wisdom of his actions. He is often surprised at his own failures and does not easily take the blame for his presumptuous mistakes. He seldom apologizes. Of the three types of men, the Command Man is most prone to think he could manage just fine without a wife . . . if ONLY he could have sex three times a week and have a cook and housekeeper who minds her own business.

## Commanding Hope

Don't despair, Mr. Command Man; you can have an amazing marriage. I know because I am this type, and my marriage has been exceedingly rich and rewarding. More importantly, it has been rich and rewarding for my wife.

**More than physical, more than emotional; it is the act of being soul mates.**

You may be uncomfortable sharing your personal feelings with anyone, even your wife. Command is a lonely thing. The sanctity of one's command must be protected from the public. It takes a while for a wife to raise her clearance level so as to be admitted to the inner sanctum of strategy and power. All this changes as a man learns to really love his wife and she learns to appreciate her husband's strengths and virtues, and accepts him on his terms.

> **The ability to persuade others to follow does not mean one is going to lead them in the right direction.**

As time passes, the King-type man will become more vulnerable to his woman than will the other two types. Because of his self-imposed remoteness he will pour all of his personal intimacy into the one person on the whole earth whom he dare trust. It is this act of becoming one flesh and one heart that is the essence of marriage. It is more than physical, more than emotional; it is the act of being soul mates. It is what God created marriage to be. It is worth any sacrifice to get to this place in your marriage. And it will be a sacrifice. Marriage in its highest form takes a great deal of giving over, especially for a Command Man.

## Exhortation to the Command Man

Even though you are a Command Man and think you need no advice, especially from an old geezer with a long beard who cannot pronounce his words with the proper English accent, I am going to tell you what you need to do. Mister, if you don't like it, choose your weapons and name the time and place. This town is not big enough for both of us. (Excuse me, please. I too am a Command Man, but I am old and set in my ways. I have these outbursts.)

I have exhorted the Visionaries and the Steady Men to diversify their image expressions. The perfect man is a proper balance of all three, as was Jesus in his humanity. I have said that a strength can become our greatest weakness by its excess and disproportionate application. I am okay with who I am. I like myself well enough. But I know I have glaring deficiencies in my lack of Priestly/Steady expressions. If I arrogantly flaunt my Command/King nature I become offensive in my insensitivity. I must give the greater part of my energies to expressing that side of humanity that is not natural to me but is extremely valuable to the people whose lives I touch. I must get out of my comfort zone and act the Priest from time to time. I must get down in the ditch and take up a shovel with the Steady Man when I would rather gather a crew and manage the completion of the job in record time. So, Mr. Command Man, the most carnal thing you can do is smugly hide behind your image and expect your wife and everybody else to come under your spell. Many grouchy, selfish men like to think their cantankerousness is the expression of a Command Man when it is nothing more than sin.

There is one Lord and one Master. And we Command Men should be humbled by our callings, using our gifts and abilities to bless the world, not to milk it. Knowing our natures and what makes us feel and think the way we do is not justification for insensitivity or lack of openness and humility; it is a warning, and opportunity to understand our deficiencies and seek the grace of God so we might live as the men God meant for us to be. It is living bigger—or smaller—than our natural gifts and inclinations that make us men of character.

## The Command Man Loser

There is a tendency for the Command Man to feel superior just because of his God-given nature, not remembering that "unto whomsoever much is given, of him shall be much required: and to whom men have committed much, of him they will ask the more." Luke 12:48 For that reason, the selfish Command Man will just get mileage out of his personality and social persona and not experience the humility that drives other men to try harder to improve themselves.

There is nothing more pathetic than a loudmouthed, over-confident, inept talker trying to lead men where he has never gone. Here we go . . . this is going to hurt. If, as a Command Man, you do not develop productive skills and you have no record of personal accomplishment, you may develop a habit of telling exaggerated stories about yourself until people just tune in for fictional entertainment. If you divorce and lose your children, leaving you with no legitimate "kingdom" of your own, you may become obnoxiously garrulous. Those who know you will have dismissed you as irrelevant years before you are aware of it, for you will still be gaining the attention of bored people with your minstrel tales. Oh, I feel your pain. Really, I do. Don't give up yet. Later in this book, I will show you a way back to productive humanity and earned honor. For now, let's get back to the heart X-ray.

You may have slid so far down the slippery slope that you think it is your right to look at pornography. You console yourself with a belief that you are sublimating unfulfilled human need. I have known Command Men preachers who fornicated or committed adultery with half the women in the church. When caught they admitted to having excused themselves with a belief that they had greater needs than other men and had served God so well that he made allowances for their gratification. Women are attracted to dominant Command Men and, like Bathsheba, are drawn into his commanding web of authority, yielding their souls and bodies to him as if he were God. They are little twits and sluts and don't even know it, and you, Mister, are a slut maker. "Her house is the way to hell, going down to the chambers of death." Proverbs 7:27

## Make Her or Break Her

If a girl has been raised by a bossy mama and a silent Steady father and has not been taught the Word of God concerning her role as a wife, she will not understand or appreciate her Command husband's great need for respect and reverence. When a wife sees her husband as overly critical or demanding, she is going to have an opinion—and an attitude. Of course, she has a right to an opinion. Only a brainless, broken woman would be without opinion. She might keep quiet but she will flare her nostrils and roll her eyes, displaying her disdain. When a self-centered Command Man sees his wife "disrespect" his command, he takes it as complete revolt. The unwise Mr. Command gets that much more demanding and self-centered. Where the Visionary might holler and openly fight, and the Steady Man will be silent and hurt, the King will withdraw and starve her out emotionally. He communicates the idea that his kingdom can get along without her. It's her move. The family either engages in a protracted cold war or the wife who doesn't believe in divorce breaks and becomes a pitiful shell.

**You do not want a slave. You want a lover, a friend, an equal partner in life.**

Early in marriage most wives will try to bring peace. She slaves, she tries to please you, and then she slowly begins to give up hope of you ever seeing her side of the matter. Many divorces happen at that point. Sometimes it takes 20 years. Some of the ladies that hang in there, suffering a perpetual lack of fulfillment, shrink as human beings, withdrawing into the shadows with their aprons on and a broom in their hands, faithfully doing all that he demands, and keeping their peace. SICKO! You do not want a slave. You want a lover, a friend, an equal partner in life. You need a spirited, opinionated help meet. You want a woman that reflects who and what you are—a leader.

**When you break your wife, you break your home. You break your children, and you break yourself. She is your rib, and a man with a broken rib next to his heart is a crippled man.**

Some Command Men are so insecure they do not want anyone knowing them well, so they shut out the one person that is most likely to gain access to their inner sanctum. They cannot rebound from criticism and are totally uncomfortable with a woman that has an opinion. As they shove her into the shadows they grow smaller until one day they are less than what they have made her become. They get no criticism, but they will never earn any praise or admiration either. They learn the art of hypocrisy and try to win the approval of those who do not know them.

When you break your wife, you break your home. You break your children, and you break yourself. She is your rib, and a man with a broken rib next to his heart is a crippled man.

A Command Man's wife wears a heavier yoke than do most women, but if you cause her experience to be rewarding she will double and triple your life's work. She will quadruple your joy and you will become more than your mama ever dreamed. Of the three types of men, your wife will most readily mold to your needs if you just give her half a chance. You are by nature dominant and a leader. Everybody is ready to follow your lead. She will as well, unless you treat her so badly you make it impossible for her to honor and respect you. If you are even close to the man you think you are, your wife will be delighted to share your yoke and pull your load, not _for_ you, but _with_ you.

It is important to note that a Command Man gone bad is likely to be abusive. His strengths can easily be directed toward destruction. He might harshly make demands and then react when things don't go his way. The smallest souls whose bitter words lose power resort to violence. The women who stay with them become so browbeaten that by the time their self-centered dictator husband turns to physical abuse they have learned to endure it with a feeling that they somehow deserve it.

There are a few men who are so cruel and violent that even when their wives do all that is required, they are still physically abusive to her and the children. I know I am shooting over the heads of some of you tyrants. You want to say what I have heard a thousand times, "My case is different; my wife provokes it; you just don't know her." Command Men are often good communicators and great manipulators, so they cause everyone to think their pitiful wife is emotionally disturbed or mean spirited, which leaves her at his mercy. Counselors need to beware. Closed doors can conceal evil things.

When your wife writes me, I will carefully instruct her in how to gather evidence against you and report you to the law. That way I may get a chance to minister to you in prison. Wife beaters don't have much to do behind bars, so they have lots of time to repent. And Command Men don't get any special respect in the slammer. I will encourage your wife to wait for you, and to receive you when you get out. Ex-cons are usually humbled a good bit. I know. I work with them every week.

Thankfully, most Mr. Command Men are not cruel or evil. They would never be physically abusive, but some are almost as destructive with silence. Command Men can control their wives by just shutting down and refusing to communicate. We have counseled women who say their husbands avoid meeting eyes, have sex only when necessary, and then keep it very impersonal. They try to communicate only through the children. It is awful being shut out. A closed door is the greatest of all insults. When he shuts her out, she loses hope. She feels worthless. No matter how hard she tries to please, she still falls short. Instead of honoring the weaker vessel, he is insulting her for being alive. This is a grave sin that God will surely judge. Such cruel evil is not to be considered. Think about how it would feel if God responded to you in that manner.

I know that most Command Men do not deserve this dressing down, but I receive hundreds of letters confirming that there are enough of you out there mentally and physically abusing your wives that these things must be said and you must face your fault and reverse course. I have never met your wife and I care more about her than you do, and I am speaking for all those abused and ignored ladies that have sent me letters with tears staining the pages. It is time to repent before God "even as Christ also loved the church, and gave himself for it; that he might sanctify and cleanse it with the washing of water by the word." You need to listen to my *Romans Verse by Verse* teaching. You can download it free of charge from our website (nogreaterjoy.org) or purchase a disc. If you don't have the money, I will send you one free of charge. Just call and request it.

## Your Guiding Verses

### Ephesians 5:25-29

25 Husbands, love your wives, even as Christ also loved the church, and gave himself for it;

26 That he might sanctify and cleanse it with the washing of water by the word,

27 That he might present it to himself a glorious church, not having spot, or wrinkle, or any such thing; but that it should be holy and without blemish.

28 So ought men to love their wives as their own bodies. He that loveth his wife loveth himself.

29 For no man ever yet hated his own flesh; but nourisheth and cherisheth it, even as the Lord the church:

### Matthew 23:10-12

10 Neither be ye called masters: for one is your Master, even Christ.

11 But he that is greatest among you shall be your servant.

12 And whosoever shall exalt himself shall be abased; and he that shall humble himself shall be exalted.

As a Command Man you have the potential to become a productive leader, but you need your help meet to stand by your side as your reigning queen. When you demonstrate to your woman that you need her, want her, enjoy her, and are willing to go the extra mile for her sake, she will be your most devoted admirer.

## The Command Man's Five Hs

- ✓ Humble
- ✓ Honor
- ✓ Have more patience
- ✓ Hesitate
- ✓ Home

> **If you fail to be a benevolent ruler at home you are not fit to rule anywhere else.**

"**Humble** yourselves in the sight of the Lord, and he shall lift you up." James 4:10 Of the three types, the Command Man is most in need of humility and the least ready to express it. Humility comes by crashing into the reality of our own fallibility.

**Honor** your wife "as unto the weaker vessel, and as being heirs together of the grace of life; that your prayers be not hindered." 1 Peter 3:7

**Have more patience** with and respect toward the other two types of men. "For who maketh thee to differ from another? and what hast thou that thou didst not receive? now if thou didst receive it, why dost thou glory, as if thou hadst not received it?" 1 Corinthians 4:7

**Hesitate** before stepping in to take charge. "Be not wise in thine own eyes:" Proverbs 3:7

**Home** is where the heart is—or should be. Exercise your impulses to rule in your own home, for if you fail to be a benevolent ruler at home you are not fit to rule anywhere else. "One that ruleth well his own house, having his children in subjection with all gravity;" 1 Timothy 3:4

## Your Theme

Your help meet will become what you make her.

## Proffered Points to Ponder

- ✓ Mr. Command will be very objective and unemotional, and he will not enjoy small talk. His vision is like a man looking from a high mountain: he sees the distant goal. Mr. Command will want to talk about his plans, ideas, and finished projects. A wise man will ask his wife to help him stay balanced by reminding him

when he needs to express empathy or listen patiently or sit still
and be quiet during a boring meeting.

✓ Most Command Men do not get close to many people—maybe
none at all. They are uncomfortable when other men try to get
inside their space. They don't like to be touched by another man.
A salesman who touches a Command Man will lose his sale. I
don't even like a man to sit next to me when I eat. If you are close
enough to touch me, you are too close. I have backed all over a
room trying to stay four feet away from some man trying to talk to
me. For clarification: I do enjoy ladies sitting next to me when I eat.

✓ Mr. Command Man will be most uncomfortable and at a loss
when dealing with the sick, helpless, and dying. Where there
is no hope, there will be no need for a Command Man. A wise
man will share those feelings with his wife and ask her to be his
stand-in. As a leader of men, it is important to have good friends
who can step in and take control when you are inadequate in
dealing with emotional issues.

✓ A born leader is a man who can, when necessary, adapt principles
or rules to circumstances for the greater good of the greatest
number of people.

✓ A wise man doesn't use his strength of personality or his gifts to
control others for his own selfish desires.

✓ A wise man knows that silly women like dominant leaders. He
will know that sharing glances with an admiring, foolish woman
always brings death to things eternal. A wise man fears God,
disease, loss of virtue, shame, and tarnishing his good name. He
keeps in mind that cute she may be, but those who follow her go
down to hell.

✓ A Command Man can presume too much in conversation and
in social settings. To say it another way, he can think of himself
more highly than he ought.

✓ A Command Man can think his viewpoint is worth more than
others'.

- ✓ He has an impulse to take charge even in areas where he has no skill.

- ✓ A Command Man tries to learn as much as he can about everything so that he is never caught at a disadvantage.

- ✓ A Command Man is more likely to carry through a rebellion started by a Visionary.

- ✓ The Visionary may explode into violence, but the Command Man is more likely to mete out controlled and thoughtful force to counter resistance. In other words, the Visionary will scream at you on the court steps but the Command Man will quietly sue the pants off of you.

- ✓ The Command Man is absolutely essential to all corporate endeavors. If it requires organization, division of duty, and delegation of authority, he is the man of the hour.

## Ladies' Wish List

Julie writes: "You ask for a wish list. Here's mine:

- ✓ I wish my husband would be more patient, less irritable, and more gentle with me and the children.

- ✓ I really wish he would not speak to me in a tone that makes me feel like I'm an idiot.

- ✓ I wish he would give me as many compliments as he does criticisms, or thank me for what I have done instead of telling me what I should be doing.

- ✓ I wish he would not treat me like I am on the same level as the children.

- ✓ I wish he would not fuss at me in front of the children, and that he would treat me with respect.

- ✓ I wish I could hold my head up and tell him I am finished with his mistreatment. Maybe someday I will, but most likely I will sneak out while he is at work and just be gone. I often think about it."

Julie

So ought men to love their
wives as their own bodies.
He that loveth his wife
loveth himself.
For no man ever yet hated
his own flesh; but nourisheth
and cherisheth it,
even as the Lord the church:
Ephesians 5:28,29

# Chapter 9

# CONTRASTING THE TYPES

## Apples, Oranges, and Apricots

As we said earlier, most men are not exclusively one type, but I have never known a man to be a balance of all three. Upon meeting a young man it is readily apparent which of the three types he is, but when you get to know him you can usually see shades of one of the other types as well.

A **Visionary/Prophet** type may have just enough Priest (Mr. Steady) in him to keep his feet on the ground, or he may have a little of the Command Man in him and be a rather bossy reformer or inventor.

**Mr. Command** may have a little Priest in him and be a very compassionate ruler or dictator, as may be. Or he may have a touch of the Prophet in him and be a creative and innovative King— for good or ill.

> **Men that are purely of one nature alone stand out like comic book characters.**

The **Steady Man** may have a little Command Man in him and make the perfect shift supervisor in a factory or a successful construction contractor or a good senator. Or he may have a little of the Visionary in him and become a Henry Ford, inventing the assembly line and manufacturing automobiles. Or, being a steady worker, he may develop new methods or tools to accomplish his trade. A small blend gives a man balance.

Men that are purely of one nature alone stand out like comic book characters. I can walk into a room and spot them standing, seated, or with their backs turned. I can hear a man's voice over the phone and usually tell you of which sort he is. Older men are more guarded and less apparent than are the younger men, perhaps because they have developed a balance over the years. Their life's work will reveal their natures, but their manner may be rounded off by years of experience or by their willingness to listen to their help meets.

Martin Luther, the reformer, was a Visionary with a little Command Man in him. Martin Luther King Junior, the civil rights campaigner, was a Priest/Steady type with a little Visionary in him, but he pressed himself to function as a Command Man—not his natural bent. Benjamin Franklin was a complete Visionary. George Bush is a Steady/Priest type with a good bit of the Command Man and no Visionary. Barack Obama is a Visionary with a touch of the Command Man.

My estimation could be off base in some cases, and if you think so, then I have been successful in communicating to you the three types.

## The Good Doctors

Yesterday my wife went to a new medical clinic run by two chiropractors. The clinic is more like a fitness center with many people in a large room, some participating in individual therapeutic exercises and others in group exercises. The doctors pass from person to person, occasionally stepping behind semipublic enclosures to adjust people. Yet even in the midst of this controlled chaos she guessed the two doctors' types as soon as she walked in the door. The one doctor looked like he would be more at home with a football in his hand than holding a clipboard and studying X-rays. He was slow, kind, and was standing behind the counter looking earnestly at the other doctor for a final decision. The second doctor, whom I will call Dr. Command, was keyed up, very aware of what was happening all over the clinic. He walked with a laidback authority that oozed confidence. A Command Man, but the bold and busy setting suggested a Visionary had been here. Where was he?

**Dr. Command Man is almost like a superhero character. He likes to save people from harm.**

When she was taken into the small consultation room, the first doctor came in. He was a gentle giant and clearly a Dr. Steady. She told him, "You look like you had rather be playing football than fixing backs." He smiled, shook her hand with his huge mitt, and began to tell her how he was accepted into professional football but Hurricane Katrina changed his plans, since that was where the team was located. This doctor was nearly 100% Priestly, so he surely was not the man who was responsible for the structure of the clinic. She didn't ask, but I bet he played defense rather than offense on his football team.

Dr. Command Man entered the small room and the congenial atmosphere was instantly gone. After a quick introduction he immediately began teaching Debi how the human body reacted to certain problems and how it could be corrected. Clearly there was no need to be friendly or conversational when there was serious business to attend to. If I had been there I would have concurred totally.

When he stopped talking, she changed the subject. "So you obviously love to communicate?" He visibly relaxed. His voice reflected his earnestness, "Yes, I have a worthy message and I like to pass it on." It was then clear that he really was a Command Man but with enough Visionary in him to dream and bring it to pass.

When she hesitated making a long-term commitment for treatment, his countenance again visibly changed and this time it was not positive. He was ticked. His Command image spoke, and without actually saying these words his message was clear, "I am the doctor here. If you want to do the right thing you will do what I say, the way I say do it." His drive to be in charge (King) and his vision (Prophet) will help him succeed. It will make him a better doctor and cause his practice to excel. He will not be satisfied with what the doctors before him have said is the best way of doing things. He will search until he finds his own answers.

Dr. Command/Visionary's choice of a secondary doctor was excellent. Dr. Steady will make everyone feel cared for, special, and safe. No one will feel rushed with his slow patience, kind regard, and willingness to speak of his own personal life. The patient will not get lost in the rush of making Mr. Command/Visionary's dreams come true as long as Dr. Steady plays a role in their recovery. It was a good working team. I told Deb to decline the program since it was obviously set up for more youthful bodies.

> **If he is a wise man, or seeks wise counsel, he will choose someone who has one purpose in life: to help her man shine brighter, climb higher, and become better at everything he does.**

Dr. Command Man is almost like a superhero character. He likes to save people from harm. He is into dramatics. At this time in his life he is not married, but when he does marry he would do well not to marry another superhero type. He would take her success as competition. His ladylove needs to be the same type as his partner, Dr. Steady. But chances are he will marry a superhero lady because those people around him that he listens to and appreciates will assume he needs a counterpart as a wife. He will listen and choose to please them. And so will begin the struggle of supremacy. If he is a wise man, or seeks wise counsel, he will choose someone who has one purpose in life: to help her man shine brighter, climb higher, and become better at everything he does. He needs a steady, hardworking servant who will not bring attention to herself in any area of life. She will knock off the brittle edges, and he does have brittle edges. People will wonder what he sees in her and why he would choose such a nondescript lady. But if he loves her and puts her at the head of his team, she will soon lose the retiring image and become a leading lady made in his image.

## Good Doctors' Wives

**Dr. Steady** is married. He probably married a nice Go-to girl that is busy doing her own thing. She will like the fact that he works for Dr. Command because she likes to get things done. For more information on the three types of women, read Debi's book *Preparing to Be a Help Meet*.

**Dr. Visionary/Command Man** would like to be married, but he rushes around too busy to take the time to get acquainted with prospective brides. He also knows there are women who would marry him for his clout or for his money. The ladies who push themselves forward will be Go-to girls, not the best match for him. Hopefully, Dr. Command will find a wife that will help him mature into the man God wants him to be. And I do hope he will use his brains instead of his eyes when he makes his choice, because the kind of lady he needs will not be dashing or daring. She will need to be a steady servant. He will need a right-hand lady for his wife, but, more importantly, he will need a woman who is there to serve him and be his cheering squad.

Remember, women are moldable; the younger they are, the more moldable they are; and the less experience they have in the world, the easier it is for them to conform to their husband's needs. Most men get married expecting their wives to just know how to please them. But now you know that if you want a good woman you must take the responsibility to love her and mold her into being that woman. That is more easily accomplished when you know yourself and your needs, your strengths and your weaknesses. It is also easier if your wife-to-be has studied and knows what God says to her as a help meet. I would advise that ALL young men require their coming bride to read, study, re-read, and discuss at great length my wife's books, *Created to Be His Help Meet*, and especially the one for unmarried girls, *Preparing to Be a Help Meet*. This is not an ad; it's just good advice.

## Contrasting the Three Types

Each type has extremes in how he relates to his wife. Good advice to one type would be inappropriate for a man of a different nature. It is important that you come to know yourself so you will understand your natural strengths and weaknesses.

## Strengths

**Mr. Command** will see men as sheep without a shepherd and organize them into a working body, helping them make use of their talents to their full potential. He is the overseer and commander where one is needed.

**Mr. Visionary** will be focused. He will see things other people don't notice. He is a fountain of ideas; nothing is impossible. He makes himself the conscience of society, judging and attempting to change things for the better. He is often radical and ready to march to his own drum. Women are rarely so focused unless they are sharing a dream with their man.

**Mr. Steady** is the man everybody likes. He is agreeable and not outwardly judgmental. He is the last to change and the first to decline getting in the public eye—appearing humble. He is the priest ready to show compassion and care for the wounded. He is the muscle and patience that builds a house, a city, or a nation. Without him the world would have many visions, a few leaders, and no one to materialize the dreams.

## Weaknesses

**Mr. Command**, if he doesn't succeed, can become an obnoxious tyrant in a very small circle that may be no larger than his family. Dictators are Command Men gone awry. He expects to be honored and to hold a place of prominence, even when he doesn't deserve it. He often appears arrogant and proud. He will boss his wife like he bosses his yardman and expect her to jump to attention.

**Mr. Visionary** will jump from one fantastic plan to another, succeed wildly, and then fail miserably, blaming someone else for it, possibly becoming radical, even violent, maybe a revolutionary. He does not always give his best energies to his family, sometimes sacrificing their comfort and security in pursuit of his vision. He reaches for the stars while she mops the floors.

**Mr. Steady** can waste away in mediocrity if he does not stir himself to creativity, and he can become a shadow to his wife's dominance if he doesn't take the reins and lead the family. He will talk when he should be working and work when he should be at home ministering to his wife and children. He will sacrifice truth for peace, and will lie to keep from hurting someone's feelings.

## Road to Ruin

**Mr. Command** can ruin his marriage by not showing love and compassion toward his wife. If he gets irritated and shows his disdain by refusing to talk or just fails to appreciate her, he is shutting the door to his marriage. No woman can continue being shut out. She will break or leave; either way it is a lose-lose marriage for both. The Command Man will think he can do better without her, but he is establishing a pattern that will follow him all the days of his life.

**Mr. Visionary** can ruin his marriage by being focused on his own dreams, thus not responsible. If he fails to put her needs before his visions he is proving he loves himself more than he loves his wife. A woman's natural drive is to have a safe haven for her children. If she feels too swamped she will leave for safer ground. He will not do well losing his family.

**Mr. Steady** probably will not ruin his marriage; instead he will just make it miserable for himself and his wife, as well as the community and the church. If he feels too uncomfortable to talk, teach, or share his feelings he will just retreat to a place he feels safe, leaving his family miserably unfulfilled. Their lives will be unexceptional.

## Compared

Mr. Command needs a lady to serve him. Mr. Visionary needs a lady to talk with him. Both Command and Visionary need their ladies to admire them. A Steady man needs a lady to walk beside him, a counterpart. She needs to know that is her role. She needs to know how she can become his colleague in life. Mr. Steady will need to find ways she can become his functioning help meet. As his help meet she really NEEDS to be getting things done.

Mr. Steady needs to learn to stand up to his bossy wife, while Mr. Visionary needs to get his head out of the clouds of dreams and go to work. Mr. Command needs to come home and tell his wife he loves her.

**Mr. Command Man** might be jealous of his wife's success and take it as a put-down. He wants her full attention, to be the only game in town. The immature Command Man who doesn't accomplish much on his own may be jealous of any success she might achieve apart from him. I have watched men publicly roll their eyes when someone happens to compliment the little lady on an achievement. In his insecurity he refuses to allow her to do something that would be helpful to him because he doesn't want her to perform better than he. When a man treats his help meet in that manner he is cutting off the one God provided to assist him in becoming more successful. Don't maintain your height by making your wife stay seated.

**Mr. Visionary** gets excited and even frantic when he is suddenly possessed of a vision. The last thing he wants at that point is for someone to tell him his idea is crazy. In the morning he may see that it's crazy, but if his wife tells him that it is unworkable before he has discovered it for himself, he will take it to be a rejection of him rather than an objective analysis by an unbiased party. Some Visionaries live on the mountain peaks of adrenaline-laced joy. They slide off into the valley of depression often enough so when they are peaking out on good feelings, they want their wives to dance and share their exhilaration. If she doesn't go up and down with him, he too may just cut her off emotionally.

> Of all the men, Mr. Visionary needs to learn to incorporate his wife into his life, for BOTH their sakes.

Of all the men, Mr. Visionary needs to learn to incorporate his wife into his life, for BOTH their sakes. And he must not take it personally when she has a mind and emotions of her own. Mister, since it is not her nature to be a Visionary, she may just be a whole lot more objective than you are. You look at the details through a microscope while she sees the whole picture. Don't cut her off for being more objective than you. It is her nature to be what she is. You are the immature one.

**Mr. Steady** is short-sighted in regard to his role as head of the family. He will take the lead if everybody is willing to follow, but if his wife balks, he will choose peace over power any day and all night. "Henpecked" and Steady Man are synonyms. A Command Man is never hen-pecked. His hen follows or gets left behind. The Visionary is too controlled by his drives to sit in one spot long enough to get pecked, but Mr. Steady will tend to sit on the nest and let the hen do as she pleases if she just lets him fertilize her eggs from time to time.

## Dumb Things Husbands Say

Now, I didn't create this list, but some of these things sound rather intelligent to me. It's the little lady's perspective that matters.

- ✓ You need to lose weight.
- ✓ Why don't you call my mom and ask her how to cook it?
- ✓ Your family is weird.
- ✓ You can't really be that dumb.
- ✓ You didn't used to think like that.
- ✓ You will feel differently when you are off your cycle.
- ✓ All the other guys' wives are cool with it.
- ✓ Who put that dumb idea in your head, your mother?
- ✓ You are not being logical.
- ✓ You are totally missing the point.
- ✓ I'll do it this weekend.

**Mr. Command can heal his marriage by focusing on loving and verbally appreciating his wife.**

✓ Hurry up with the kids and clean up, because I've got plans for you.

✓ Not now! I'm trying to watch the news.

✓ Shut the kids up before I come and shut them up myself! I can't even hear this show.

## Healing Your Marriage

**Mr. Command** can heal his marriage by focusing on loving and verbally appreciating his wife. Cherish her to the point of serving her and she will have the energy to stand beside you in all things. You must court your little lady and make yourself vulnerable before her. I know this is hard, but it becomes much easier when you bring her to the place where you can trust her with guarded areas of your heart. Both of you need to be assured that each has absolute goodwill toward the other. You will do well to encourage her to tell you how you make her feel. It is not about your intentions; it is about what she receives on the other end. You are never right on any issue until she is secure in love.

**Mr. Visionary** can heal his marriage by attending to his wife's needs and security first. You need to regularly put aside your wild ideas long enough to make sure she knows you are doing what is best for the family. You must force yourself to patiently listen to her concerns. Your good arguments make cold bed partners. Your zeal and vision will not feed the family or assure them of their importance. Learn to sit on your "brilliant brainstorms" and trust your wife's caution. You don't have to disassemble the only family car to construct a tractor. Give it a few days and discuss it with her. You might change your mind before you cause too much consternation.

> **Mr. Visionary can heal his marriage by attending to his wife's needs and security first.**

> **Mr. Steady can heal his marriage by first stepping forward to take the lead and then teaching his wife to be productive, resourceful, and successful.**

Is it worth the trouble for couples to learn to function as one? Yes. God designed her to be your helper. Remember, she came to you as a kit to be assembled. You took her out of the box and complained that she did not work properly. God gave you the directions in Ephesians 5. You must sanctify and cleanse her so you can present her to yourself as a fully functioning help meet. She wants to be your helper: " . . . but she that is married careth for the things of the world, how she may please her husband." [1 Corinthians 7:34]

**Mr. Steady** can heal his marriage by first stepping forward to take the lead and then teaching his wife to be productive, resourceful, and successful. She will be happy when you take her by the hand and lead her to become a productive individual.

Unless the wife of a Steady Man is rather laid back and steady herself with not much ambition, she will not find enough self-expression just sitting around waiting on her husband to bring a little excitement into her life. So if you don't want her using her energies criticizing you, you should encourage her to develop productive hobbies or activities that enhance the family in some way.

Mr. Steady wants to be nice to his wife, so he leaves her at home sitting and feeling useless. You are not being nice; you are abdicating responsibility. She might get her way, but it will not satisfy her. Your lack of leadership will frustrate her. She will either get nasty-spirited, try to control others, or go out and get her own projects going that leave you at home to cook for yourself.

I will say again, God calls a wife "help meet" for a reason. A woman was designed to be doing something productive, something that will make her feel she has value beyond housemaid and baby birther. She was created to be your helper. Are you helping her help?

## Wish List

This wish list is drawn from our letters.

- ✓ I wish that when I talk he would listen, hear what I am saying, and then communicate and empathize.
- ✓ I wish he would give 100% to the marriage and family, not just work and play.
- ✓ I wish my husband would lead us in prayer and family devotions.
- ✓ I wish he were more spontaneous, more dates with me, and talk with me.

✓ I wish he would talk more about feelings, not just concrete statements.

✓ He doesn't take time alone with me. He makes me feel pushed away.

✓ I would love it if he would look into my eyes and listen with interest when I talk to him.

✓ I wish he would not apologize too soon, and not use the words, "If I did that, I'm sorry. Well, if I did that . . . if that's what you thought I meant . . . I'm sorry you took it that way . . ."

---

**Who can find a virtuous woman?**
**for her price is far above rubies.**
Proverbs 31:10,11

---

Chapter 10

# THREE KINDS OF WOMEN

## Knowing Her Strengths and Weaknesses

In my wife's book for single women, *Preparing to Be a Help Meet*, she draws a picture of the three kinds of girls and how they relate to their husbands. She calls them **Go-to Girls** (Command), **Servants** (Steady), and **Dreamers** (Visionaries). As we said earlier, men are very fixed in their natures from birth, but the girls seem to develop their types as they grow and mature. In many cases, their type is not as readily identifiable until later in life. If a girl marries young, or before she has extensive independent experience, she can readily mold into the counterpart her husband needs. God created the female to be the helper, so, following marriage, most girls will quickly adapt to their husband's needs regardless of their types.

Couples seem to be best matched in complementary pairs—opposites on the color wheel, red and green, purple and yellow, blue and orange. A man strong in one trait is best served by a woman strong in an area where he is weakest. A Command Man and a Go-to Girl can end up competing with one another. I am a Command Man so I appreciate the strengths of a Servant and a Dreamer.

As a rule I don't much like Go-to/Command women and would need to make quite a bit of adjustment if I were married to one. There was never any danger of that, because in my youth I never would have given an aggressive woman any attention. I had a first and only date with several Go-to Gals. But I am sure they eventually made some Steady Men a very congenial mate. The Steady Men, unless they are insecure, are usually drawn to Go-to Girls.

Understanding your nature and that of your spouse will enable you to know her weaknesses and strengths so you can help her develop her full potential rather than taking offense at her particularities. As a woman matures and meshes her life into her husband's, the lines blur as to her type. If she is a Servant then she takes strength from her husband and becomes stronger and more confident. If she is a Dreamer, she learns to temper her ideas to fit his needs, thus becoming more of a Servant. If she is a Go-to Gal she learns to enjoy serving while still possessing her aggressive approach to life. It is up to the man to lead his wife to become all he needs her to be.

## Dreamer/Visionary

This next list came from our readers. It is the combined wisdom of several letters.

- ✓ A Dreamer likes to make things happen.
- ✓ She is creative.
- ✓ She is not as concerned about details, but is given to an active imagination.
- ✓ She is driven and focused.
- ✓ She is not always patient with those who are not as efficient, but is a great person to have around when something needs to be done.
- ✓ She cares deeply about people and issues but would rather do something about it than sit around thinking.
- ✓ She has strong intuitions and impressions, many of which turn out to be correct.

## Servant/Steady

- ✓ A Servant woman is extroverted, friendly, warm, and cheerful.
- ✓ She is hospitable and loves to visit and get to know new people.
- ✓ She is very conscious of needs and opportunities to help others.
- ✓ She is often emotional, very compassionate, and has strong beliefs, opinions, and convictions.
- ✓ She needs a strong man to keep her feeling balanced.
- ✓ A Servant woman is always trying to serve and give.
- ✓ She is not very good at pacing herself, sometimes overexerting and overextending, and is prone to discouragement, exhaustion, and burnout.

✓ She's very sympathetic and understanding, quick to take blame, and very burdened with the problems and needs of others.

## Go-to Girl/Command

✓ A Go-to Girl often is dignified.

✓ Perhaps the most misunderstood of the three categories, a Go-to woman takes life seriously.

✓ She has great attention to detail and is very conscious of what is appropriate and what's not.

✓ She does not like excitement, sudden change, too much activity, and unpredictability.

✓ She thrives on consistency, loves peace, and is a woman of principle.

✓ She has a great deal of inner strength and can be very loyal, committed, confident, and creative.

✓ She can be emotional but does not express her feelings easily.

✓ She is a dignified woman that has strong opinions and high standards but is easily discouraged by failure.

✓ She responds well to encouragement but becomes insecure when criticized.

## One Reader Wrote:

"A key to understanding these three types of women is to discover what motivates them."

✓ A **Dreamer** wants to make everything work and look good.

✓ A **Servant** woman wants to make everyone happy.

✓ A **Go-to** dignified woman expects everyone, especially herself, to live up to high ideals.

The dominant strength of each has the potential to be her greatest weakness. As their individual goals are different, so are their needs.

✓ A **Dreamer**/Visionary woman needs a focus or a project. She needs to feel that she has something important to do.

✓ A **Servant**/Priest woman needs to feel appreciated and that the people she is ministering to are being helped.

✓ A **Go-to**/Command dignified woman needs to be put at ease so that her creative potential can thrive.

Chapter 11

# WHAT SAITH THE SCRIPTURES?

Below are the most significant Biblical passages on marriage from a man's perspective. I am not going to offer a detailed commentary on all of them, but the texts are printed for your perusal and highlights are noted. You will find it helpful to organize a Bible study for men around these passages.

**God was married to Israel just as Christ is betrothed to the church.**

### Isaiah 54:5-8

**5** For **thy Maker is thine husband**; the LORD of hosts is his name; and thy Redeemer the Holy One of Israel; The God of the whole earth shall he be called.

**6** For the LORD hath called thee as a woman forsaken and grieved in spirit, and a wife of youth, when thou wast refused, saith thy God.

**7** For a small moment have I forsaken thee; but with great mercies will I gather thee.

**8** In a little wrath I hid my face from thee for a moment; but with everlasting kindness will I have mercy on thee, saith the LORD thy Redeemer.

**Marriage is a one-flesh union until death. (Romans 7:1-3)**

### Mark 10:7-9

**7** For this cause shall a man leave his father and mother, and cleave to his wife;

**8** And they twain shall be one flesh: so then they are no more twain, but one flesh.

**9** What therefore God hath joined together, let not man put asunder.

## Keep it in your pants.

### Proverbs 5:15-23

**15** Drink waters out of thine own cistern, and running waters out of thine own well.

*[Satisfy your sexual thirst at your wife's fountain.]*

**16** Let thy fountains be dispersed abroad, and rivers of waters in the streets.

**17** Let them be only thine own, and not strangers' with thee.

*[Don't share sex with anyone else.]*

**18** Let thy fountain be blessed: and rejoice with the wife of thy youth.

**19** Let her be as the loving hind and pleasant roe; let her breasts satisfy thee at all times; and be thou ravished always with her love.

**20** And why wilt thou, my son, be ravished with a strange woman, and embrace the bosom of a stranger?

**21** For the ways of man are before the eyes of the LORD, and he pondereth all his goings.

**22** His own iniquities shall take the wicked himself, and he shall be holden with the cords of his sins.

**23** He shall die without instruction; and in the greatness of his folly he shall go astray.

*Ecclesiastes 9:9* Live joyfully with the wife whom thou lovest all the days of the life of thy vanity, which he hath given thee under the sun, all the days of thy vanity: for that is thy portion in this life, and in thy labour which thou takest under the sun.

## Don't divorce.

### Malachi 2:14-17

**14** Yet ye say, Wherefore? Because the LORD hath been witness between thee and the wife of thy youth, against whom thou hast dealt treacherously: yet is she thy companion, and the wife of thy covenant.

**15** And did not he make one? Yet had he the residue of the spirit. And wherefore one? That he might seek a godly seed. *[He made them one flesh for purposes of producing a godly seed]* Therefore take heed to your spirit, and let none deal treacherously against the wife of his youth. *[Don't divorce.]*

**16** For the LORD, the God of Israel, saith that **he hateth putting away** *[divorce]*: for one covereth violence with his garment, saith the LORD of hosts: therefore take heed to your spirit, that ye deal not treacherously.

**17** Ye have wearied the LORD with your words. Yet ye say, Wherein have we wearied him? When ye say, Every one that doeth evil is good in the sight of the LORD, and he delighteth in them; or, Where is the God of judgment?

## She owns your body; don't withhold it.

### 1 Corinthians 7:1-6

**1** Now concerning the things whereof ye wrote unto me: It is good for a man not to touch a woman.

**2** Nevertheless, to avoid fornication, let every man have his own wife, and let every woman have her own husband.

**3** Let the husband render unto the wife due benevolence: and likewise also the wife unto the husband.

**4** The wife hath not power of her own body, but the husband: and likewise also the husband hath not power of his own body, but the wife.

**5** Defraud ye not one the other, except it be with consent for a time, that ye may give yourselves to fasting and prayer; and come together again, that Satan tempt you not for your incontinency.

**6** But I speak this by permission, and not of commandment.

## Do not grow bitter.

### Colossians 3:18-19

**18** Wives, submit yourselves unto your own husbands, as it is fit in the Lord.

**19** Husbands, love your wives, and **be not bitter against them**.

**1 Peter 3:1-13** (printed and discussed below)

**Ephesians 5:25-33** (printed and discussed below)

## God's Marriage Outline for Men

The volatile apostle Peter must have learned a lot from his own marriage experience, for he gives us six verses commanding a woman to submit to her husband, followed by seven verses defining a man's responsibility to his wife. We won't scrutinize the passages containing God's command to wives. This book will fill up all too quickly just looking at what God says to husbands.

### 1 Peter 3:7-13

**7** Likewise, ye husbands, **dwell with them according to knowledge**, giving **honour unto the wife**, as unto the weaker vessel, and as being heirs together of the grace of life; that your prayers be not hindered.

**8** Finally, be ye all of **one mind**, having **compassion one of another**, **love** as brethren, be **pitiful,** be **courteous**:

**9 Not rendering evil for evil**, or **railing for railing**: but contrariwise **blessing**; knowing that ye are thereunto called, that ye should inherit a blessing.

**10** For he that will love life, and see good days, let him **refrain his tongue from evil, and his lips that they speak no guile:**

**11** Let him **eschew evil, and do good; let him seek peace,** and ensue it.

**12** For the eyes of the Lord are over the righteous, and his ears are open unto their prayers: but the face of the Lord is against them that do evil.

**13** And who is he that will harm you, if ye be followers of that which is good?

Drawn from 1 Peter 3, above, here is a Biblical outline of how a husband should relate to his wife. This list enumerates a husband's responsibility to his wife. Note the passage is addressed to husbands in particular (v. 7).

1) **Dwell with them**—no divorce or separation.

2) Dwell with them **according to knowledge** that they are the weaker vessel. It would take at least three full-time servants to do what most wives are called upon to perform alone.

3) **Giving honour** unto the wife, as unto the weaker vessel.

4) Have **one mind** and function so as to maximize your relationship as heirs together of the grace of life.

5) **Love and show pity and be courteous**.

6) Do **not respond to railings** with railings or to **evil with evil**, but rather blessings.

7) **Refrain your tongue** from evil and guile.

8) Avoid and **flee from evil**, and **do good**.

9) **Seek peace**.

These nine points would form the basis of a good Bible study.

## Marriage, the Divine Reality

Think about it: of all the possible analogies God could have employed to describe his relationship to his church, he uses the husband and wife's physical merging into one flesh and bone (Ephesians 5:25-33). Note the following verses.

**John 3:29** He that hath the bride is the bridegroom: but the friend of the bridegroom, which standeth and heareth him, rejoiceth greatly because of the bridegroom's voice: this my joy therefore is fulfilled.

**Revelation 19:7-9**
**7** Let us be glad and rejoice, and give honour to him: for the **marriage of the Lamb is come, and his wife hath made herself ready**.

**8** And to her was granted that she should be arrayed in fine linen, clean and white: for the fine linen is the righteousness of saints.

**9** And he saith unto me, **Write, Blessed are they which are called unto the marriage supper of the Lamb**. And he saith unto me, These are the true sayings of God.

**Revelation 21:9** And there came unto me one of the seven angels which had the seven vials full of the seven last plagues, and talked with me, saying, Come hither, I will shew thee **the bride, the Lamb's wife**."

**Revelation 22:17** And the **Spirit and the bride say, Come**. And let him that heareth say, Come. And let him that is athirst come. And whosoever will, let him take the water of life freely.

The following nine verses express how a husband is to love his wife.

**Ephesians 5:25-33**
**25** Husbands, **love your wives**, even as Christ also loved the church, and gave himself for it;

**26** That he might sanctify and **cleanse it with the washing of water by the word**,

**27** That he might present it to himself a glorious church, not having spot, or wrinkle, or any such thing; but that it should be holy and without blemish.

**28** So ought men to love their wives as their own bodies. He that loveth his wife loveth himself.

**29** For no man ever yet hated his own flesh; but nourisheth and cherisheth it, even as the Lord the church:

**30** For we are members of his body, of his flesh, and of his bones.

**31** For this cause shall a man leave his father and mother, and shall be joined unto his wife, and they two shall be one flesh.

**32** This is a great mystery: but I speak concerning Christ and the church.

**33** Nevertheless let every one of you in particular so love his wife even as himself; and the wife see that she reverence her husband.

In your study of the passage, note that it begins with "love your wives" and ends with, "Nevertheless let every one of you in particular so love his wife even as himself . . . " In other words, the nine verses are bracketed by the command for husbands to love their wives. Everything in between is an elaboration of that command—defining how love is expressed. The word *love* appears six times in the nine verses.

✓ **How does a husband love his wife?**

The same way Christ loved the church.

✓ **How did Christ love the church?**

He gave himself for it. He lived and died for the church.

✓ **What is Christ's goal for the church, and a husband's goal for his wife?**

To sanctify and cleanse her.

✓ **By what means did Christ sanctify and cleanse the church, and how should a husband sanctify and cleanse his wife?**

By washing her with his words. WOW! Blow me away! A husband can sanctify and cleanse his wife with his words!

✓ **For what purpose does Christ—and a husband—wash his bride?**

That he might present her to himself not having spot, or wrinkle, or any such thing (that is ugly or unpleasant) but that she should be holy and without blemish. He didn't marry a perfect bride, but he is in the process of removing all spots and blemishes in anticipation of presenting her to himself. Through love acted out he is preparing her for himself.

✓ **How should a man love his wife?**

Just as much as he loves his body as expressed in his feeding and protecting it.

✓ **A wife is a member of the very body of her husband.**

For the Scripture tells us to leave our father and mother and become one flesh with our wife.

✓ **So a man should love his wife just as a wife should reverence (honor, submit to) her husband.**

Chapter 12

# WASHING OF THE WORD

We must examine Ephesians 5 (above) more closely. Clearly the subject of this passage is earthly marriage, but it is also an analogy of Christ and the church. It is like one of those drawings in which you view a distinct image and then suddenly see a completely different image drawn with the same lines. The longer you view it the more it changes back and forth. This passage is the story of earthly marriage, of husband and wife, but it is also the story of Christ and his bride. One is a figure for the other. They are mirror images.

> **Ephesians 5:
> An analogy of Christ
> and the church**

God's comparing his relationship with the church to a man and his wife is not a random metaphor God chose for its convenience and similarity to the point he wanted to make. Marriage was created in the image of God's relationship to his people. Just as the physical bodies of men and women reflect the image of God, the sexual relationship reflects the communion of the human spirit with God's spirit. The final heavenly state will be a climax in the spirit when God and his bride merge into oneness.

"Marriage is honorable and the bed undefiled" because it is created in the image and likeness of heavenly intercourse. One entire book in the Bible, the Song of Solomon, is dedicated to a bride's erotic desires for her beloved.

> **Marriage was created
> in the image of God's
> relationship to his
> people.**

The nature of marriage is that two shall become one flesh. In Ephesians we read of the relationship of the church to Christ, "For we are members of his body, of his flesh, and of his bones." Ephesians 5:30 The analogy leans heavily on the physical union of a man and woman with its over-the-top emphasis on body, flesh, and bone union. Eve was created from a bone taken from Adam's side, prompting Adam to respond, "This *is* now bone of my bones, and flesh of my flesh." Genesis 2:23

## By Divine Design

Our sojourn here on earth, with all of its sin and pain, is not just an unfortunate cosmic mistake from which we are trying to dig our way out. God commenced a grand project in the Garden of Eden. Even as he placed the perfect couple in that pristine environment, commanding them to "be fruitful and multiply," he knew they would not resist the temptation to act independently. He knew they would sin, plunging the world into a tragedy that would drag on for millennia. But it was and is by divine design. The program is on schedule and is producing the results God anticipated. (See my book *Divine Design* for a full discussion of God's eternal purposes worked out in humankind.)

> **God commenced a grand project in the Garden of Eden.**

God is generating a family of like-minded sons and daughters. His son Jesus is the prototype. God desires much more than he is able to create. He cannot create character. He cannot create people with experience. He cannot create a free will that chooses only righteousness. So he created (or allowed to come into existence) an unstable environment that is a mixture of order and degeneration, of pleasure and pain, of good and evil, of success and failure, of justice and grace, of life and death. At the center of it all are millions of souls with the opportunity to rise or fall, be good or bad, to ascend to a state much higher than their creation, or to degenerate to a despicable and deplorable depth of depravity. Those who recognize their weakness and call upon him for deliverance will find strength to rise beyond themselves and conform to the preordained image of God's son. The man Christ Jesus is the first of many sons whom God will bring into a state of glory—a glory that far exceeds the original paradise. It is not as Milton wrote, "Paradise Restored." It is far beyond paradise. It is sonship arrived at through a process of overcoming.

The male and female combination, properly functioning, simulates the entire human experience and creates a synergy where the sum is greater than the parts, where the end is better than the beginning, were testing produces triumph, where two mortal souls merge into a oneness that expresses the image of God in a way that would never have been possible in a single act of creation.

Most men are ignorant of the grand program of which they are a vital part. They drag around complaining and blaming, wishing for something better, thinking they got the short end of it. They speak and act as if it is not right that they should have conflict and trial. Life was hard enough, and they got married for their pleasure, only to discover that it too is a battleground where character is tested and a man is stretched to his limit and then beyond. Over half of the men bail out of their marriages because they are not men enough to rise to the challenge, to win in the game God placed them in, to grow as a human being, to become a fit member for the kingdom of God.

Mister, life is bigger than your happiness, or should I say gratification. If you just want to squeeze the lemon once, expecting sweet lemonade to come out and fill your glass, you will throw away a lot of lemons and never get a satisfying drink. God doesn't give us a perfect anything. Not a perfect body, not a perfect mind, nor a perfect wife. We inherit life in a broken state, and we are broken to match. God is looking for overcomers, and a true overcomer is more than a survivor who takes care of self. To truly overcome one must not live unto himself; he must live to bless others. He must be a savior and a sanctifier, just as is God's prototype son Jesus. Your ministry, your calling, the job you are here to do, begins with sanctifying your wife. You are called to make her all that God wants her to be, to die for her if need be, and, much more difficult, to live for her in the everyday humdrum of life. That is why God said, "For if a man know not how to rule his own house, how shall he take care of the church of God?" 1 Timothy 3:5

> **To truly overcome one must not live unto himself; he must live to bless others.**

Ministry begins at home and advances no further until you have mastered the high calling of husband and father. The person you are at home is the real you. The public you is an edited version designed to deceive. Your worst moments with your wife are the truest expressions of who you are. Knowing that causes me to be aware that I am in need of repentance and forgiveness.

> **Ministry begins at home and advances no further until you have mastered the high calling of husband and father.**

## Cleanse Your Wife

**These three verses are the most important in the entire Bible regarding marriage.** I will print them again and again. You should have them memorized by the time you finish this book.

> ### Ephesians 5:25-27
> **25** Husbands, love your wives, even as Christ also loved the church, and gave himself for it;
>
> **26** That he might sanctify and cleanse it with the washing of water by the word,
>
> **27** That he might present it to himself a glorious church, not having spot, or wrinkle, or any such thing; but that it should be holy and without blemish.

**A husband's ministry on this earth is parallel to Christ's ministry.**

A husband's ministry on this earth is parallel to Christ's ministry. As Christ came to love an imperfect bride and receive her while still in sin, so a husband receives an imperfect bride. As Christ gave himself for the church, a husband is to sacrificially give himself for his wife. As Christ is the head of the church with the responsibility of loving, sanctifying, and cleansing her, likewise the husband is the head of his wife with a lifelong ministry of sanctifying and cleansing her.

This is God's great plan, conceived in eternity past, the means by which he brings us into conformity to his heart. It is heaven's clinic, the place where two sinners join hands and hearts as they become "heirs together of the grace of life."

Marriage is a high calling, an opportunity to discover the power and wisdom to grow beyond self-interest as we learn to live for another. It is the place where we can daily forsake all and make ourselves small on behalf of one whom God loves.

I say it again: in marriage the total is greater than the sum of its parts. When the two become one, they are much more together than they would ever be apart.

> ### Ecclesiastes 4:9-12
> **9** Two are better than one; because they have a good reward for their labour.

**10** For if they fall, the one will lift up his fellow: but woe to him that is alone when he falleth; for he hath not another to help him up.

**11** Again, if two lie together, then they have heat: but how can one be warm alone?

**12** And if one prevail against him, two shall withstand him; and a threefold cord is not quickly broken.

Marriage properly ordered is the quickest path to obtaining wisdom, grace, mercy, patience, faith, compassion, and humility—especially humility. If it were not for the constant presence of that other human being in our life we could live in a delusion. In our solitude we could call a half measure a whole, we could believe that mediocrity is perfection, that lack of conflict is peace, that distant sympathy is compassion, that sharing with a friend is transparency, and that liberal giving is sacrifice. We could live our entire life alone and be convinced that we are mature and emotionally balanced. The closeness of marriage creates a friction that either builds a fire that destroys everything or rounds off the edges and sharpens our spirits. God made marriage not only for the joy it brings but for its ability to expose our weaknesses and remind us of our fallibility. In marriage we go deeper, climb higher, reach further, and develop beyond the perceived limits of our humanity. It is heaven's incubator where we hatch into eternity. "Whoso findeth a wife findeth a good thing, and obtaineth favour of the LORD." Proverbs 18:22

> **Marriage properly ordered is the quickest path to obtaining wisdom, grace, mercy, patience, faith, compassion, and humility— especially humility.**

I could ask, "What is your marriage doing for you?" But the more pertinent question is, "What is your marriage doing for your wife?" Is she being perfected or rejected? Are you causing her to aspire to greater things or expire in fatigue? Is she climbing or declining? Loving or loathing? Does she serve you with joy or with a sense of duty? Does she know she is your treasure or does she feel used and abused? Your job as her husband is to cleanse her, not offend her with words of criticism.

If you fail to perfect your wife, you not only fail her, you fail God; you fail the entire human process. You fail the kingdom of God. Since God chose marriage to illustrate his ministry to the church, to fail in marriage is to defame the ministry of Christ. To fail to sanctify your wife is an opportunity lost for eternity.

STOP! Don't commit depressicide. God has a solution, and I am going to tell you what it is.

## Wash With Words

Look at the passage again and this time focus on verse 26.

### Ephesians 5:25-27

**25** Husbands, love your wives, even as Christ also loved the church, and gave himself for it;

**26** That he might sanctify and cleanse it with the **washing of water by the word,**

**27** That he might present it to himself a glorious church, not having spot, or wrinkle, or any such thing; but that it should be holy and without blemish.

> **We sanctify our wives the same way Jesus sanctifies the church— by our words.**

The passage implies that a wife needs sanctifying, cleansing, and washing, for she has spots, wrinkles, and blemishes. The goal of this sanctification is "that he might present it to himself a glorious church." Again the assumption is that Christ, and by extension husbands, married imperfect brides and must engage in a sanctifying process so one day they can present their brides to themselves in a sanctified state.

We sanctify our wives the same way Jesus sanctifies the church—by our words. Christ's words to the church wash away impurities. Listen to his words. "Come unto me, all ye that labour and are heavy laden, and I will give you rest. Take my yoke upon you, and learn of me; for I am meek and lowly in heart: and ye shall find rest unto your souls. For my yoke is easy, and my burden is light." Matthew 11:28-30 What beautiful words, inviting the lowliest and most needy to come.

As Jesus ministered, " . . . all bare him witness, and wondered at the **gracious words** which proceeded out of his mouth." Luke 4:22

"[T]he **words that I speak unto you, they are spirit, and they are life**." John 6:63 The song says, "Sing them over again to me, wonderful words of life . . . ."

The words of Christ cause us to sing with grace in our hearts. "Let the **word of Christ dwell in you richly in all wisdom**; teaching and admonishing one another in psalms and hymns and spiritual songs, singing with grace in your hearts to the Lord." Colossians 3:16

When Israel went astray after other gods and came under severe judgment, God represented himself as a husband abandoned by his wife, saying, "Therefore, behold, I will allure her, and bring her into the wilderness, and **speak comfortably** unto her." Hosea 2:14 God saw that restoration of his bride began with alluring her with **comfortable** words.

## Speaking Healing Words

This can be the first day of your renewed marriage. You may not see fruit right away, but you must begin by cultivating the fallow ground with healing words. "A man hath joy by the answer of his mouth: and a word spoken in due season, how good is it!" Proverbs 15:23 Wives are always in season for "good words." They are hurt by our words. You have been hurt by her words, have you not? Where does it stop? It stops when one party (that's you) starts speaking comfortable words, gracious words, words that are spirit and life. The tongue can be a world of iniquity or it can be a tree of life. The power is in our words.

> **This can be the first day of your renewed marriage.**

> **James 3:6** And the tongue is a fire, a world of iniquity: so is the tongue among our members, that it defileth the whole body, and setteth on fire the course of nature; and it is set on fire of hell.

> **Proverbs 15:4** A wholesome tongue is a tree of life: but perverseness therein is a breach in the spirit.

Put your fiery tongue away like a man puts away his weapon. End the conflict by absorbing some blows without returning fire. Stop trying to win the argument and start trying to win your wife. Stop getting in the last word, and start getting in some pleasant words.

## Spots, Wrinkles, and Blemishes

The ministry of Christ to his bride is that of removing spots, wrinkles, and blemishes. I print the text again because it is so very important that you maintain your focus on what God says.

>  **Ephesians 5:25-27**
>  25 Husbands, love your wives, even as Christ also loved the church, and gave himself for it;
>
>  26 That he might **sanctify and cleanse** it with the washing of water by the word,
>
>  27 That he might present it to himself a glorious church, **not having spot, or wrinkle**, or any such thing; but that it should be holy and **without blemish**.

Note once again, the context for this passage is "Husbands, love your wives, even as Christ loved the church, and gave himself for it . . . " The purpose of the passage is not to reveal how Christ loved the church, but to give us an example of how a husband should love his wife. We have seen how he should sanctify and cleanse her with his words. Now we examine the nature of a husband's ministry.

I just love the Word of God. It is composed of perfect words, in the Received Text that is. The same cannot be said of commercial versions like the NIV and 200 other English perversions. The Holy Spirit has inspired this description of a man's ministry—spots, wrinkles, and blemishes. Everything that is wrong with your wife is summed up in these three words.

**Spots are foreign matter that stains.** They are not inherent. They are the result of carelessness or misuse. They stand out because they do not belong. They speak of a former event when something went wrong and the stain is left on the garment for all to see.

**Wrinkles result from disuse.** They are there to testify that the garment has not seen the light of day. It has been safely tucked away and not had a chance to get spotted by the world. A wrinkled garment is a protected garment, but apparently not well favored.

**A blemished garment is one that has an inherent flaw**. It was never perfect. It has always been marred by nature. Blemished garments are not usually put on the front shelf. They are not worn on special occasions. They must be kept at home and used for practical purposes lest the wearer be embarrassed in public.

WOW! Isn't God smart? And he never even got a degree in psychology. Consider all that is wrong with your wife: She is either **spotted** by the world through experiences that have left her with guilt, shame, or emotional issues, or she is **wrinkled** from having been cloistered like a slave and never allowed to develop as a person. She is wrinkled with hidden talents and gifts never developed. She is a wasted resource. Her husband soars higher while she stoops to scrub floors. Or a wife may be **blemished** from birth or from limitations placed upon her in her developing years. Her very personality is flawed, or her social skills are clumsy, or her motherly instincts are missing, or she is gawky and clumsy by nature. She could have a low IQ or be physically or mentally impaired. There are many ways a woman can come to maturity with blemishes that are part of her very body and soul.

A proud husband may be ashamed of his wife's moral spots or be embarrassed by her social wrinkles; or he may have pity on her for the imperfections of her blemishes. Know for certain, his dissatisfaction is quite apparent to her, exacerbating the problems, causing her to either retreat or fight for the respect she deserves, leaving both in an unhappy marriage.

I know of no young bride coming to marriage without some spot, wrinkle, or blemish. Some are unspotted by the world, but wrinkled from lack of experience. Others may be spotted but far from wrinkled. Still others may be neither spotted nor wrinkled, but blemished. Unless you marry a 60-year-old widow that has already gone through a sanctifying process, your new bride will need sanctifying in one or more areas, and the process won't be complete on your first anniversary.

## Spots

> **2 Peter 3:14** Wherefore, beloved, seeing that ye look for such things, be diligent that ye may be found of him in peace, **without spot, and blameless**.

> **Jude 22-23** And of some have compassion, making a difference: And others save with fear, pulling them out of the fire; hating even the **garment spotted by the flesh**.

> **1 Timothy 6:14** That thou keep this commandment **without spot**, unrebukeable, until the appearing of our Lord Jesus Christ:

A woman who comes to marriage other than as a virgin is spotted. It matters not what others see; the stain is on her conscience. It affects her self-image. Even if her only fornication was with her eventual husband, the stain is the same, for the shame was hers before marriage and she did not leave it at the altar. A divorcee comes into marriage with many stains. A large number of women were molested when they were children, and that stain runs much deeper than the adult fornication stain.

In our modern age, some girls are stained by sexting and immodest dress and behavior, or exposure to sexually suggestive or explicit movies and music. Some girls come to marriage having experimented with homosexual acts in their early teens.

Others will testify to none of the above, but the stain comes in little shades, thin layer after layer through their associations with unrighteous friends and peers. It is impossible to attend a public school and not be stained. When you touch something, it touches you, and every relationship is reciprocal. Lot lived in Sodom but did not share their immorality. Yet the Bible says Lot "vexed his righteous soul from day to day with their unlawful deeds." [2 Peter 2:8]

Your wife may have a "vexed" soul. If she failed to "keep this commandment without spot" and now wears a "garment spotted by the flesh," with your help she can be "found of him in peace, **without spot, and blameless.**" Jesus is the great washer of spotted garments, for I have personally witnessed thousands who "have washed their robes, and made them white in the blood of the Lamb." [Revelation 7:14] It is called "the washing of regeneration, and renewing of the Holy Ghost." [Titus 3:5] The writer of Hebrews asks a rhetorical question, "How much more shall the blood of Christ, who through the eternal Spirit **offered himself without spot to God**, purge your conscience from dead works to serve the living God?" [Hebrews 9:14] He who had no spot offered himself to God as a substitute for all who have soiled their garments with sin and shame. He died as if he were the spotted one, suffering the full consequences of all sin. He now offers his unspotted robe in exchange for soiled ones. He bore our shame so we can bear his holiness. The God who "calleth those things which be not as though they were" Romans 4:17 stands ready and willing to call you and your wife spotless. It is not a matter of undoing the past or of making amends. It is a free gift of righteousness that can be received without precondition.

### Romans 5:17-20

**17** For if by one man's offence death reigned by one; much more they which receive abundance of grace and of the gift of righteousness shall reign in life by one, Jesus Christ.)

**18** Therefore as by the offence of one judgment came upon all men to condemnation; even so by the righteousness of one the free gift came upon all men unto justification of life.

**19** For as by one man's disobedience many were made sinners, so by the obedience of one shall many be made righteous.

**20** Moreover the law entered, that the offence might abound. But where sin abounded, grace did much more abound:

It is not a matter of doing; the work of redemption has already been done by Christ. You must believe to receive. It is not a matter of great faith; it is just a little faith placed in a big God that washes away spots and stains. Where your wife's sin (spots) abounds, your grace should much more abound as does Christ's.

> **The work of redemption has already been done by Christ.**

## Washing Away Deep Stains

I know many of you want to tell me that your wife is, in fact, a believing Christian but still has latent guilt and insecurity hanging around from her past. I understand that some people have a difficult time letting go of deep scars even after God has forgiven them. I know it is our nature to form opinions about ourselves from past experiences and to interpret our present in terms of a dead past. But the solution is the same. To the degree that we believe in the forgiveness and cleansing of the Lord Jesus Christ, our consciences are purged from dead works. Unregenerate sinners and saved, soiled souls alike need the same washing. Keep coming to the living well and the spots will disappear from the conscience.

Here, Sir, is where you come in as her sanctifier and cleanser. God cleanses with his words and so must you. Your spotted wife needs to hear words of forgiveness and assurance. I am not saying you need to forgive her. I assume you have already done that. If not, stop reading right now and go apologize for any part you had in her guilt and for failing to make it clear that you treasure her greatly. But if the air is clear between the two of you and her conscience is spotted in a very personal way, you should become a channel of assurance that she is forgiven by God and is indeed a worthy human being. We tend to form opinions about ourselves from the depths of other people's eyes. Just one rejection or criticism from you can set her back six months. You must maintain an atmosphere of acceptance through the words you speak. Your tongue can be a world of iniquity or a fountain of peace. The power to remove your wife's spots is in your hands and it is your responsibility to do so. She will need more than your grace and opinion; you must also instruct her in the Word of God so she knows God forgives her as well.

**You are your wife's sanctifier and cleanser.**

Don't feel cheated for having a spotted wife. It is your opportunity to glorify God by emulating his role as sanctifier and savior. It is your calling as a husband. God has entrusted you with this task. She is his child and he wants her cleansed even more than you do. He died to make it possible and expects you to live to make it practical.

## Spotted Bride Made Clean

Dear Mr. and Mrs. Pearl,

I would like to share with you some of my story in case you find it of use for your men's book.

I had a childhood that left me very lacking as a wife, mother, and functioning adult. My father was manipulative and abusive mentally and physically. Both of my parents put on a religious act for the public that was a cover-up for their lazy selfishness, which created an angry and chaotic home. Many predators (including my brother) took advantage of our dysfunction to sexually victimize me and my siblings.

I was gentle, timid, sensitive, and always had a great desire to please others. As a child I felt that I was stupid, I couldn't do anything right, and I was never good enough to earn love or even be noticed. As a teenager I became calloused to my parents' emotional manipulation and I was rebellious to authority. I found that I could win favor in social circles by putting on my own act and so I became skilled in my own methods of manipulation.

This was the environment that I came out of at eighteen when I met and married my husband. I was introspective, thoughtful, able to reason, and my abusive history had matured me in many ways. But emotionally I was still a disabled child. I could not handle conflict and had learned to either lie or submit to abuse.

There was not a honeymoon period for us. My sweet husband was forced into a role of being a parent in many ways. He had to force me to dress modestly, practice safe habits, and not allow myself to be taken advantage of. I acted compliant in his presence while rebelling and dishonoring him behind his back and then lying to avoid conflict or blame. In addition, I was entrenched in depression, grief, and self-pity. David had to get tough and force me to do the most basic responsibilities—cleaning, cooking, and being active.

**God has entrusted you with this task.**

Despite all of the conflict and ugliness that I presented David with, he never withheld his love or approval from me. He constantly affirmed that he thought I was beautiful. He jumped on every opportunity to praise me. And even when things were at the worst, he would find something about me to brag to his coworkers, family, and even strangers in the store.

The Lord is really the one responsible for my healing, which is even still taking place, but I know that David is a blessing God gave me even when I had turned my back on him. Through my wonderful husband I have learned so much about the love that my Heavenly Father has for me.

We have now been married for six and a half years and experience a wonderful unity in our views, dreams, and goals. I have read your wife's book and am working on being the help meet I know my husband deserves. I continue to struggle with my old habits of depression and just plain selfishness, but I have been greatly affected by hearing what you say on joy and parental attitudes, and I am excited for the benefits my family will reap as I practice it more every day!

Thank you for speaking truth,

David's help meet

## Spotted Bride's Husband Speaks

Dear Mr. Pearl,

My wife did not ask me to contribute to her letter, but I think some clarification is needed.

My wife is speaking honestly of her deep inner struggles, but I assure you that she is far more than she presents herself to be. Her difficult childhood planted seeds in her that are now showing fruit of strength in character. She has a quiet and enduring spirit about her. Before I proposed, I knew that once this young woman was transplanted to good soil and tended well, she would bear fruit that would feed me and our children well. And I was right! I married this woman because I could see pure gold under only a thin layer of debris.

I believed then, as I do now, that all husbands should call out the woman of God in their wives. I expected more than just "performance" from her. I required her to be what God requires from all of us, and I gave her a great deal of love through the process. That is all I did.

As a side note, I would admonish any husband who is "disappointed" in his wife's performance. Many husbands expect their wives to do dog tricks for their own selfish pleasures. We do not have any Biblical directive to require that and therefore have no authority to demand it. And if a wife does happen to perform under those conditions, it will not bring the satisfaction that one would expect. He will see her expression of being prostituted and used. That only brings an awareness of failure to a man's sense of mission. Instead, a man should think less highly of himself and then submit HIMSELF to the authority structure that God has delineated. Then, and only then, is it natural and easy to see where he has responsibility to fit and craft his wife into a beautiful piece of "functional art."

By the way, I have gleaned a great deal from your example and found a sort of father figure in your writings. You live out and put on paper what I have dreamed about. You give me confidence to stand on what I have long been ridiculed for believing. Thank you for defining it so clearly.

And thank you for creating such a wonderful role model for my wife,

David

## Wrinkle

A wrinkled garment is an unused garment. It has been placed on the shelf and left unattended. It was valued enough to keep but not valued enough to wear. Most wives come to marriage wrinkled, and most stay wrinkled through their entire life. One wrinkled lady writes:

Mr. Pearl,

I've heard foolish men making comments about their wives' weight, features, appearance, cooking, etc. Don't they realize when they are doing that, they are cutting off their own arms? When my husband comments on my beauty, I feel like a flower opening up and blooming. I flourish like a healthy blossom receiving all the optimum nutrients and growing conditions. Men should know they get what they grow.

Debra

Again I print the text so your understanding will be rooted in what God says. My job is to explain the sense of it that you might understand what you read (Nehemiah 8:8).

### Ephesians 5:25-27
**25** Husbands, love your wives, even as Christ also loved the church, and gave himself for it;

**26** That he might sanctify and cleanse it with the washing of water by the word,

**27** That he might present it to himself a glorious church, **not having** spot, or **wrinkle**, or any such thing; but that it should be holy and without blemish.

My wife came to marriage somewhat wrinkled. She had many talents and gifts that were never developed. I think she was also a little blemished. She lacked confidence in any public setting where she felt outclassed. Like me, she was raised in a very rural environment in the Deep South. Her experiences never took her far from home or from her roots, and she lacked confidence in many areas. In the early years of our marriage, it aggravated me to see her crumble in social settings. I had been an evangelist since I was seventeen and had traveled extensively, meeting people of every class. I had also attended a nationally acclaimed art academy and then went on to get my BS degree in another college. I had seen enough to know that every man, regardless of his station, is frail and limited in scope, so no one intimidated me. But I watched her distort the truth in public to avoid conflict. I observed her get run over intellectually by people who thought more of themselves and less of her. I had much more faith in her than she did in herself.

She had the opposite problem from most women today. She had been raised in a very conservative Independent Baptist home and church, coming to marriage expecting to obey and serve. And she did. Except for those occasions when she suddenly blew up, she was the perfect servant. Several years passed with little progress in her self-confidence. It was three years before we had our first child. When Rebekah was about four years old and Deb was teaching her to read and write, she observed that Rebekah seemed to see and write letters backward. So she called Memphis State University and asked to speak to a child development professor. Amazingly a man returned her call. When she described the problem, he told her it was dyslexia. "Dis-what-e-ah?" He suggested a book, so off to the library Deb went and found several books on reading disabilities. Concerned for our daughter, she devoured the information and then launched her own program. She had me make a small box to hold sand and then guided Rebekah as she wrote with her finger in the sand.

Over the next two years, she became an expert on dyslexia. She spent many hours in the library reading and studying many things. My part in all this was to encourage her, to assure her that she could do it, that she was capable; and sometimes I had to babysit or build sand boxes or whatever her latest experiment called for.

She didn't stop with a study of dyslexia; she followed her imagination down many paths and wanted to try everything. Homeschooling became a laboratory of discovery. I remember spending two days making a beautiful tofu press that got

> **I had much more faith in her than she did in herself.**

used twice. I helped her capture swarms of wild bees and built hives for them. She became a student of everything, reading an average of four or five books a week, but she still lacked public confidence, often yielding her superior knowledge to more dominant women. It aggravated me even more to know that she was the master but allowed herself to be treated with condescension.

As more children came along and her homeschool class grew, she created her own curriculum. In trying to relate to the children the recent history of the civil rights movement under Dr. Martin Luther King, she searched for a children's book but found none, so she wrote her own, even drawing pictures and coloring them. The kids loved it, and others who read it thought it was wonderful.

Seeing an opportunity for her to develop her talents, I encouraged her to attend a night course on writing and publishing. I kept the kids and she came home excited, telling me all the fascinating things she was learning. So I told her she should publish her book *Listen to My Dream*. She drew the characters and I painted them. We went to a local printer to get guidance on sizes and methods. We published 5,000 copies and I encouraged her to fly to Atlanta and meet with the King Foundation. Over the next year she traveled alone and met with many people including lawyers, heads of large denominations and chain stores, and the King Foundation. The first 5,000 sold quickly and we reprinted. The public school system ordered books for every fifth grade teacher, and the public libraries began to carry her book. We spent our meager savings promoting it, and just when she was negotiating an order for 1,000,000 books, the King Foundation shut us down, demanding an exorbitant percentage.

It was a heady ride. She became famous in her own right, granted in a small circle, but she earned the respect of many people in high places, and it changed her. She would never again allow herself to sit on the shelf and gather wrinkles. We were poor for the endeavor but richer in spirit. It would be years before I would sit down to write *To Train Up a Child*, but when it was finished she knew exactly how to get it published, and when it proved to be popular in our small circle she knew how to offer it to a larger audience. The wrinkles were all worked out after 20 years of marriage and I like her even better. I have presented her to myself without spot or wrinkle or blemish.

**Is your wife meeting her full potential?** Today she is a tigress. She won't back down from the Queen of England or a hostile CNN reporter. She will lecture a college professor or tell a doctor how to better treat his patients. She has grown to be a more versatile help meet. She has been my able partner and associate in business and ministry. I have allowed her to be my help meet and she has risen and risen and risen to the occasion. I don't know what her limits are and she doesn't acknowledge any. Sexy, brains, creativity, and personality—what more could a man ask for? Well . . . maybe a good crabbing expedition in the middle of the night.

What about you? Is your wife meeting her full potential? Does she have contributions to make to the church and community that have been stifled by cloistering? Some men are so insecure they do not want their wives to grow, lest they stand taller. Wives confined to diapers and dishes can grow weary and discontent, feeling they are trapped on an endless merry-go-round where every day is the same and the scenery never changes. Provide opportunity for your wife to grow as a person. You cannot decide her interests. She must discover them by trying many things. When something lights her fire, she will brighten and become enthusiastic in the pursuit of it. When that happens provide the means for her to pursue her interests.

One caution is called for: A wife's interests and the pursuit of them should never detract from the family. She should not abandon the home to seek personal fulfillment. The family should be made better by her personal development.

## Without Blemish

A garment that was made with imperfections is blemished as is one that suffered fundamental structural degradation.

**Ephesians 5:25-27**

**25** Husbands, love your wives, even as Christ also loved the church, and gave himself for it;

**26** That he might sanctify and cleanse it with the washing of water by the word,

**27** That he might present it to himself a glorious church, not having spot, or wrinkle, or any such thing; but that it should be holy and **without blemish**.

A wife that is blemished has a fault that may be constitutional in nature or so ingrained in her soul or body as to be inseparable from her person. A blemish is not the result of sin. There is no blame in it. In many cases there is no cure for it. The cure is in learning to live with it, or even developing it as an asset.

My wife came to me with one blemish. She is deaf in one ear—apparently from birth. She developed it into an asset by learning to sleep with her good ear down when the house was too noisy. I thought her extreme hick accent was a blemish until the day I heard a very cool guy say he thought it was delightfully cute and charming. I have watched her charm a shop owner into selling to her at half price. She can entertain a crowd all day long with her colloquialisms and manner. It took Loretta Lynn to the top of the charts. I have heard that some of the country singers try to mimic the accent. So, there you are. I married a famous country singer that can't sing and was not yet famous. But she is cute. And country gals do it better.

## The Cackler

I know another fellow who married a talented woman, but she had some obvious blemishes. He was ashamed of her in public. If there were 100 people in a public place you could hear her laughing above everything. She sounded like a hen that just laid a double-yolked egg. He was a quiet man with lots of dignity, but she seemed to take no notice of the social tone around her, being totally unaware of her intrusive laughter. And she laughed at inappropriate moments. There were other uncouth mannerisms that caused him to be ashamed to take her into public.

The worst thing about it was that she felt his rejection. He didn't tell her what bothered him; he just showed exasperation and displeasure at her presence. She grew angry and belligerent, further acting in embarrassing ways.

This went on for years, and there was talk of divorce. She even left him for a while. But slowly my friend came to treasure his wife for other virtues he saw in her and expressed his gratitude and admiration for her motherhood and her cooking and housekeeping skills. She began to relax in public and didn't have a need to be in the center of everything. She stopped laughing like a babbling chimpanzee and gained some grace and dignity. As he responded, she responded and a cycle was set in motion as they both matured.

The last I saw of them, she was still a little gawky, but nothing like before, and he is more accepting of her lack of social skills. He has worked the blemishes out of her, and their marriage improves with age.

## The Girl No One Ever Noticed

About ten years ago, a carload of young people just passing through stopped by for a visit. There was one girl that sat in the middle, slumped down on the couch with her long, naturally blond hair covering her face. I noticed her for her inconspicuousness. She seemed broken, self-diminishing. When they all stood up to leave, I saw that she was well over six feet tall, but she stooped and slumped as if to make herself shorter. Her thin body looked like a pretzel standing there in the background. I never could see her face, for she kept it turned away and shut down like a blank computer screen. You seldom see people that blemished. In her mid-twenties, she was the girl no one ever noticed.

About two years later an acquaintance stopped by with his new bride. She stood beside him like an oversized shadow, seeming fearful and apprehensive. He bragged on her and complemented himself for obtaining such a treasure. After several years of marriage, I saw them again. This time she was standing up straight like she was proud of her height. She laughingly calls her husband "Little Man." He looks up at her with delight and they now have several handsome kids. They exercise together. She filled out in all the right places and her face now looks at you with interest. She is no longer a shadow and is actually quite attractive, something no one else could see until her husband loved her as she was and took her with her wrinkles and blemishes. She has grown under his sanctifying grace. And she has helped temper some of his rough edges. He still needs some work, though.

I don't really know the nature of her blemishes, but I am sure they go back a long way. I do know she was not molested. She was virtuous in every way and highly moral, but something in her soul was blemished. Her husband/savior has redeemed a life that was sinking into the recesses. She now blooms and would catch the eye of any man. That's God's work done God's way, and it never lacks God's supply.

God receives all of us just as we are with our blemishes, gawkiness, and clumsiness, whether we are too tall, too short, too dumb, slow-witted, one-eared, paralyzed, deaf, blind, or poor. He fills up his house with just such, and reminds us that "not many wise men after the flesh, not many mighty, not many noble, are called: But God hath chosen the foolish things of the world to confound the wise; and God hath chosen the weak things of the world to confound the things which are mighty; And base things of the world, and things which are despised, hath God chosen, yea, and things which are not, to bring to nought things that are: That no flesh should glory in his presence." 1 Corinthians 1:26-29 Can we love any less or demand any more? Are we better than God? If he is willing to receive all and then dedicate his life to sanctifying us, who are we to expect a heavenly marriage without engaging in a patient sanctifying process?

**Likewise, ye wives, be in subjection to your own husbands; that, if any obey not the word, they also may without the word be won by the conversation of the wives; For after this manner in the old time the holy women also, who trusted in God, adorned themselves, being in subjection unto their own husbands: Even as Sara obeyed Abraham, calling him lord: whose daughters ye are, as long as ye do well, and are not afraid with any amazement.**
1 Peter 3:1, 5-6

Chapter 13

# OBEY INDEED?

## How Do I Get My Wife to Obey Me?

In 1 Peter we read the noted exhortation to women, "Likewise, ye wives, *be* in **subjection to your own husbands**" and " . . . in the old time the holy women also, who trusted in God . . . **being in subjection unto their own husbands**: Even as Sara **obeyed Abraham**, calling him lord:" I can hear a man saying, "Yeah, a woman needs to know her place." I answer, "There is no need; you will remind her often enough."

I have received a thousand letters from men asking the same question, "How do I get my wife to obey me?" Likewise, at speaking engagements men have come up and made similar statements, "I have shown my wife the Scripture that says she is to obey me, but she will not listen." I have responded, "What passage of Scripture tells a man to demand that his wife obey him?"

"Well, it says 'Wives, obey your husbands.'"

"No, it says, 'wives **submit** yourselves unto your own husbands,' but to whom is the passage addressed?"

"To wives," they hastily answer.

"And who is commanding wives to submit to their husbands?"

"God is," they confidently assert.

I respond, "So God commands the wife to submit, but where does he command the man to command his wife to submit?" Where in the New Testament do we read of how a man is to rebuke a rebellious wife? God commands wives to submit, but he never even suggests that husbands are to assume the right of demanding submission. I have been married 40 years and have never told my wife it is her duty to submit to me. I feel it would be a cheap shot indeed to use God's command to women to settle a marital dispute. It would be taking undue advantage to use divine leverage against another human being. I would feel like the pope or a cult leader to control another by invoking God and the Bible. I know it is my responsibility to earn her respect and gain her confidence.

My wife is telling your wife to obey her own husband, and so she should. "The aged women . . . teach the young women to be sober, to love their husbands . . . obedient to their own husbands . . . ." Titus 2:3-5 And when I teach the Bible to the church and come across a passage where God commands a woman to submit to her husband, as God's voice I teach the ladies to submit to their own husbands. But this book is not directed at wives. They got hit pretty hard in *Created to Be His Help Meet*. It is our turn, men, and we are not going to cop out by throwing all the burden on the little lady.

## Not Created to Obey?

Though it is none of our business what God says to wives, it will serve us well to examine all the Scripture carefully so as to adjust our misconceptions.

In the creation account neither God nor Adam said anything about Eve being created to obey. God made her so Adam would not be alone, so she could complete him and help him in soul and spirit, not so he would have a servant.

> **Genesis 2:18** And the LORD God said, It is not good that the man should be alone; I will make him an help meet for him.

After Eve's creation Adam responds prophetically, defining the historical significance of the moment. <u>Notice he makes no allusion to her obeying him</u>.

> **Genesis 2:23-24** And Adam said, This is now bone of my bones, and flesh of my flesh: she shall be called Woman, because she was taken out of Man. Therefore shall a man leave his father and his mother, and shall cleave unto his wife: and they shall be one flesh.

But after Eve initiated the first sin and then lured her husband into disobedience, God placed a curse upon Satan, nature, Adam, and upon Eve.

**Genesis 3:16** Unto the woman he said, I will greatly multiply thy sorrow and thy conception; in sorrow thou shalt bring forth children; and thy desire shall be to thy husband, and **he shall rule over thee**.

Paul's letter to Timothy reveals further consequences of the curse, describing why women are not allowed to hold the highest office in the church or to gain ascendance over men in a church setting and why their husbands are to rule over them.

### 1 Timothy 2:11-15

**11** Let the woman learn in silence with all subjection.

**12** But I suffer not a woman to teach, **nor to usurp authority over the man**, but to be in silence.

**13** For Adam was first formed, then Eve.

**14** And Adam was not deceived, but the **woman being deceived** was in the transgression.

**15** Notwithstanding she shall be saved in childbearing, if they continue in faith and charity and holiness with sobriety.

Since Adam was "not deceived" by Satan's lies and Eve was, no doubt due to her female nature which rendered her more gullible than Adam, God has commanded men to not again put themselves in the place of granting leadership to women. They are the first to be swept away with cultish dogma.

But don't get haughty, men; just because God "busted" the woman down in rank due to her being deceived into listening to the enemy, that does not leave the man as her slave owner. Rather it places a responsibility upon man to now bear the full burden of leadership—leadership, not ownership.

## Curse on Child Bearing

The curse on Eve was two-fold.

**Genesis 3:16** Unto the woman he said, **I will greatly multiply thy sorrow and thy conception; in sorrow thou shalt bring forth children;** and thy desire shall be to thy husband, and he shall rule over thee.

For her disobedience God first cursed Eve with multiplying her sorrow through more frequent conceptions. Most mammals can conceive only once or twice a year, not every month as can the daughters of Eve. That is a Biblical doctrine not well received—or even known. And if we men had to go through it just one time, we would agree that it is a curse.

> **The curse on childbearing is lifted if the wife and husband develop a relationship of faith, charity, holiness, and sobriety.**

Frequent conceptions lead to more sorrow through more miscarriages, more stillborn babies, more sick and dying infants, and finally more sorrow from children going astray and disappointing by their sin and suffering. The greater emotional burden falls on women due to their created natures as nurturers.

But Paul indicates a wonderful thing. The curse on childbearing is lifted if the wife and husband develop a relationship of faith, charity, holiness, and sobriety.

> **1 Timothy 2:15** Notwithstanding **she shall be saved in childbearing**, if they continue in faith and charity and holiness with sobriety.

In a marriage where the wife does not do as did Eve in leading them into rebellion, and where the husband and wife continue in a state of faith, charity, holiness, and sobriety, a Christian couple will avoid the curse on childbirth. The promise is, "Notwithstanding she shall be saved in childbearing." That word *notwithstanding* means "in spite of, even though, although, regardless of the curse, even though there is a curse in force it will not apply to a couple walking after the Spirit of God."

You might want to read the above section again. It will be long time before you again see it in print or hear it in a sermon. I wasn't born in Zion, but I can read.

## Cursed to Be Ruled

The second part of the curse on Eve is the subject at hand. For her sin of being easily deceived, Eve was cursed to be ruled by her husband.

> **Genesis 3:16** Unto the woman he said, I will greatly multiply thy sorrow and thy conception; in sorrow thou shalt bring

forth children; and thy desire shall be to thy husband, **and he shall rule over thee**.

It is most significant that the first mention in the Bible of Adam ruling over Eve comes after their fall as a part of the curse. Just as Eve is cursed to be ruled, Adam is cursed to be the ruler. Which is the greater burden?

It is absolutely true that Adam was first formed and then Eve, and by nature Eve is Adam's help meet. Adam is not Eve's help meet. But there is no indication that circumstances in a sinless world would have required Eve to submit to Adam; there would have been no need. When Eve was deceived and led her husband into sin, the dynamics of their relationship to God, to nature, and to each other changed. As the weaker vessel her desire would now be to her husband and he would rule over her—like it or not, for better or for worse. The curse as to ruling is still in place and conditions remain the same, with men ruling over their wives who otherwise would have been partners in paradise. The curse lives. Look at Saudi Arabia, where a woman's testimony is worth half of a man's. Look at wife abuse in America and the entire Western world.

It is the presence of sin that makes the Ten Commandments, government, capital punishment, and the hierarchy of power in the home necessary. Eve was not created to be under rule. She earned the curse of subjection.

The general subjugation of women is not due to the application of a religious precept, Christian, Muslim, or otherwise; it is inherent in all cultures in every century from the beginning of human history and down to the present. Women don't seem to like it, and men in general take advantage of it.

## Domestic Subjection Only

In the Christian world there exists a general concept that women are privates walking among an equal number of captains, all of whom must be saluted and obeyed. The curse did not place women in the position of surrendering to the rule of men in general—only their husbands. Peter addresses wives, telling them to be in subjection to their "**own** husbands"—not to every husband and not to every man, just their husband. Just in case we missed it, he repeats the phrase in verse 5, "their **own** husbands."

**1 Peter 3:1, 5** Likewise, ye wives, be in subjection to **your own** husbands; that, if any obey not the word, they also may without the word be won by the conversation of the wives; For after this manner in the old time the holy women also, who trusted in God, adorned themselves, being in subjection unto **their own** husbands:

Paul also emphasizes the fact that wives should be subject to "**their own** husbands," not to men in general.

**Ephesians 5:24** Therefore as the church is subject unto Christ, so let the wives be to **their own** husbands in every thing.

It is quite clear. The Holy Spirit did not want any misunderstanding on this issue. Knowing the propensity of men to rule over everything, and the vulnerability of women—"the weaker vessel"—he inserted the word *own* after *their* in **every** text where he commands a wife to submit. I know of many churches that assume a general policy of women being in subjection to men in general. It reminds me of the old European class system where the lower class should "know their place." Likewise, in the Old South, blacks were told to "know their place." Old social customs also dictated that children "know their place." In each case it is an attempt to protect elitists in their privileged positions. It is fear that creates and perpetuates layered social order. The top of the food chain fears loss of prestige and control, and the subjugated fear the hands that feed them. The system loses its cultish powers when all believe in individual dignity and equal worth before God.

> **Love never enslaves; rather it seeks liberty and free expression for all.**

Love never enslaves; rather it seeks liberty and free expression for all. If God gives worth and dignity to men, women, and children, by what right does another human being take that dignity away? Again I say, marriage is a corporation requiring a hierarchy of authority, and God has designated the man as the head, but his headship is limited to his family alone.

A woman may choose to obey God and therefore her husband, as did Abraham's wife Sarah, but there is no connection between the political structure of a marriage and the population in general.

## Not Created to Serve

My wife is telling your wives to serve their husbands. I am thankful she serves me, but we need to keep in mind that being born a man is not a license to be served. I have worked on construction sites off and on since I was ten years old. There are times when you must leave one of the regular hands in charge of the construction while you get materials or bid on another job. Some employees are so immature that they see their leadership role as a chance to tell other people what to do rather than as a responsibility to get the job done correctly. They get heady with power and act the fool to the detriment of the project, making it very difficult for the other men to obey them. The job suffers and the designated foreman blames the workers.

> **The leadership role God gives a man in marriage is not a privileged position; it is a great responsibility requiring sacrifice and service.**

Likewise the leadership role God gives a man in marriage is not a privileged position; it is a great responsibility requiring sacrifice and service. I am embarrassed by the attitude and actions of many preachers and laymen alike. Some misguided men see the world as divided into the served and the serving—male and female. Women are not created to serve men any more than men are created to serve women. There is nothing in Scripture that suggests the female gender is to be subjugated by the male.

Both are created to meet the needs of the other, which means that each voluntarily serves the other, but to reduce either to the role of servant is a perversion of nature. Your wife is not your assistant. She assists, but not as a business assistant or domestic servant would. Her assistance is first on the level of the soul and spirit, which may then result in gracious, voluntary serving. If not, you have no right to intimidate her and certainly no power to constrain.

Upon marriage, my wife immediately commenced serving me, but it was years before I would learn that it was a gift from someone who wanted to bless me, not a woman doing what women are supposed to do. For years I thought it was all about me. I was the head and she was the . . . well, she was there to make me happy and successful, to help me do whatever I wanted to do. It was her role to be happy serving. Somebody has to be boss, and, imperfect as I was, God appointed me to be the head of the home and her to . . . you know, cheerfully do her duty. I knew that when a woman gets right with God she stops complaining and nagging and starts serving her husband without question. But then, I acquired my views from my culture, not from God.

## Your Helper, Not Your Slave

The people at No Greater Joy work for me. I am their boss. Many of my employees are smarter than I, and most of them have talents and abilities I do not possess. I trust them to fulfill their respective jobs, and I seek their advice in their area of expertise, often deferring to their judgments in a matter. Sometimes they even question a decision I make. I counter-challenge them and expect them to argue their point. I would be foolish to treat their opinions lightly. I would be cutting off my own success if I didn't treat them with respect.

**You are not her master; you are her partner in sanctification.**

You are not her master; you are her partner in sanctification. As head of the family, you are responsible to be an example and to patiently encourage your wife to grow as a person and to help her understand and perform her duties as your chief helper. Your role in marriage is not that of enforcer; it is that of an encourager.

## Submit, Not Obey

Several passages in the Bible instruct wives to submit to their own husbands, but obedience is only mentioned twice, and each has its own unique context. Following is one of the many commands that a wife should be in subjection, but it provides an example of Sarah going even further in an act of obedience.

> **1 Peter 3:1, 5-6** Likewise, ye wives, be in **subjection** to your own husbands; that, if any obey not the word, they also may without the word be won by the conversation of the wives; For after this manner in the old time the holy women also, who trusted in God, adorned themselves, being in **subjection** unto their own husbands: Even as **Sara obeyed Abraham**, calling

him lord: whose daughters ye are, as long as ye do well, and
are not afraid with any amazement.

The Bible records just two occasions in which Sarah obeyed Abraham,
so one of them will of necessity be the event to which Peter is referring.
The second episode is not significant; he commanded her to prepare
a meal and she did. Of course, if your wife doesn't prepare meals that
verse will be more relevant to you. The first event recorded in Genesis
12 is no doubt the experience in question.
When visiting Egypt, Abraham feared that
Pharaoh would see his beautiful wife Sarah
and have him killed so as to make of her an
eligible widow, so Abraham commanded
her to lie, saying she was only his sister.

> **Your role in marriage is
> not that of enforcer; it is
> that of an encourager.**

Sarah obeyed Abraham, lying as he commanded, calling him "lord." And
though she was in jeopardy of being taken to Pharaoh's bed, she was
"not afraid with any amazement" at the position her lying husband
had put her in. Her faith was justified when God intervened and struck
the Egyptians with diseases. Pharaoh divined that it was God's judgment
on his nation and discovered the ploy. He so feared God that he released
Abraham and Sarah and after a stern rebuke sent them away unharmed
with their goods.

Why make an issue between the very similar words *obey* and *submit*?
Because though they can be used interchangeably in many contexts, they
are different in connotation, not only in English but also in Hebrew and
Greek. (I make reference to Hebrew and Greek for those of you who are
foolishly enamored with two of the original languages.) A quick review
of every use of these two words readily reveals a wonderful distinction.
We get the same results in any language. Webster's accurately represents
the differences, as does Strong in his Greek word definitions, not that we
can fully trust either of them. Get a concordance or look them up in a
Bible program and read every use, noting the differences. That way you
won't have to take my word for it or A. W. Strong's or Webster's, or any
one of your favorite mothballed Greek scholars.

I won't go through all the proofs. It would be too long. You can research
it as you will. **Obey** has a much lower threshold than does **submit.** It can
be impersonal and devoid of heart motive. In Scripture, the winds and

the sea obey him. Devils obey him. A slave obeys his master. A child, through constraint, obeys his parents. Servants obey their masters. We are commanded to obey magistrates. The church is to obey them that have the spiritual rule over them. We put bits in horse's mouths and they obey us. Sarah obeyed Abraham in a very difficult situation. You could call that blind obedience, much like a slave renders to his master, or a child renders to his parents. No questions asked, no answers given.

Though God commends Sarah for her extraordinary obedience, (I must say it again) **the Bible never commands a wife to obey**. It commands much more than obedience—it commands her to submit. Submission is a voluntary attitude of cooperating. Strong is correct in saying that the Greek word behind "wives **submit**" was a "Greek military term meaning 'to arrange [troop divisions] in a military fashion under the command of a leader.'"

> **Submission is a voluntary attitude of cooperating.**

When Hagar fled from her jealous and oppressive mistress, "the angel of the Lord said unto her, Return to thy mistress, and **submit** thyself under her hands." Genesis 16:9 Not just grudgingly obey. She had never stopped obeying; she just treated Sarah with disrespect. She was told to return and **submit**, that is to willingly and with all her heart place herself under the authority of her mistress.

Paul employs the same Greek word in the book of Romans. "For they being ignorant of God's righteousness, and going about to establish their own righteousness, have not **submitted** themselves unto the righteousness of God." Romans 10:3 The word **obey** would not be an appropriate synonym to replace *submitted* in this passage—"have not [obeyed] themselves unto the righteousness of God." To *submit* to the gift of righteousness is the opposite of *obeying* unto righteousness. Those striving to obtain righteousness through human means were not submitting to God's offer of righteousness through Jesus Christ. I know many misguided souls who are obeying God but not submitting to the gift of righteousness. A wife could obey her husband without an ounce of submission.

Look at 1 Corinthians 16:15-16 and 1 Peter 5:5. They carry the meaning of "voluntarily conforming to and assisting."

Consider the dual use of *submit* in this passage. "**Submitting yourselves one to another in the fear of God. Wives, submit yourselves unto your own husbands, as unto the Lord.**" Ephesians 5:21-22 Again *obey* could not be used as a synonym in either setting. It could not read, "[Obeying] yourselves one to another" or "Wives, [obey] yourselves unto your own husbands." Christians, men and women in the church, are told to submit to each other. That means a voluntary yielding of ourselves to the service and blessing of all concerned. We do not obey each other in the church; we submit to each other.

The words *obey* and *submit* used in parallel in the book of Hebrews confirms they are not close synonyms. "**Obey them that have the rule over you, and submit yourselves: for they watch for your souls, as they that must give account, that they may do it with joy, and not with grief: for that is unprofitable for you.**" Hebrews 13:17 **Obey** and then on a higher level **submit**. Obedience is good, but submission is from the heart.

View all 16 uses of *submit* in the entire Bible and you will confirm to yourself that when God tells wives to "submit themselves" to their own husbands, he is saying something quite different from "obey the old man." Slaves, children, and dogs obey. Love submits for purposes higher than fear of disapproval. Obedience can be given to someone you fear or hate, but submission is the act of joyfully giving one's self.

**Obedience can be given to someone you fear or hate, but submission is the act of joyfully giving one's self.**

Every use of submit (in all its forms) is immediately followed by a reflexive pronoun (yourselves, themselves, himself, etc.,) indicating that the verb's action is being done to the submitter. The submitter is the one getting the action of the verb. Whereas when the verb "obey" is used, the one being obeyed gets the action.

Some husbands demand obedience and get it, but they never get submission. It reminds me of the little boy who refused to sit down until he had been firmly spanked, at which point he sat down. When later challenged by his brother he said, "I might have been sitting down on the outside, but I was standing up on the inside." I know you do not want to settle for having your wife obey you on the outside while still standing up on the inside.

You should also do personal or group Bible study on the word *rule*, as in "he shall rule over thee." You will be shocked that Biblical ruling is quite different from the modern concept of "divine right" ruling.

## Contrary Commander

Mr. Pearl,

I hope you tell the men, Love is not "God says you are to obey me, so it's my way or the highway. You need to read Debi Pearl's book and get yourself in order." My husband (a pastor) has actually said this, and somehow does not believe this is contrary to his vows. He is a tyrant that robs me (and the children) of giving him the gift of submission, because he demands it angrily. I do not feel loved; I feel owned. And my four-year-old wants to know why Daddy hates him.

Kim

No doubt this husband is a carnal Command Man, for there is no way someone so self-centered could come to be regarded as a spiritual leader other than by lazy parishioners who are deceived by his commanding presence. A Steady Man would rarely be such as spoiled, insecure jerk. A Visionary might speak in such a manner if he were provoked, but he would apologize soon enough and try to make up for his error; whereas the immature, self-centered Command Man actually believes in his divine right as a man.

Wise up, Mister. You are an embarrassment to the rest of us men. I wish there were another category to put you in—man, woman, and *other*. You are not God and you have no right to command your wife to obey you. Any man criticizing his wife and suggesting she read *Created to Be His Help Meet* is anything but Christ-like.

She rightly and wisely observes that you have robbed her of "giving [you] the gift of submission." It is impossible to give that which is taken from you by force or intimidation. You cannot demand a gift, or love, or marital submission; it is given voluntarily to those who do not deserve it and is an act of grace and mercy. You, Sir, have made yourself higher than God by angrily demanding to be obeyed. Not even God gets down on his children like that. Her submission to you is between her and God.

Until you change your attitude, you will never have her heart, and without her heart you will never have a marriage that is fulfilling. Abraham Lincoln would write her a proclamation of emancipation.

> **There is no Scripture in which God commands wives to exercise indiscriminate obedience toward their husbands.**

There is no Scripture in which God commands wives to exercise indiscriminate *obedience* toward their husbands—discriminating *submission*, yes, but not blind *obedience*. And there is certainly no Scripture that licenses a husband to assume a position of expecting obedience. When exhorting the young preacher Titus concerning young wives (text above), Paul didn't even tell the preacher to command the young women to be obedient to their husbands; he told Titus to tell the aged women to do it. That is why my "aged" wife wrote *Created to Be His Help Meet* and not I. She is in a position to teach the delicate subject since she is not the one seeking to be obeyed. It is totally inappropriate for a man to teach his wife to obey him or even to submit to him. On the outside it looks extremely self-serving. How can it not be?

## Letter from Loveless

Dear Mr. Pearl,

My heart is to honor God. After reading the lady's *Created* book I started making a real effort to serve and bless my man, but he takes the "wanna" right out of me. He never says "Thanks" or "You look great" or "You are the best cook," or even, "I can see you were busy today because the house is so clean." He does give me plenty of instruction and rebuke when I don't do a thing just as he wished. I try so hard to do as he says, but he never mentions that I have done well. When I am a good helper I wish he would say so. Just one little word would mean so much.

Debra

## Not-So-Dear, Thankless Tyrant,

When a woman does what she can to serve and honor her man and he greedily consumes her sacrifice with unthankfulness, he is destroying both his wife and his marriage. It will not be surprising if your wife grows bitter over the years. Your perpetual presumption upon her passive acquiescence could be borne only by a martyr.

Jesus said, "Well done, thou good and faithful servant." Mr. Wife Abuser, why can't you express a little gratitude and appreciation? Yours is not just a wife problem; it is a heart problem. I can imagine how your children are going to turn out, and it's not good. If it is within your power to bless another human being with a few words, with a smile, with an appreciative pat, and you don't do so, you are lower than the skunk that gets in the henhouse and eats the chickens that lay the eggs the children would eat. It doesn't matter what you think you have communicated; the bottom line is how you have made her feel. It is your duty to make her feel cherished. God commands you to cherish your wife. Anything less is disobedience to God. God says you are to wash her with your words. Start raining down grace and mercy on the poor woman.

> **Every woman deserves to be loved, and you are the only one in position to love the mother of your children.**

Every woman deserves to be loved, and you are the only one in position to love the mother of your children. If you don't love her, your children will grow up under the tutelage of an unloved woman—sad, angry, and bitter. It is hard enough to get it right when two people cherish and honor each other, but when they are bleeding the life out of one another, what hope is there the children will grow up to be emotionally stable human beings? None. You make your bed, and your children and grandchildren will lie it, and five generations from now they will wonder when the family lineage became dysfunctional and destructive. It is happening on your watch. Only you can change it. Your great, great grandkids living in foster care or an institution won't know or care that you blamed your wife. Blame is the path evil takes when it doesn't want to bow at the altar of repentance.

## These Are Hard Sayings

I know I am hard on you. I am hard on myself. I am not, as some writers, using up good paper to "encourage" you to adopt a few positive principles that will enhance your happiness and supplement your satisfaction. I am as a prophet calling you to repentance, for life is a battle between this compromised human nature that is ugly beyond belief and the Holy Spirit of God seeking our sanctification. "Man at his best state is altogether vanity." Psalm 39:5 "They are all gone out of the way, they are together become unprofitable; there is none that doeth good, no, not one." Romans 3:12 This is an eternal contest between good and evil, and the consequences are forever. Life is a great test designed to perfect us or reject us from God's everlasting kingdom. Every day is opportunity to start over, but every moment counts for us or against us, looking to the time when "God shall bring every work into judgment, with every secret thing, whether it be good, or whether it be evil." Ecclesiastes 12:14 If we never learn to love and forgive and minister life to our wives, how will we fit in God's kingdom of overcomers?

> **Every day is opportunity to start over, but every moment counts for us or against us, looking to the time when "God shall bring every work into judgment, with every secret thing, whether it be good, or whether it be evil."**

## A Man Should Be Humbled

A man should be humbled and a little ashamed that God commands another human being to submit to him. Wives must submit now because Eve proved the female gender to be unequipped to take the lead. But Adam submitted himself to her will when he voluntarily ate of the fruit. I feel we should apologize to our wives for the burden God has placed upon them. Mister, our primary concern and the focus of our energies should be upon obeying God and living such a wise and exemplary life that our wives want to submit to us. A woman's submission to her husband is a costly gift that should be received with reluctance and reverence.

A woman who obeys her husband is looking beyond his frail and fallacious soul to the God who stands behind him. "Wives, submit yourselves unto your own husbands, **as unto the Lord**." Ephesians 5:22 Her obedience is humility before God ("as unto the Lord"), not a duty fulfilled for the sake of the man. Somehow religious men have gravitated into the same error as the former kings of England, thinking God granted them a divine right to be reverenced and obeyed regardless of their deserts. She can only obey her fallible husband "as unto the Lord, not unto men."

So, men, let us pay close attention to what God says to us, recognizing that our wives are God's servants, not our servants. "Who art thou that judgest another man's servant? to his own master he standeth or falleth. Yea, he [she] shall be holden up: for God is able to make him [her] stand." Romans 14:4

---

**A woman's submission to her husband is a costly gift that should be received with reluctance and reverence.**

---

Chapter 14

# LEAVE AND CLEAVE

We have received hundreds of letters like the following, so I cannot write a book to men without addressing the common failure to obey the first prophetic utterance upon the earth, which is the most fundamental precept of marriage—leaving your parents and establishing an independent family.

**Genesis 2:24** Therefore shall a man leave his father and his mother, and shall **cleave unto his wife**: and they shall be one flesh.

Jesus reinforced this foundational principle of marriage.

**Matthew 19:5** And said, For this cause shall a man leave father and mother, and shall **cleave to his wife**: and they twain shall be one flesh . . .

---

**Meaning of *cleave*:** Genesis 2:24 says, "Therefore shall a man leave his father and his mother, and shall cleave unto his wife: and they shall be one flesh." *Cleave* is an interesting Hebrew word. It is *dabaq* and is used 54 times. Thirty-two times, it is translated "cleave" in the English; five times it is translated "follow hard," meaning someone is running and the other person is pursuing him, very intent on catching him and is right behind him, will not slacken his pace, and is near to grabbing him. It is translated "overtake" three times, connoting that the pursuer followed after until he came along beside the person. Then it is translated "stick" three times, as in two things sticking together. It is translated "keep fast," don't turn it loose. Then it is translated "together" two times, "abide" as in stay there one time, then "close" one time, "enjoined" one time, "pursued" one time, then "take" one time. So if we take all these together, what could we sum them up as? *Cleave* unto your wife means stay close together, be inseparable. It means mingle, follow hard, stay right close by, keep fast, hold on to, don't turn loose, be near to your woman. So God commanded that man was to leave his father and mother and cleave unto his wife only.

"That thou mayest love the LORD thy God, and that thou mayest obey his voice, and that thou mayest cleave unto him . . . " Deuteronomy 30:20 That is that same Hebrew word *dabaq*. Just as we are commanded to cleave to God, God commands us to cleave to our wife. It's a sacred and a holy thing, the same word used with both God and wife, equating our passion for our wife with our passion for God.

**We have received many letters like the two following.**

Dear Mr. Pearl,

I would like to see a whole chapter devoted to the subject of leave and cleave. I feel betrayed because I am loyal to my man, but his loyalty is divided. Just for the record, my man is a godly man (seminary trained, even). His mom's word seems to be law even about the way we raise our children. If I say, "I think we should . . ." or "I thought we decided to . . ." He will say, "Yes, but my mom thinks . . ." It often feels like there are two women in this marriage and I am the lesser.

Joan


Dear Mike,

I have a wonderful, loving husband and I am thankful to God for him. He is the Steady Man! However, you have got to address the issue of mother-in-laws. My steady husband is a people pleaser; he will give anyone the shirt off of his back and will not ask why. He has always been a good and obedient son to his parents. However, my mother-in-law is a very controlling person. Everyone knows this to be true. My husband works with his father, so our lives are directed by him through his mother. His dad says, "Your mom says that your wife should or shouldn't . . ." My husband usually will not stick up for me because he wants to keep peace and please his parents. My father-in-law says bad things about me in front of me as if I weren't there. One day he might say I am withholding the children's affections from their grandmother, so I let the kids go visit, then the next day he says G-Mama has to be the real mom because I sure am not. No matter how I try, my mother-in-law regularly finds fault with me. My husband says just to pretend it was not said. He says he knows they are just sour.

So I am bullied by my in-laws. I have spent most of my marriage crying every day from new insults. I wish with all of my heart that my husband would protect me. I do listen to my husband and I obey him.

As much as I love him, many times over the years I have considered leaving because I just can't stand being constantly criticized, but then they will have proven their point of how evil I am. In-laws can tear a marriage or a heart apart. I have spent my whole marriage sad.

Thank you,

Daughter of Eve

> **Marriage is leaving father and mother to establish a two-person union, not a three or four.**

## A Disgusted Michael Answers

Excuse me while I spit and gag. I wish you men could see the disdain on my face. I am sorry; I just cannot respect a man that allows his wife to suffer criticism at the hands of his parents. One criticism one time would be two too many. I would pack my ditty bag in the pick-up truck, grab my wife and kids by the hand, and say to my parents, "See you next Christmas." Hang the job and security; wife comes first.

Jesus was clear: Marriage is leaving father and mother to establish a two-person union, not a three or four. Mister, instead of cleaving to your wife, you are cleaving to your parents like a nursing child. What are you afraid of? Does life scare you so badly that you are willing to settle for half of a marriage and 10% manhood?

**This is how I would counsel the lady with the outlaw in-laws:**

**Dear Abused Lady,**

> Your in-laws do not respect you because you do not respect yourself. You have considered divorce, which God forbids, but you have never considered self-defense, which he condones. When you stand firm on your principles you can "train up in-laws in the way they should go, and when they are old they will mind their own business."

> You said your father-in-law says bad things about you in front of you, and you stand there silently and take it. Your husband doesn't say anything because he doesn't respect you either. When one of your in-laws speaks disparagingly of you in your home, immediately point to the door and with authority tell them to "Get out, and don't come back until you have a civil tongue in your head." It will feel so good. When your father-in-law says your grandmother

must be the mom because you are not a fit mom, announce that grandmother will not be allowed to receive visits from the kids for the next month while you practice being a "good mom."

## Honor to Whom Honor Is Due

Dear Pearls,

How do we set boundaries gently while maintaining relationship and honor with our parents? My mother-in-law redecorates my home to her liking, meddles in our finances, belittles my husband, telling him he's foolish to spend money this way and that. My other stepmother throws fits when we aren't "fair." Both women want 100% loyalty and subjection from us. My mother examines the kids for bruises and marks, and uses the "examination" as a tool to threaten calling the DHS when things don't go her way. Help us.

A Reader

## Michael Answers

Dear Lady,

God tells you to submit to your husband, but there is nothing in the Bible that remotely suggests you should submit to your mother-in-law. You need not respect her any more than she respects you. When she tries to "decorate" your house, tell her you are happy with it the way it is and sweetly decline. When she insists, you insist. When she gets huffy, keep your dignity and quietly ask her to leave and not come back in your house until she is willing to respect your domain.

How could she meddle in your finances unless you give her the reins? Gently tell her in so many kind words that it is none of her business.

As to your mother examining the kids for bruising, I do hope you are not bruising them; if you are then you are out of control and need to seek counsel. But if her threats are an attempt to intimidate you into surrendering to her will, tell her in no uncertain terms that her visiting privileges are terminated until further notice. If I had a parent or in-law that without provocation threatened to call child protection on me, I would move to a different state and not leave any forwarding address. Where are the men, that a cantankerous old battle-ax can intimidate a family?

## Mice or Men?

You won't believe this one, but I print it because it is a common absurdity.

Dear Michael,

I am thirty years old. I would like to know when, if ever, is the authority of the old parents no longer in force over an adult son, especially if the mother is not in authority to her husband? Although I am not married, I have been on my own for many years, and I am well established in my career and ministry. My mother is a divorcee, so I have provided for her over the years. My dad has not been a part of my life for many years. Mother can be very spiritually manipulative. I have met a young woman whom I believe would make an excellent wife and mother to my children. She is not only a good choice, but she has my heart, and I believe I have hers. Her family is wonderful. They would be all for our marriage. My mother, on the other hand, does not like the idea. A while back, my mother did pick out a wife for me. She was sure this was the girl God had for me to marry. I was willing to talk to the girl's parents, although I was not in any way attracted to her. As it turned out, the girl was already asked for and soon married. Do I, as a grown man, submit to my mother, or should she, a woman without a head, submit to me?

The Last Straw

## Michael Answers

Should you submit to her or should she submit to you? Neither. There is one statement you made that I do question. You said you were a "grown man."

## 49 Going on 16

Mike,

I am 49 years old and have a question in regard to obeying my father. I would like to sell my house and move from the area, but he does not feel I should, and he reminds me that if I want God's blessing I must honor him. When am I free to make my own decision?

M. C.

## Michael Answers

I can't believe I am reading this. It gets crazier all the time, but I have enough letters like it to decorate 50 Halloween trees. Otherwise, I would think this letter a joke—49 years old and you still obey Daddy? Is there a powerful cult out there in Crazy Land persuading grown men to abdicate their God-given duties to take responsibility for their own lives?

I said I would answer it, but I don't need to. It is like the personal testimony of the man who burnt his pants off starting a fire in his lap. What could I add to the story that would make it more instructive?

## What Does the Bible Say about Obeying Parents?

### Ephesians 6:1-4

**1 Children,** obey your parents in the Lord: for this is right.

**2** Honour thy father and mother; (which is the first commandment with promise;)

**3** That it may be well with thee, and thou mayest live long on the earth.

**4** And, ye fathers, provoke not your **children** to wrath: but **bring them up** in the nurture and admonition of the Lord.

The children that were to obey their parents were still being *brought up* in "nurture and admonition." It is emotionally sick for parents to expect their grown children to obey them. And only an emotionally crippled adult would allow his life to be dictated by his parents.

It should be the goal of every parent to bring his children to the point of making independent, wise decisions. If parents have earned the respect of their child, the grown child will want to continue to consult his parent in matters of importance, but the final decision is his.

In the time of Israel's wandering in the wilderness, we find that a person 19 years old and under was not considered a responsible adult, but upon turning 20 he would die for his own sins. A Jewish child was considered to be two years old with the commencement of his thirteenth month. In our reckoning, the nineteen-year-old would be eighteen. So the Biblical age that divides a child from an autonomous adult is 18.

## Honor the Old Reprobate?

Dear Mike and Debi,

My husband and I are struggling with issues with his family. He was abused by his dad as a child, and now his brother has been charged with abusing children. His family wants to get together, but I fear for my children. My husband is undecided. He knows all those things happened, and are continuing to happen, and we could be putting our children at risk regardless of how hard we try to watch them. He wants to show honor to his dad, but does forgiveness and honor mean subjecting yourself and your children to them? Family is the ugliest thing in our life, yet we are commanded to honor and obey.

M. D.

## Michael Answers

The Bible does not command adults to obey their parents, and honor has nothing to do with subjection to another. Your children come first. Personally, I would break off all contact with the old reprobate and "honor" him from afar. If your husband does decide to get together, make sure the children are never out of your sight, and never allow them to sit in the "devil's" lap. When your children are old enough to understand— four years old—warn them to never sit in his lap or allow him to touch them in any way. On judgment day, you won't suffer any loss for having not trusted your children to a criminal, but you will suffer loss now and forever if on your watch your children are molested because you didn't have the backbone to offend a sinner who offends children and should be cast into the sea with a concrete block tied to his head. I say that with the greatest love and Scriptural authority. (Matthew 18:6-10)

Where are the men? Has this false doctrine of patriarchal authority so eroded common sense and supplanted personal responsibility that reprobate parents should be unconditionally reverenced as God?

**Has this false doctrine of patriarchal authority so eroded common sense and supplanted personal responsibility that reprobate parents should be unconditionally reverenced as God?**

What makes you or your husband think you should forgive an unrepentant sinner for a crime that deserves the death penalty? Get my audio titled *When Forgiveness Is Sin.*

Mister, why do you put your wife in this position? "Judge righteous judgment." John 7:24

## Backbone

Dear Pearls,

My dad left my mother for a lady he met on the Internet. My mom is not blameless in this situation, for she nagged him to death for the past ten years. My sister and I have taken some very hard looks at how we treat our husbands since all this happened. Our dilemma is in trying to honor both parents without taking sides. Both parents are trying to win our favor over the other. Also, my dad wants us to let him and his live-in lady take our children places. How can we honor him and yet say no? Are we being judgmental?

## Michael Answers

You've got the question backward. It is not how can you honor him and still say no. The question is, having said no, how can you honor him?

You can make a judgment without being judgmental. Wise judgment is the duty of every moral agent. A person without judgment is a conglomerate of flesh without humanity. Jesus said, " . . . judge ye not what is right?" Luke 12:57 He also commanded us, "Judge not according to the appearance, but judge righteous judgment." John 7:24 Likewise, Paul said, "But he that is spiritual judgeth all things, yet he himself is judged of no man." 1 Corinthians 2:15 I would just as soon my children ride on the hood of the car as go anywhere with either one of them. Their feelings would be my last consideration. Again, Where are the men?

# Chapter 15

# ISSUES

## Sucking the Devil's Tit

(Lady, if that title offends you, remember this is a book written by a man to men. If you can't handle the flack don't take the flight. I am talking men-talk, not women's Bible studies. Your husband is a little thick-headed, so I am screaming it like it is.)

Dear Mr. Pearl,

My husband is sneaking around doing porn again. I know it is so for two reasons: he has gone weeks without having sex with me and because the other day porn came up when I was on his computer. This time was different because it had a young girl on it. We have four young daughters. He recently started horse-playing with them. They love the attention but sometimes it definitely looks off-color. I am now scared of my own husband. What can I do to protect my children? I am willing to see my husband behind bars to safeguard them. Do I threaten him? Could a daddy, a Sunday school teaching, homeschooling daddy, really sexually mess with his own daughters? Please help me do the right thing before it is too late.

Sharon

I go into prisons every week and minister to "daddies" who molested their daughters or sons. You can spot them from across the yard. They are the nervous guys that are careful not to get in the wrong place. They get the longer sentences. The murderers may get out in six to ten years, but not the child-handling weirdos; they are there for 20 years or longer. The prisons are furnished with streetwise men who despise child molesters. Most of them have children and they hate a pervert to hell. Every once in a while they get bored and decide to kill one.

One of my best students, a man that loved the Lord and wrote beautiful poetry, was strangled to death in his cell by seven men who thought it their mission in life to purge the world of another child molester. The man had long since repented, having been in prison 15 years, and though God had forgotten his sin, the white supremacists never forget. If prisoners feel such hatred and need to punish such men, just imagine how God feels.

**You don't eat at Satan's table without being poisoned.**

When we get letters like this we make sure the lady knows how to protect her children and how to get the evidence to put her man behind bars a long time. Even if this daddy has not yet sexually handled his daughters, he is skirting on the edge of this diabolical sin and will eventually indulge. You don't eat at Satan's table without being poisoned. Sometimes it is a slow erosion over time, but often it is the first bite, ending in death and suffering for many.

A few months ago a young single woman contacted one of the local girls and told her she needed help getting away from her "over-protective" parents. She said her dad was coming into her room while she slept and was touching her privates in a sexual manner. The really disgusting thing was that every weekend her dad was going from church to church giving

**The day of reckoning always comes. Sin will find you out.**

testimony and singing. I can feel the damnation of God on that lying hypocrite. We arranged for the girl to meet with the sheriff and tell her story. We sat with her as she poured out the vileness. He starting using her as a tiny child of 3 years old, holding her down and forcing his penis into her mouth until she thought she was choking to death. For years she lived in silence and fear. The day of reckoning always comes. Sin will find you out. He hated himself and repented often. He thought he was forgiven. But his pornography always drove him back to his daughter. Damn to hell!

"And whosoever shall offend one of these little ones that believe in me, it is better for him that a millstone were hanged about his neck, and he were cast into the sea." Mark 9:42 And might I say for all the little children, "Good riddance."

Dear Pearls,

My husband isn't interested in regular sex any more. I know he has watched porn that portrays anal sex, so now he wants to try it all the time. Because he hears at work that it is okay, he thinks maybe it is. It is dirty, disease ridden, and causes damage to the bowels. It is what queers do. As his wife, he says it is my duty to obey him in this. I hate it. It makes sex seem evil and has changed my attitude toward him. He will not listen to me but he might listen to you.

Janice

## Michael Answers

Dear Lady, God has never commanded a wife to obey her husband to the point of sin or degradation. You are not a slave and he is not God. You must "obey God rather than men." Acts 5:29

**Your wife is not your slave and you are not God.**

Mister, there are lots of men hanging around the toilets at the interstate rest stops who would just love your sexless sex. They invented it and can't imagine why you would prefer it on a woman when it was designed by the devil to be used on a man.

Mike,

Pornography is a HUGE struggle with men these days because of its availability on the Internet. Porn is an enormously private sin. Nobody has the guts to talk about it. I graduated from a Christian university. They do their best to "block" sites, but any computer guru (myself included) can find a way around it. As I am not sure I will ever completely conquer my sin, I keep my household Internet free. I've erased my hard drives of any remnants of porn and had my wife go through and delete any song or movie that she deemed inappropriate as well. I still get hit with the urge EVERY time I am on the Internet. Since I ordered and listened to your *Sin No More* and *Men Only* MP3 I say a prayer for God to protect me before I sit down at a computer. I have two daughters, age five months and two and a half years. I would not forgive myself if my sins influenced them to put themselves into situations comparable to the images I've seen on the Internet. If I were reading a book on how to be a better man, these topics would need to be chapter 1.

Jim

**Monster lusts are constructed of many little lusts.**

Men face powerful lusts—driving, demanding lusts that do end-runs around their wills and mock their spiritual resources. Prayer proves feeble. Faith is stripped of all its boldness. The heavens appear empty. The doctrine of Sinful Nature has no better proof than the shattered wills of men controlled by lusts. After being dragged helplessly into the darkness a number of times, all men, "Christian" or otherwise, become theologians or philosophers, readily explaining their plight by voicing the one doctrine they believe with all their hearts, "I am controlled by my sinful nature, and cannot do other than sin." The Apostle Paul had a similar experience: "I am carnal, sold under sin. For that which I do I allow not: for what I would, that do I not; but what I hate, that do I . . . . Now then it is no more I that do it, but sin that dwelleth in me. For I know that in me (that is, in my flesh,) dwelleth no good thing: for to will is present with me; but how to perform that which is good I find not. For the good that I would I do not: but the evil which I would not, that I do. Now if I do that I would not, it is no more I that do it, but sin that dwelleth in me." Romans 7:14-20

How does a man's condition so degenerate that he can say with Paul, "It is no more I that do it, but sin that dwelleth in me"? Monster lusts are constructed of many little lusts. When a man allows small, manageable lusts to linger for a while, he is deceived into thinking he can be their master. He takes his lusts out of their secret place for his momentary pleasure and then puts them away before they get too big to control. And the lie seems to have validity for a while; he can indulge in the little pleasures of lust and still maintain self control—still be a "good man." But what he doesn't realize is that he has not been feeding a swarm of little independent and manageable lusts; he is feeding the monster that lies beneath the surface, growing larger and more powerful with every morsel it is fed. The day will come when he again casually opens the door to his will and invites a little lust out to play, but instead the monster that has been brooding beneath the surface will leap out of its secret den, no longer content to eat the respectable scraps in secret and then retreat to its resting place. It demands a full meal, gorging itself on the blackest of human passions until its belly is bloated with its gluttonous indulgence. Only after its appetite is satiated will it lessen its grip on the will and retreat to its dark den. The vessel of fulfillment is left feeling helpless and afraid, cautious and guilty. The ugly beast has established its dominance. But it is not yet through. The man has tasted unbridled, illicit pleasure. He will want more. The beast lives.

How does the man rationalize his dastardly experience? He thinks himself the victim of his sinful birth, but he determines to do better before it happens again. He thinks he must "have more faith," "pray more." But in time, he falls back into the habit of tossing small morsels past his conscience into the mouth of tiny, controllable lusts. The monster rebuilds his power base one thought at a time, one glance, one TV commercial, one magazine picture, one wandering of the imagination. Like a volcano building up pressure, there will be another eruption of lusts. The day of no return draws near.

## The Serpent

Many years ago I read of a man who kept a boa constrictor for a pet. He had received it as a gift on his thirteenth birthday. It was then about two feet long and very cute. As it grew, he would take his pet out of its cage and let it wrap around him. Several years passed and the snake grew to be about sixty pounds and twelve feet long. The young man loved to spring a surprise on new friends. When the moment was right, he would slip into the den and take the boa out of its cage, allowing it to wrap around his body several times. It was cold and slick, the scales making a dry sound as it slithered over his flesh, the mouth parted slightly, the tongue darting out to taste the air. It always had the desired effect, eliciting oohs and ahhs.

A friend asked him, "Aren't you afraid it will squeeze you to death?" The master of the snake laughed as he replied, "I have owned him since he was a baby. We understand each other, and I know how to handle him." But even as he spoke he remembered earlier experiences. When the snake was only about six or seven feet long it would occasionally wrap around an arm or leg and squeeze frighteningly hard, yet the snake's master was stronger and able to forcibly remove the tight coils. But there was that one really scary time when the serpent was about ten feet long and weighed about thirty pounds. It had been crawling around its master's body for over an hour when it suddenly wrapped itself around his neck and began to squeeze. It took some effort, but he was able to subdue it and place it back in the cage. For over a month he was fearful to release it, but as his confidence returned he allowed it out, but he took more precautions, never allowing it to wrap around his neck. That had been nearly two years ago and nothing had happened since, so he knew he was the master.

> **Lust is like the baby snake. It never comes to us full-grown. If it did we would fear it and flee.**

About a month later a friend brought over several young people from the university, wanting to see the "big snake." As the serpent slithered out of the cage and up the arm of its master, it made its way right around his head and neck and back around again. The master quickly attempted to make adjustments, but the tail executed two quick turns around his shoulders, pinning his arms. The guests all hooted with delight as snake and master slumped over the couch face down. They made comments about how beautiful it was and how powerful it had become. They began to ask questions but got no answer. Some laughed as others became alarmed. But what did they know about snakes? It was all a good show. And then the entwined twosome rolled over on the floor, leaving the master face up. They were horrified to see his face purple and his eyes half popped out of his head. They were afraid and ran around in panic. One of them finally ran to the kitchen and grabbed a knife. He tried to stab the snake, but found it not as easy as he thought. After about ten minutes the paramedics arrived and there they found a dead snake master wrapped in the tightly bound bloody coils of the serpent—master no longer.

Lust is like the baby snake. It never comes to us full-grown. If it did we would fear it and flee. It comes with just enough thrill to make it exciting, but with no power to control. As we feed the lust, it grows larger and larger. Living with it, we don't see what is happening. We keep believing that we will always be its master. It scares us from time to time, but the thrill brings us back. Then one day we discover we are no longer its master. The death it brings may even enhance the eroticism. We no longer flee. We seek out its binding coils.

In time, as repeated offenses sear the conscience, many men become accessories to the pillage of their moral souls, freely opening the door to lust, beckoning him enter even before he knocks. It is then that God gives them over to "vile affections" and "uncleanness" and finally "to a reprobate mind, to do those things which are not convenient . . . Being filled with all unrighteousness, fornication, wickedness, covetousness . . . Without understanding, covenant breakers, without natural affection, implacable, unmerciful: Who knowing the judgment of God, that they which commit such things are worthy of death . . . ." Romans 1:26-32

> **Don't tell me you are a helpless victim; you fed and nurtured the serpent that took your life.**

If this is your lot, don't tell me you are a helpless victim; you fed and nurtured the serpent that is taking your life.

## Dating Yourself

Dear Mr. Pearl,

Please warn against masturbation. It is a kind of unfaithfulness and denial of the spouse. My husband grew up sneaking around looking at porn and masturbating. While we were dating he was hot after me, but shortly after our marriage he went back to his "loving himself." I try to make him understand it is a slap in my face that he prefers doing himself over making love with me. He hears but doesn't hear.

Sue

Dear Ms. Pearl,

I NEED YOUR HELP! I am a new wife (less than two years) who is currently reading your book *Created to Be His Help Meet*. I have found this book to be life-changing. However, the answers that I need on intimacy are not in your book. My husband can go for extended periods without sex or touching unless I initiate or when he sees that I am depressed. This situation has really hurt my self-esteem and some of my respect for him. It is difficult to believe this is the person who pursued me with persistence as a single man. He has a history of pornography and masturbating from his youth. So basically, he continues to find pleasure in himself. It leaves me with nothing but excuses. I have stopped initiating sex with him due to the pain of the rejection. I want a MAN in my bed at night, not a boy playing with himself.

Joan

## Masturbating Monkey

In Thailand there are parks and temple sites filled with a particular monkey. Tourists go there to laugh at them. The monkeys hang around in the trees above the spectators and masturbate, throwing their semen on anyone who gets close enough. The very writing of it is disgusting, but then they are just animals acting on instinct. We cannot expect them to act out of reason or self-restraint. They feel like it; they do it, with no dignity or pride. They aspire to nothing higher than sensual satiation of carnal desire. Are you a masturbating monkey? To say you can't help yourself is to confess that you are unworthy of humanity. It's God's joke that AIDS came from monkeys.

It is bad enough as is, but have you gotten into child pornography yet? It is a rung on the ladder you are climbing. It's just a matter of time. You need to locate a millstone and a rope. You are going to need it.

**Mark 9:42-48**
**42** And whosoever shall offend one of these little ones that believe in me, it is better for him that a millstone were hanged about his neck, and he were cast into the sea.

**43** And if thy hand offend thee, cut it off: it is better for thee to enter into life maimed, than having two hands to go into hell, into the fire that never shall be quenched:

**44** Where their worm dieth not, and the fire is not quenched.

**45** And if thy foot offend thee, cut it off: it is better for thee to enter halt into life, than having two feet to be cast into hell, into the fire that never shall be quenched:

**46** Where their worm dieth not, and the fire is not quenched.

**47** And if thine eye offend thee, pluck it out: it is better for thee to enter into the kingdom of God with one eye, than having two eyes to be cast into hell fire:

**48** Where their worm dieth not, and the fire is not quenched.

**Luke 12:5** But I will forewarn you whom ye shall fear: Fear him, which after he hath killed hath power to cast into hell; yea, I say unto you, Fear him.

## Stupid Is as Stupid Does

Mr. Pearl,

I know you have many letters to answer so I feel bad bothering you again, but I need to ask this for my sake and some other women who are dealing with this. My husband read the "Pornography: Road to Hell" article and he said that the article applied only to men who were actually masturbating and having sexual fantasies (fantasies meaning thinking about having sex with her). That to be adultery it had to involve sexual fantasies and masturbation and your article only deals with that, not men who just look at women for a rush. He is struggling with the true definition of lust/adultery. He wanted to know if your pornography article is only directed at those who act out sexual fantasies with porn, or is it also to those who are looking for a rush (he calls it like an adrenaline rush) by looking at women, because he doesn't feel like what he did fits into the same category as men acting out or having fantasies. He feels God got his attention before he went any deeper. How is a wife to get through this when I feel cheated and disgusted when I look at him? Thanks again for help.

Rainy

Mister, you can describe your pornographic addiction as an adrenaline rush, but until Hugh Hefner is taken out of hell and cast into the lake of fire no man is going to believe you. I have heard some doozies in my time, but your excuse is the most bizarre lie I have ever heard. You must think your wife is really stupid. I didn't sojourn my sixty-six years in a vacuum. I began ministering to street people, drunks, dope heads, and hippies when I was sixteen years old. I have spent decades ministering in boys' homes and prisons. I ministered to Sailors and Marines for twenty years. They don't call them seamen for nothing. I have heard it all, packaged a thousand different ways, but your lame excuse is actually a statement that you are losing your mind. You are an ordinary sinner held captive by your own lust and you have no excuse, for I have seen thousands come to Christ and find complete deliverance from all manner of perversion. I have watched sodomites become saints and prostitutes become preachers' wives. I have seen the sexually addicted delivered from damnable desires and drawn into the service of God.

Why keep traveling down a road that takes you where you do not want to go? When will you turn around? It doesn't get easier; quite the opposite. The heart grows harder with every click of the mouse, and your soul is diminished with every flicker of the screen. "But exhort one another daily, while it is called To day; lest any of you be hardened through the deceitfulness of sin. . . . To day if ye will hear his voice, harden not your hearts, as in the provocation." Hebrews 3:13, 15 In the provocation God killed 3,000 souls.

To the rest of you porno freaks, you should know your wife may be one of the many who have written to my wife telling how she longs to be loved, to be held, to be the object of your desires. She is brokenhearted and feels diminished when you go into the dark place to love yourself (That is the term so many women use). "Love yourself"? How disgusting!

No man needs pornography, for God has "given unto us all things that pertain unto life and godliness." 2 Peter 1:3 God commends natural sex between a man and his wife, saying, "Let thy fountain be blessed [ejaculation]: and rejoice with the wife of thy youth . . . let her breasts satisfy thee at all times; and be thou ravished always with her love." Proverbs 5:18-19 "Marriage is honourable in all, and the bed undefiled: but whoremongers and adulterers God will judge." Hebrews 13:4

## Your Hand, Your Help Meet

The normal man is gifted with erotic desires toward the opposite sex. "But every man hath his proper gift of God, one after this manner, and another after that." 1 Corinthians 7:7

**1 Corinthians 7:2-5** [T]o avoid fornication, let every man have his own wife, and let every woman have her own husband. Let the husband render unto the wife due benevolence: and likewise also the wife unto the husband. The wife hath not power of her own body, but the husband: and likewise also the husband hath not power of his own body, but the wife. Defraud ye not one the other, except it be with consent for a time, that ye may give yourselves to fasting and prayer; and come together again, that Satan tempt you not for your incontinency.

The term *help meet* takes on a glow of reality when we consider that our beloved spouse is there to "meet" our sexual needs. A pervert that views pornography has joined himself to a digital screen and becomes one flesh with flashing bits of lies and deceit. God created Eve to excite Adam and meet his desires, but the devil created pornography to be a man's help meet. It helps him conform to Satan's lust and degradation. God brought the man and woman together and said "the bed is undefiled" . . . "let her breasts satisfy thee at all times", but the devil says "Your hand is your help meet; let it satisfy thee at all times." Maybe you should put your wedding ring on the middle finger of your right hand.

I wrote a book called *Holy Sex*, showing God's perspective on marital love. It is an unconventional commentary on the Song of Solomon and other erotic Bible passages. Also, get my audio series *Sin No More* and learn how to overcome all sin all the time.

## Now I Know He Loves Me

Dear Brother Mike,

A wonderful thing happened at our house. My husband decided to lock the computer down. I am so thankful. I would like to tell other men, do not be ashamed of Internet protection! Sometimes when I have to enter a password for my husband to be able to access a sports page, he says he's sorry. I respond cheerfully and say, "I'm not!!!" What a blessing and peace of mind! I have more respect for men who have Internet protection than those who don't and think they can handle things on their own . . . what foolishness! Our marriage is so much better now and my husband comes to me for his needs. I am so glad to give myself to him. His sin was eating my heart out and he knew it yet kept sneaking around. Then he listened to *Sin No More* and decided to have a professional come out and lock the computer down tight with only me knowing the password. For the first time I knew he loved me, cared for my hurt, and put me over his own lust. The difference with our children has even been remarkable. Our marriage was saved, as I had reached the end and had made secret plans to go back to my parents. Porn is so very evil.

Tammy

"And be not conformed to this world: but be ye transformed by the renewing of your mind, that ye may prove what is that good and acceptable, and perfect, will of God." Romans 12:2

## Blogging and Bogging in Sin

Dear Mr. Pearl,

I am writing to warn other men, and hopefully help someone avoid the immeasurable pain and damage I've done to my family and myself and by such a seemingly small sin and mistake.

Keep in mind when you read this that we were a "Christian" family, in church all the time, upstanding, admired members of a small farm community, and homeschooled our daughters from the start.

I started a blog on a website about five years ago. This was not an evil site, and actually had many Christians writing on it, many involved in witnessing to others, and involved in some good theological discussions. My blog was about aspects of my faith, daily and family life, and photos I took.

My wife and daughters were aware of it, and read it.

On this site there was the capability of leaving comments on other members' sites and emailing/instant messaging them. For many it was a little world-wide "community" and all very fun and exciting meeting new and interesting people, and responding and getting involved in other people's lives. It certainly hooked me in. I felt God had given me an opportunity to share my faith with non-believers and be involved in encouraging other Christians. I developed Internet relationships with men and women all over the country and world. Some got to be very close and personal. And you can probably already see where this is headed.

One married, professing Christian woman in another state became particularly friendly and we slowly began sharing more personal information. Seemingly innocent and even "godly" at first; we talked about our struggles in our faith and family life. Mind you, all this was over the Internet with no face-to-face contact, or even pictures shared.

> **At some point, about a month into the "relationship" it crossed a line, and I knew it.**

At some point, about a month into the "relationship" it crossed a line, and I knew it. Whatever it was I felt was lacking in my own marriage she was providing: admiration, attention, excitement, etc. We began leaving more flirtatious comments and messages, and the relationship really became the focus of my life at that point and an intense addiction. She even brazenly mailed a gift to my house.

At this point my wife obviously began to take notice and was hurt and offended, but I stubbornly and deceptively excused it all away, saying it was all completely innocent. The guilt, however, was tearing me apart. I remember one of my daughters getting up late at night to use the bathroom, and seeing me at the computer emailing the other woman. I remember working at a jobsite alone and sobbing, wondering how it could have come to this. It had all started so innocently and with good intentions.

I finally confessed the whole thing to a family member and another older Christian friend. They both told me I had to completely cut the relationship off. I again stupidly and stubbornly refused, not wanting to "hurt" and reject this other woman. I thought we could just stay friends. That stance would come back to haunt me. I told my wife about it and it broke her heart. Even though there was not a bit of physical contact, let alone sexual, and not even an actual picture of who it was I thought I was "in love with," it was an adulterous affair by Jesus' own definition in Matthew 5:28.

Because I would not immediately and cleanly break off all contact I did even more damage. When I finally saw the light, it was too late.

## I lost everything for an Internet relationship.

I was living in a beautiful house I had built with my own sweat and blood, but was completely unwelcome there and despised by my wife and two teenage daughters. We went to the "Christian counselors" (who may have done more damage) but it was all for naught. My daughters became more and more angry and rebellious, and whatever other existing problems were in my home were compounded. And even though I thought for a time that my wife had forgiven me, and even though I knew I absolutely wanted to stay married to her, it all came crashing down a couple months later.

My wife found a way to legally throw me out of my house, and hired the biggest, baddest divorce attorney around. I went through a whole year of divorce court hell. I lived out of my work truck, stayed in others people's homes, and when it was all over I had lost a beautiful country home on five acres that was completely paid for, my first brand new car (completely paid for), another vehicle, a cabin on 19 acres in another state, a timeshare on an island, and $50,000 in the bank that was supposed to be the start of my retirement. And I had to write out a check for $15,000 in child support. None of this money had come easy, either. I've earned my living by hard physical labor as a carpenter.

And worst of all by far, I lost a marriage of 23 years and two daughters that I love more than anything else in this life. I have not seen my girls or even heard their voices in over three long years now. They want nothing to do with me, and I don't know if I'll ever get to see them again.

I cannot even begin to describe the pain and loneliness that separation has caused.

And for *what*? An "innocent" little Internet relationship and a few moments of false admiration and titillation from a lady that I wouldn't know from anyone. She might be a gross-looking sicko that played me. Satan sure did.

"Be not deceived; God is not mocked: for whatsoever a man soweth, that shall he also reap."

A Fool

## Video Games

Mr. Pearl,

Please speak to men about the dangers of idleness by way of video gaming. My husband has been obsessed with video games for 15 years. He will spend up to 8 hours straight playing one game. He professes Christianity but has neglected to raise his children under the fear and admonition of the Lord; that has been left up to me, as have **Satan's toys.** all homeschool issues, home maintenance, auto maintenance, bills and finances, medical appointments, etc. It's all on me because he is busy with video games. He has confessed to me that on three occasions God has convicted him of his gaming issues, but that changed nothing. He has skipped work and church at times to stay home and game. This puts a tremendous burden on me to be responsible for everything while my marital child plays. It sets a bad example for the children. He has never taken care to teach them godly things, but literally from the time they could walk he sat the boys down to learn Playstation. Guess what my boys want to do now when they get up first thing in the morning? Yep, Playstation!

Aside from the practical burdens I carry alone, I also feel a tremendous burden to be "my brother's keeper." I grieve for the state of his soul, knowing that he will have to give account for all of these years of life wasted on video games when God blessed him with a family to be responsible for. When confronted with this issue he responds with intense anger. Once when I found out that he had been closing himself in the bedroom looking at nasty female pictures on a game I got rid of the game. He was so angry that he threatened me that I had gone "too far" and he wanted out of the marriage. After that I moved the Playstation to the front room where he could no longer hide what he was doing. He said I had gone too far over that too. Now he stays in a constant angry pout because with the game system in the front room he can no longer play for so many hours straight.

Once when I was praying to God about this issue, God spoke to me that the video games are a god to my husband, an idol that has come before Him. Now my children and I feel like we have to tippy toe around his mood. We have hidden certain video games all over the house so that he cannot find them. The children have to wait until he is at work to pull these games out and play them. He thinks that I threw these games away and he is mad about that too.

At Christmas time when my oldest son was little, my husband would tell me that my son had told him that he wanted certain video games for gifts and that he wanted them really bad. So I would buy them as gifts for my son. When my son got old enough he told me that had not been the truth, that those were the games that his dad had wanted. I spent years buying "gifts" that I thought my son wanted based on my husband's greed and lies to get his games.

This is such a problem in our home that I have often prayed to God that my husband could be delivered from this stronghold and even considered counseling for myself and my children. I know other wives who also have similar (but not as severe) issues with their husbands and the computer. In our home the children and I speak of my husband's "media god" or his "game god." Sadly, my children can easily recognize this god in his life, but even though my husband claims Christianity, my oldest son and my daughter do not believe that he even really believes in the one true God's existence.

Please Help,

Helen

**Proverbs 12:12** The wicked desireth the **net** of evil men: but the root of the righteous yieldeth fruit.

**Proverbs 29:5** A man that flattereth his neighbour **spreadeth a net** for his feet.

## Why Pastors Lose Their Families

I am including this section because we received a huge number of letters from pastors' wives feeling trapped and helpless, asking us to address this subject.

**1 Timothy 3:5** For if a man know not how to rule his own house, how shall he take care of the church of God?

Dear Mr. Pearl,

My husband serves our congregation too well. He is so compassionate. But at times I feel I should call his cell phone posing as a parishioner so I can get him to pay at least that much attention to the children and I. Yes, he is home at night. He loves the children and does devotions at dinner with them. He is a loving, dedicated husband and father, but he is spread so thin. He has a full-time business in addition to pastoring our church.

Our conversations are almost always interrupted by the ringing cell phone. He can't just let it ring. He has to answer. He listens and offers help. He'll see to it that members of the church get something fixed or he helps pay for it to be fixed, yet he never seems to get to the things he has promised to fix in our home.

What about our family? What about my interests, the children's interests and needs? He'll remember that someone in the church has something going on at a certain time, but will forget that he promised to take us to an event or help with children's doctor visits, etc. I know he has wonderful intentions, but he often neglects to keep the promises he makes to us.

I know it could be worse. It could be bars and porn that keep him from us. I feel like a monster being jealous of church. But at times that is just how I honestly feel and so do the kids.

Jealous


Mr. Pearl,

My husband is a pastor. He loves being a pastor. He lives, eats, and breathes the church to the exclusion of his family. I wish he could become aware that his children see him as there for everyone but them, that they can't count on him to keep his word to them, only to the church members.

You ask for a wish list; here's mine.

> **I need him to love me; I need him to look into my eyes, and I need to see love.**

✓ I wish he could see that our oldest son resents the church (and lumps God in with it) at only 10 years old. I wish he could see that his family should come first and that WE need him.

✓ I wish my husband could understand that every time he throws angry, childish temper tantrums—complete with yelling, slamming, and throwing things—my respect for him drops another level.

✓ I wish my husband could understand that when he doesn't have a conversation with me for weeks on end, doesn't hug me, or tell me he loves me, or even treat me with the same respect he'd show an outsider, that when he wants to be intimate it makes me feel cheap, not loved.

✓ I wish he didn't leave me to carry the burden of the entire household and children alone while he "ministers" to his church, leaving no energy for his family.

✓ I wish he could see how hypocritical he looks to his children (yes, and to his wife) when he preaches about a godly home, yet doesn't live it—never having family devotions or prayer time, and spending all of the time he is home in front of the TV, yelling at the kids if they get in the way of his seeing or hearing the TV.

I am not a perfect wife or a perfect mother and I realize that. I can honestly say that I have taken Debi's book to heart and am really trying. I feel so overwhelmed, like I can't take one more step on my own. I want the best for my children and my home but I can't do it alone. I NEED my husband. I need him to pray with me (and yes, I've asked). I need him to love me; I need him to look into my eyes, and I need to see love.

Karen

Dear Mike,

Computer games are stealing my marriage and church. It has caused my husband to put God and family second. He thinks he is doing his job because he goes to church and preaches, doesn't drink or smoke, doesn't watch bad TV, homeschools, limits the children's computer usage, doesn't hang out with his buddies, etc., but he leaves the child raising to me. And when he is home he believes it is sufficient family time to just be in the same house. Our church is failing due to failing marriages. Satan is having a field day while our men play games.

Rachel

Dear Mr. Pearl,

One thing I would like for all fathers to understand is how much they are adored, loved, and needed by their kids. We have a three-year-old son who sits in his father's chair at the table when Papa isn't home. One day I asked him why he sat there. He announced, "Because I am a Sir."

An example of how important papas are happened last night. I asked, "Alex, what did you do today?" It had been a busy day; Alex and I played with a LeapPad we got from the library, made Kool-aid, watched an educational DVD, cleaned, played, worked in the kitchen, and after my husband got home we went to Bible study and to the library. His answer was, "I watched Muzzy. I helped make Kool-aid. And Papa played with me!" The emphasis added doesn't do justice to the way his face lit up when he said that. Fathers, please don't be too busy for your children.

Sue

## Closing Thought

**Now I will say a word to you pastors.** This is one subject I know well. Before I married I often preached ten to fifteen times a week, and that was just the beginning of my ministry. I witnessed on the streets and taught Bible studies and held prayer meetings, organizing large groups to go out and minister in fairs and parks. There were times that my head didn't hit the pillow until daylight. I burned the candle at both ends and in the middle at the same time. My only concern was getting more wax. By the time I was 21 I was pastoring an Independent Baptist Church in Millington, Tennessee. I still maintained a busy schedule with many outside preaching and ministering activities. I put off getting married because I wanted to be free to do God's work.

> **I knew that my wife would be my first and foremost ministry.**

I looked forward to marriage, but I knew that it would change my life and my ministry, for I had read the Bible and believed what it said, "But I would have you without carefulness. He that is unmarried careth for the things that belong to the Lord, how he may please the Lord: **But he that is married careth for the things that are of the world, how he may please his wife.**" 1 Corinthians 7:32-33 I knew that marriage would mean giving up much of my activity.

When I was about to turn 26, I finally married my sweet Deb. Life changed. No more all-nighters—except at home. I gave up a lot of my hectic ministry and became a husband, caring for the things of the world, how I may please my wife.

When children came along I ministered at about 20 percent of the former level. I have continued to minister all my life, paying my way by the sweat of my brow, financing my ministry with my own labor.

As the children got big enough, I took them everywhere, including on the street to preach. People otherwise inclined to refuse a gospel tract will always take it from a five-year-old. My children learned to witness for Christ by the time they could talk, and it was something we shared together. They went to Bible studies and prayer meetings as well as fishing and hunting and hiking. They became my constant companions and never felt deprived of my presence. Except for about a two-year period, the kids grew up without a TV in the house, and I never watched anything that they couldn't watch, which wasn't much—*The Waltons*, *Little House on the Prairie*, and *Gunsmoke*.

Before I married, when I attended the Memphis Academy of Arts, I listened to a conversation between a teacher and a student ambitious to become a great artist. The student asked, "What does it take to be a great artist?" The teacher answered, "You have to eat art, think art, and sleep art." The student asked, "Well, what does your wife think about that?" His answer was an epiphany to me, "When my wife married me, she married an artist." It was a life lesson that shone like the Word of God from heaven. I knew that when I married, my wife would marry a husband, not an artist, not a preacher, not a man of any preoccupation. I knew that she would be my first and foremost ministry. God says I should care for the things of the world, how I may please my wife. A preacher has no right to place his affections anywhere else. According to the Scripture, a minister should be "One that ruleth well his own house, having his children in subjection with all gravity; (For if a man know not how to rule his own house, how shall he take care of the church of God?)"

1 Timothy 3:4-5 Remember, ruling is not bossing. Any tyrant can do that.

If you put your wife and children first, you will turn your entire family into ministers and you will find that the visual aid you create will accomplish far more than all your sermons.

## Created to Be God's Bride

Mr. Pearl,

I have had a heavenly marriage, but it has been mostly the fruit of my husband. When I married, my husband received a woman who, in spite of her love for Jesus, had been indoctrinated as a feminist during her schooling. I knew very little about my Biblical responsibilities as a wife. But my husband knew what his role was—to love me as Christ loved the church and gave His life for her. He seems blind to my faults, has never uttered a critical word (even though I often deserved one), and daily expressed his gratitude for having me as his wife. He is servant-hearted and serves me and our children unselfishly. There have been times (mostly out of ignorance) I have not submitted, and he has loved me anyway. There have been times I have been disrespectful and he has loved me anyway. There have been times I pushed him away intimately, and he has loved me anyway. I have heard him pray every night for the 13 years we have been married that he would love me just like Jesus would if Jesus were in his shoes. I'm starting to understand that Jesus really does love me with the same fault-blind, passionate, unselfish, servant-hearted love that my husband has shown me. More and more I'm becoming the bride my husband deserves. But my husband is proof that if only one partner in a marriage is capable of behaving God's way, that's all it takes for an amazing union.

Cindy

## A 20-Cow Lady

**A man sent me this delightful story. He didn't give the source.**

Mr. Pearl,

I came across a very interesting story that touches on a concept many men seem to miss—husbands cleansing their wives' spots and blemishes. This story appeared in an older book I found at a thrift store. I can't find the book, so I will recount the story from memory. I believe it to be fiction, but am unsure.

Many years ago (decades) in Hawaii, there lived a very wealthy, shrewd businessman who happened to be single. There also lived a man with two single daughters who were of marriageable age. The younger daughter was known throughout the town for her beauty, but the older girl was very plain, if not unattractive and dull. She stood and sat with her hair covering her face and her shoulders slumped. She could be in the room with several others and you would never know she was there. One day the shrewd businessman came calling at the man's home about his daughter. Now at that time, a husband would pay for a bride in cows. A normal bride would command 2 cows, but an exceptional bride could bring as much as 4 cows. Everyone in the town started guessing what the wealthy man would pay for the young, beautiful bride. Soon, the townspeople were surprised to find that the man was actually calling on the older, plain sister. Some wondered again what he would give. Perhaps he'd only pay 1 cow since he was so shrewd. Others said he was goodhearted, so maybe he would even offer 3 cows. All were shocked when they found out he'd paid 10 cows for her! The town was filled with disbelief. He disappeared with his new bride for a year, and when he came back, the townspeople were in awe. The man looked the same, but who was this beautiful, poised woman with him? Could it be the same bride he left with? Indeed it was the same woman, but with confidence, grace, and beauty far superior to her sister's. A buzz filled the air. They said that the man had really gotten a bargain. This woman wasn't worth 10 cows; she was worth 20!

**To slightly alter a famous poem by Edwin Markham that I memorized in college:**

> She drew a circle that shut me out,
>
> Heretic, rebel, a thing to flout,
>
> But love and I had the wit to win,
>
> We drew a circle that took her in.

> This was published in pamplet form in 2001 under the title
> ***Pornography: Road to Hell*** by Michael Pearl.
>
> With the increase of pornography use, we felt it essential to add
> this to our book.

# PORNOGRAPHY: ROAD TO HELL

Our magazine *No Greater Joy* is a publication dedicated to child training and family. It would seem that a dissertation on pornography should be confined to a different format. But we receive many letters from wives concerned about their husband's pornographic indulgence. The letters we receive are from homeschooling, no birth control, go to church, "put on a good front" families. Wives want to know how they can train up their children to follow the Lord when their husbands are secretly following porn queens. At one large meeting of several thousand "Christian" men, over 50% of those present confessed to having "used pornography" in the previous seven days. Most ministers avoid ever mentioning this shameful subject. Of those that do, the majority treat it as a "weakness" that Christians should "overcome with counseling." I disagree. We too have avoided addressing the subject because of its sensitiveness. Some of you who live in isolation (thank God that you do) may be offended at my frankness. But you must understand that the lives of many families and the souls of their children are at stake.

**If you isolate yourself in a room and indulge in pornography, you are not sick; you are evil.**

I would want my children to read this article. The degree to which they understand the words would be a general guide as to how much they are ready to consider. I would then discuss it with them, according to their maturity. It's your choice. Just be apprised of the fact that most kids are exposed to some form of pornography by the time they are ten years old.

Now I am speaking to you, fathers. If you isolate yourself in a room and indulge in pornography, you are not sick; you are evil. You are having intercourse with a computer, or with the pages of a publication. In effect you are having an erotic experience with the editor–probably another man. While you are fantasizing with that commercially produced image, know that there are thousands of others engaged in eroticism with the same image, at the same time as you. You are part of a disgusting group of perverts, all piled onto the same image together. And somewhere there is a sexually dysfunctional editor enjoying the extent of his erotic powers.

**You are copulating with yourself.**

You are not oversexed. You are not even sexed. You are alone. At best you are copulating with yourself. Don't tell me that you are getting yourself primed for a conclusion with your wife. It is the priming that draws you back again and again, not the conclusion. You are a pervert. A real man is bigger than his member. He is big enough to say "no" to his passions. A man whose passions are stimulated to the point of being all-consuming is not a man of greater prowess. He is a man whose soul has shrunk until his little member is the strongest thing left. God created us with sexual drive, but he also gave us a steering wheel and a brake to direct and control our drives. If you can't control yours, it is not a statement of the strength of your drive, but of the weakness of your soul. You are wasting away to the level of an alley cat. Adam fell, but you are falling even further. You are plunging your soul into eternal destruction, moving as far away from God as you can get. You are lost and helpless by choice. You do not deserve sympathy or understanding; you deserve condemnation and scorn. You are not a victim; you are a perpetrator. You

**While you justify yourself, your own conscience condemns you.**

justify your addiction by pointing to the many who have fallen as you have, but you are condemned by the many who have not fallen, and by the many who were once where you are but have since repented and been restored to normalcy.

While you justify yourself, your own conscience condemns you. You sneak around like a thief as you lie and deceive. Your whole life is dedicated to the dragon. Your body is being consumed as your soul is being digested. You are having communion with the devil— bowing in worship of the flesh. You are a disciple of evil. You have chosen to be part of a group that defiles their own flesh, *"that worshipped and served the creature more than the Creator, whose god is their belly, whose glory is their shame (Romans 1:25; Philippians 3:19)."*

Very few ever return from the pit into which you are sinking. You have taken the downhill slide into Hell, and there is absolutely nothing to stop you except your willingness to apply the brakes. The problem is that you are more addicted today than you were one year ago, and you will continue to fade into the shadows of debauchery until you are one with the evil on which you feed. You are on the road of no return and every day you are less likely to reverse your course.

> **The lust you have created is never satisfied. It is an itch with no scratch, only more itch.**

The lust you have created is never satisfied. It is an itch with no scratch, only more itch. Pornographic satisfaction is like the pot of gold at the end of the rainbow–always just out of reach. The lust of pornography draws a man ever deeper into the dark tunnel of promise until he discovers he has missed life and love. Pornography destroys your ability to "make love," and replaces it with the cunning wit to use and abuse. There comes a point when any attempt at a normal relationship is nothing more than assisted masturbation. Your world grows ever smaller until you are alone with your semen. You stink of self. You do not deserve a woman.

You have nothing to be proud of. You are not a bull. You are a dog. There are millions just like you. Most are not as hypocritical as you are. Some of them hang around bars, nightspots, and porno shops; but take note, you feed on the same diet. Your soul is a receptacle of the same putrefaction. You may yet join them, sharing not only the same books and videos, but also the same dirty motel rooms with their indigenous occupants.

*"Stolen waters are sweet, and bread eaten in secret is pleasant. But he knoweth not that the dead are there; and that her guests are in the depths of hell (Proverbs 9:17-18)."*

So your wife is frigid? Don't tell me that pornography is a substitute for a good woman. I was not homeschooled and protected. I am sixty-six years old. I preach in state prisons every week and have done so since I was eighteen. I have ministered in coffeehouses and rescue missions and on the street since I was sixteen. You might convince yourself that you are forced to your actions by an unresponsive wife, but I don't buy it. I have known of porno-freaks that got married to good women, but found that they liked to be alone better than sharing. We have talked to women who are willing and ready, but their husbands prefer their own company. Pornography and a wife are not alternate ways to fulfill the same drive.

> **The drive for pornography is a cultivated, perverted passion that has nothing to do with love and marriage.**

The drive for a wife is a natural drive, whereas the drive for pornography is a cultivated, perverted passion that has nothing to do with love and marriage. If a pornographer were to marry a porno queen, he would quickly become dissatisfied with her and crawl back in his little hole, alone with his imaginations and the images created by an industry that makes its money not by satisfying its customers, but by keeping them dissatisfied and hungry for the artificial. Your secret world is revolting to real men who know how to love one woman and dedicate the rest of their energies to creative living.

But the most destructive thing about your sin is the effect it has on your children. We live in a spirit world of both righteous and fallen angels.

> **The children of godly parents are protected from unclean spirits by being under their moral umbrella.**

We are surrounded by evil spirits seeking the moral destruction of every human soul. The children of godly parents are protected from unclean spirits by being under their moral umbrella. But when a father gives his mind over to wicked lusts, he removes the hedge of protection around his family and invites impure devils into his home. Wishing them away will avail nothing. Any prayers you pray for their safety are negated the moment you open the pages of a pornographic book or glare at an electronic image. When you tune in to electronic pornography you have established a two-way link with the spiritual underworld. When you lie in bed at night and conjure up wicked images, the devils won't stop with your mind; they will gleefully rush into the bedrooms of your children and assault their little souls and bodies. Evil thoughts will come to their minds–thoughts you have been thinking that are telegraphed to them by the devils. Your defenseless children will be taken captive, and you are the one that threw the gate open to the enemy.

If sodomy is sin, pornography is its "significant other." If the Bible be true when it says that those who commit fornication (Greek *porniah*, the root of our English word *pornography*) *"shall not inherit the kingdom of God (Galatians 5:19-21),"* then the future of any and all pornography users is the suffering of eternal damnation. And in Ephesians 5:6, again speaking of fornication (por-niah/pornography), he says, *"Let no man deceive you with vain words: for because of these things cometh the wrath of God upon the children of disobedience."* If you think you can indulge in pornography and still be a Christian, you are blindly hoping against the clear statements of Scripture. Disciples of Christ read their Bibles, not the dirty books of sodomites and lesbians. Every time you retreat into your world of lust, you shut the door in God's face. You are dangling your soul and the souls of your children over the fires of eternal damnation.

**Any prayers you pray for your children's safety are negated the moment you open the pages of a pornographic book or glare at an electronic image.**

I have not been as hard on you as God will be in the day of judgment. You have only one hope, and that is to repent toward God. I did not tell you to repent of your sin of pornography, because as an unregenerate man you will not find the power to forsake your first love. You must repent toward God. This you can do while still in the slavery of your sin. To repent toward God is to prefer God and his righteousness above everything else. It is to desire his holiness in your life—to hate the sin that binds you. Make no mistake. The man that repents toward God is a desperate man, a man that longs for the holiness God will bring into his life. The man that repents toward God will experience restless nights and skipped meals in his search for God. A man that repents toward God will find no pleasure or peace in anything until he can rest in God alone. It will not do for you to walk down an aisle and pray a sinner's prayer. It will not be sufficient for you to ask for prayer, or to confess your sins, or go to counseling. You must go directly to God through the Lord Jesus Christ with no hope and no confidence but the mercy and grace of God.

**I have not been as hard on you as God will be in the day of judgment.**

*It is a fearful thing to fall into the hands of the living God,* but it is a blessed thing to stay there until you are forgiven, and cleansed, and then empowered to walk in holiness. The dragon can be killed by Christ alone. Whom Christ makes free *shall be free indeed.* I have seen God save and deliver lesbians, sodomites, and porno freaks as easily as he saves children. Christ is sufficient.

I have done you a service by increasing your guilt, by bringing the law down on you like it will be in the day of judgment. Your conscience will not be satisfied by anything less than your exposure and punishment. The good news is that Jesus Christ took upon Himself the shame of your sin. God laid on Him your iniquity. God made Jesus to be sin in your place. He was treated as if He was the pornographer, the guilty sinner. He died the death you should die. Your sin has been paid for in the sufferings of Christ. If you repent toward God, God will forget your sin as if it had never happened. He will put away your sin and remember it no more. He will remove the guilt and free you from sin's power.

It will take years for the temptations to go away. The devils will return every day and night to offer you the opportunity to rehearse the sin you have laid down, but God will deliver you from yielding to the pull of temptation. The gospel of Jesus Christ is the *power of God unto salvation to every one that believeth. He is able to save to the uttermost those that come unto God by him.*

The next move is yours. Are you so far gone that before the week is out you will return to that dirty place, or will you repent toward God and see your perversion come to an end? I wrote this for one reason–to see some children saved when daddy repents toward God. It's your move. Your children, your wife, and your God are waiting.

This is an excerpt (updated) from the book *Holy Sex* by Michael Pearl first printed in 2004.

I didn't want to end on a negative note. This is a most delightful view of holy sex.

# HOLY SEX

## Erotic Pleasure Is Created in the Image of Worship

God patterned everything he created after his own nature, including all aspects of erotic pleasure and reproduction. For the Bible tells us that by observing creation, we can gain knowledge of the Creator (Romans 1). All that is material and finite was created in the image of his nonmaterial self. By attentive searching, we can discover the association of each thing God created with some aspect of his image.

Time, with its past, present, and future, was created in the image of his infinity. Matter was created to reflect the very existence of God. He created energy in the image of his power, vast space in the image of his boundlessness, motion in the image of his activity. The mind was created in the image of God's wisdom, the will in the image of his self-determination. The human body was created in the image of God's connection with physical creation. Music was created in the image of God's soul. Color was created in the image of his beauty. The senses of sight, touch, smell, taste, and hearing were created in the image of God's experience of himself. The gift of speech and writing was created in the image of the second person of the Godhead—the "Word." The human spirit was created in the image of God's Holy Spirit. Sex, where body, soul, and spirit merge into oneness, was created in the image of communion within the Godhead. Erotic pleasure was created in the image of worship. Copulation, conception, and birth were created in the image of God's creative powers.

Anyone who has experienced both the height of pure spiritual worship and pure erotic pleasure knows that one is the image and the other is the reality. Even if you have never dared consider it, now that it is brought to your attention, you must know that it is so.

The heights of worship transcend erotic pleasure in degree, but not kind. Pure worship occurs when one loses consciousness of self and focuses upon the person of God with wonder, humility, admiration, love, and devotion. The state of worship is the most intense period of concentration one can know. It is almost an out-of-body experience—certainly out of this world. It is the height of purity, wholeness, peace, joy, and love. It is a state of being from which one never wants to leave.

If you still haven't come to accept my stated conclusion, then tell me, what did God create that is in the image of worship, if not erotic pleasure? And what then does erotic pleasure reflect of God's nature? What does its very prominence on the pages of Scripture and in the physiology of the human race say about the Creator who designed it?

The Song of Solomon exalts erotic desire and fulfillment to a plane that has led most commentators to conclude that it must necessarily be an analogy of love between Christ and his church. Have they not seen the very reality the Holy Scriptures have so plainly stated? It must be that writers rush so quickly to the spiritual plane that they fail to draw their reader's attention to the plain sense of the text. If I appear bolder than others, nonetheless, I stand on historical ground in my interpretation of this song. If the many commentators are correct in viewing this as a picture of Christ and his church, then consider that it was God who chose and carefully crafted an erotic song to represent worship.

If the only worship you have experienced has been ritualistic and structured, or if the only sex you have experienced is selfish and dirty, you will not be able to understand the analogy of erotic pleasure to worship, which God so clearly "pictures" in his inspired word. If this is the case with you, don't be discouraged; there is a way of cleansing and recovery, which we will come to shortly.

## Objection That the Song Is Not Meant to Be a Discussion of Sex

If this was not meant to be a discussion of sexual pleasure, the author of the song should have flunked his writing class. Why seduce your audience with clear images of erotic pleasure if you want to lead their minds to something entirely different? If we should say, as do others, that this erotic description is meant to be an analogy of Christ and the church, we have not weakened the erotic content of this book; rather, we have elevated it to the dignity and holiness of that which it typifies. One chooses an analogy for two reasons: first, its similarity to the thing it is to depict, and second, its familiarity to the audience. The reader cannot draw the parallel unless he first thinks upon the typical. If you object to considering the sexual content of the Song of Solomon as important and practical for all married couples, you, of all people, need it most. Have you ever wondered why you don't smile as much as some of us do?

## The Association of Smell and Taste with the Sex Drive

It is clear from several passages that the author of this song speaks metaphorically of the bodies of the main actors as fruit, flowers, wine, aromatic herbs, spices, honeycomb, milk, and fountains of waters to be consumed. Their nostrils are filled with odors of each other, and everything pleasant they experience through their senses reminds them of the love they share.

He compares her **breasts to clusters** *of grapes,* and says the "**smell of thy nose** *[is]* **like apples; And the roof of thy mouth like the best wine**" *(Song of Solomon 7:7-9).*

She says of him, "**Thy lips, O my spouse, drop as the honeycomb: honey and milk are under thy tongue; and the smell of thy garments is like the smell of Lebanon**" *(Song of Solomon 4:11)*. Out of a desire to taste him deeply, she explores the inside of his mouth with her tongue, comparing the taste of his mouth to *honey* and *milk.*

In 4:11-5:1 he compares her to a garden of sweet fruit and spices, and she responds by calling upon the gentle cool breezes to blow upon her fruit until the **spices flow out**. He then is attracted to the flowing juices of her body and comes to drink and eat.

Science has established the organic link between pleasant odors and sexual drive. But before science ever came along, every young male could tell you that when he smelled gardenias or honeysuckle, he thought of some lovely female in his life or of the one in his dreams. Why do young men bring flowers and candy? Why do young ladies anoint themselves with sensual odors? Why do couples eat by candlelight with flowers in the center of the table? Because smell and taste are stimuli to the sexual drive.

The book of Proverbs gives an account of a woman attempting to seduce a man into a sexual encounter with these words: "**I have perfumed my bed with myrrh, aloes, and cinnamon. Come, let us take our fill of love until the morning: let us solace ourselves with loves**" (Proverbs 7:17-18).

Scientific studies have revealed that natural body odors are more seductive than the most expensive chemical perfumes. After that, domestic spices like cinnamon have proven to be highly stimulating. Take an apple pie to bed and . . . well . . . look out!

As strange as it seems, clinical studies have proven that artificial perfumes actually diminish the sex drive. The clinicians jokingly call commercial perfumes "pesticides." However, a man or woman can be conditioned to identify the odors of gaudy perfumes with erotic experiences, but it must be a learned response—a taste this author never acquired.

> **Here is the key. You must determine that, for the glory of God, you will be the kind of husband you should be even if it never changes your wife.**

If you want to cut through all the cultural conditioning and get back to natural responses, there is no odor so intoxicating as the pure, natural odor of your spouse, and no taste so sweet as the head-to-toe delicacy of your God-given mate. Many a lover has said to his or her mate, "You look so good, I could eat you," and then proceeded to do just that.

If you have a hang-up about sex, you didn't get it from the Holy Spirit; you got it from a world that has never learned to handle something so wonderful and powerful as pure, heavenly eroticism. When is the last time you, like the lady in our song, washed yourself, anointed your body or your bed with stimulating, natural odors, ate and drank something pleasant, dressed provocatively, adjusted the lights, undressed provocatively, and then "went to heaven?" God created Adam and Eve, said it was very good, brought the first naked woman to the first naked man, and commanded them to copulate. It is what he gave to the sons of men as their "**portion in this life**" *(Ecclesiastes 9:9)*. He created marriage " *. . .* **to be received with thanksgiving of them which believe and know the truth**" *(1 Timothy 4:3)*, "**And whatsoever ye do, do it heartily, as to the Lord, and not unto men**" *(Colossians 3:23)*.

## What is Natural Sex? What is Perverted?

I have been amazed on several occasions by individuals who ask me how a man could live with his wife and not lust after her. I am always shocked. I know how this twisted outlook comes about, but given my holy experience, it is always unbelievable to have someone reveal that he thinks marital sexual activity is evil. In our present society, perversion is more common than normalcy.

We will not list and discuss the many forms of perversion. This author, in spite of the fact that he has ministered on the streets and in prisons for 40 years, could not name ten percent of the possible perversions. We can come to our point more directly by discussing that which is natural. Romans 1:26-27 speaks of the **natural use of the woman**. The passage reveals that same-sex activity is **against nature**.

There are married couples who abstain from certain forms of perfectly lawful and natural foreplay for fear that it is unnatural, while there are unbelievers who justify all manner of aberrant perversions, professing that to them it is a natural desire. So how do we determine what is natural to the sexual relationship of a married couple?

God's book on sex doesn't take us very far into the bedroom of this couple. But several things are clear. She dressed and undressed to attract him. She put on natural odors that were seductive, prepared her bed with the same, put on jewelry to attract him, and prepared herself with deep erotic imaginations of him. They delighted in the nakedness of the other, as seen by their joyful description of the beauty of all parts of their bodies. They tasted each other as fruit, and drank of the other as wine and water. He lay all night upon her naked breasts. She admired his thighs, belly, and testicles. He admired her hips and bare belly, seeming to be attracted to her pubic hair. They came together with complete abandonment and joyful passion. It is totally natural for married lovers to taste each other from head to toe. There is something so pure and uncomplicated in their total absorption with each other.

Sexual expression that is good and natural will come to the innocent couple spontaneously. It doesn't need to be taught. Various forms of sexual foreplay and expression are rediscovered with each couple in the normal course of their growth and experimentation.

If your bedroom gets boring, try the trampoline at night, or a lonely hilltop on a windy autumn day. Camping trips can be a trip, and you simply must find a lonely place and skinny-dip together. The kitchen, the carport, the wood-shed or the barn, all are natural and good places. Some of your pleasures will be discussed and planned, and some will be spontaneous, catching both of you by surprise. Just be careful not to surprise the kids, the neighbors, other swimmers, or mountain trail hikers.

Love and commitment only produce what is natural. It is never violent, abusive, or degrading. If a man truly loves a woman, he will approach sex as a way to satisfy her, to elevate her person, to thrill and bless her. Good sex can be quiet and tender one time and rowdy and rambunctious another, but it always leaves one mellow and pure in spirit. It is as clear as spring water and as holy as a prayer meeting.

## Baggage

Problems arise when people come to marriage with baggage—hang-ups—or when they have their thinking twisted through exposure to Hollywood, pornography, or deviant behavior learned in the company of others already perverted.

There is a natural threshold of sexual expression that completely satisfies the deepest longings of the human body and soul. Though physical sex is a beautiful form of expression, true satisfaction is ultimately found in the spirit. This is true in every facet of human existence.

But the wicked will never find spiritual satisfaction. Therefore sex never satisfies them. They can satiate their hunger, but they can never rise to true satisfaction. Old forms of expression grow dull, and they must dare to experiment with new and forbidden things that have nothing to do with expressing love.

Here is where the devil has his field day. By coupling degrading or violent acts with the sexual passion, these offensive acts take on the excitement of sex, and in time seem to be a part of it. The more daring and deviant the acts, the greater the thrill. For those people, there comes a time when sex without all the alien trappings ceases to be sex. The powerful appetite for sex becomes the sanctuary and point of entry for all forms of alien behavior. It will be impossible to communicate this concept to a pervert, for his perversion has worked its way upstream until it has polluted the very fountains from which flow his human personality.

I know that many of my readers are waiting for me to list the forms of acceptable and unacceptable foreplay. By way of principle, I will say that any activity that does not spring from love and contribute to love is wrong. Love never involves coercion. It doesn't produce guilt.

It is possible for you to "feel" guilt that is inappropriate. A misinformed mind, caused by former associations, can come to view the holy as if it were profane. Removing that false guilt is one of the purposes of this study. Your exposure to the Word of God on this subject will automatically begin the process of freeing you from false guilt.

## Perversions

As to specifics: the rectum is for waste disposal and is never meant to be part of sexual expression. That is the reason God placed it out of sight, deep in the buttocks. No innocent young couple would ever "discover" the other's rectum or find satisfaction in their own being fondled or penetrated. The idea of rectal penetration came about because queers found it the closest thing to the female vagina. Rectal sex is sodomy, and it is sick. A wife should refuse to participate. A man whose interests lie in that direction should decide whether he wants to be a queer or a husband—one or the other. Men, don't use your wife contrary to nature—and, wives, don't be so used.

All forms of bondage, blood, beating, or inflicting pain are perversions that are learned, not natural desires. Such things are a simulation of rape and violence. Even in their mildest forms, these deviations are fantasies in violence and perversion, the practice or pretense of evil, preparation for crimes worthy of death. The person who desires such things is lost to true love. He will spend eternity in bondage, suffering the fires of Hell. A wife should refuse to participate.

It goes without saying that all sexual activity between same-sex partners is perversion, as is all sexual activity outside of marriage and all adultery and incest. The use of pornography is tantamount to indulging in adultery, fornication, homosexuality, bestiality, incest, child molestation, and every deviant thing it portrays. Pornography is anti-love and hijacks erotic pleasure, elevating it to a place of deity. It is the devil's substitute god, an act of dark worship. It ceases to be sex and becomes an extension of masturbation. One who uses it reminds me of a rabid dog eating himself. If you are participating in one of these perversions, you have divorced God and are courting Hell.

## So You Were Wounded When You Were Young

It is a common excuse; a wife says, "I don't like sex because I was wounded when I was young. I was abused as a child. I had several ugly experiences." In effect, she is saying, "I am hurt; I am not normal; don't expect me to love and be loved as God intended, for I am broken. Please excuse me from my duties and the opportunity to experience pleasure."

God anticipated your excuse, and so recorded the fact that the lady of this song came from a disadvantaged background, was raised by people who were angry with her, and made fun of her (1:6).

Others have accepted the forgiveness of God, thrown away their bitterness, and acted as God intended. You can, too. The path to healing is to know the truth and then act accordingly, regardless of how you feel. **"Commit thy works unto the LORD, and thy thoughts shall be established"** *(Proverbs 16:3).*

## Guilt

**"Every sin that a man doeth is without the body; but he that committeth fornication sinneth against his own body"** *(1 Corinthians 6:18).* This passage puts sexual sin in a category all by itself—sin against one's own body. It leaves a weight on the conscience like nothing else. This is not an abstract doctrine; it is universal experience. Guilt is one word that preachers and psychiatrists never need define for the public.

Experience has proven that no sin has the power to permanently stain the conscience as does sexual sin.

Many bank robbers fleeing the scene with a bag of money have been shocked when the bag suddenly exploded with red dye. All the money and the robber are indelibly stained. At that point the money is rendered unusable and the robber is marked for all to see. Likewise, when young people violate their consciences and steal a little sex, whether it is in the form of pornography, same-sex experimentation, voyeurism, or teenagers "making love," their consciences are permanently stained. Outside of God, the only way to make the stain go away is to gravitate into a world where everyone and everything is stained red. The citizens of such a society learn to be comfortable with the stain and eventually come to deny that red exists.

Though few people live in a world that is all red, most adults are marked with some stain. Many studies report that more than half of all married women who are capable of doing so do not come to a climax when they have sex. Counselors reveal that it is very common for married women carrying the baggage of guilt to find sex repugnant, that is, until they are lured into an extramarital affair, at which time they "feel" young again, and it is all so exciting as before. However, when the new wears off and the stain of guilt grows darker, the freeze once more creeps into their bed. Again sex seems dirty, and they are nauseated by it. They do not know the source of their sexual dysfunction. Some turn to pornography, some to alcohol or drugs, others to sex therapy, counseling, or further extramarital affairs. The stain spreads; the soul grows cold; and they take to watching soaps and listening to romantic songs that fantasize of true love.

It is very common for women to say that they become nauseated when they know their husband wants to "do it." Wives reveal how they wait until their husbands are asleep before going to bed, or they rush to bed before he does and pretend to be asleep—anything to avoid sexual activity. Others tell their counselors that they just lie there cooperating, but not participating, and try to think about something else.

This frigid state is most often a result of the guilt they unconsciously associate with sexual activity. In a similar way, when I see an orange and think about eating it, the muscles in my jaw involuntarily constrict. Likewise, when I see a dental chair, I can feel the vibrations in my head. The association of two things occurring at the same time conditions the person to view them as one and the same—an orange and constricting jaw muscles, dental chairs and vibrations, sex and shame.

When I was a child, I loved chocolate-covered cherries. Nothing in the world could compare. But on one occasion when I had spent the previous week in bed with the flu, someone gave this sick boy a whole box of chocolate-covered cherries. I had never eaten more than one or two cherries at a time. This was an indulgence of preposterous proportions. I ate half the box before I began to throw up the soured, acidy syrup. To this day when I see a chocolate-covered cherry, I am nauseated. I will eat one if you make me, but it is not pleasant. I like cherries, and I like chocolate, but I am conditioned now to sincerely feel that chocolate-covered cherries are "sinful." Just one experience is all it took. I know that I have an unreasonable phobia. I am now an old man, and it makes me sick to write about it. For all these years I have been controlled by that one negative conditioning experience.

In a similar manner—though on a different level—a person can be induced to associate sex with guilt and sin. It happens like this: A young girl knows she should not engage in sex before marriage, but she is overcome with passion; so she sneaks around like a thief and violates her conscience. Later, she feels guilty and tells herself that she will not be a "bad girl" again. But in time, passion overrides the conscience, and she once again succumbs to the temptation.

Two things are happening at the same time: She is feeling guilty, and she is having sex. Sex and guilt become synonymous in her subconscious mind. But while "love" is young, the passion is still stronger than the guilt. Yet there comes a time, after she is married and the passions of sex have been satisfied, that guilt will come to the surface and be stronger than the passion. The guilt and shame will shut down her sexual responses, and she will view her husband's advances as I view chocolate-covered cherries—something to be regurgitated. The more often guilt and shame smother her sexual responses, the stronger grows the shame and her inability to respond to his advances. She will grow into a confirmed state of frigidity.

Now you know the rest of the story. You weren't born broken. You broke yourself.

Most men respond to guilt differently. Rather than freezing up and withdrawing, they become demanding and aggressive. They seek more sex more often, and it takes on the form of dominance and exploitation, rather than sharing and loving. They cease to care for the ladies, but continue to use them as a "necessary evil." In extreme cases, guilty men take out their feelings of self-condemnation by punishing the objects of their lust. That is how the "F" word came to be used as an aggressive, threatening curse. The man who uses it, uses women and views sex as an act of dominance and violence.

The world of sexual exploitation and guilt is a dark pit where the sex drive no longer resembles the marvelous vehicle of passion God created. It is a vortex spiraling downward into the fires of lust and hell. For many, there is no return. The lower you descend, the less likely you will ever believe there is any other way. The Garden of Eden gives place to the whorehouse of horrors. Paradise turns to pain. What God wondrously created the devil commandeers, and the end does not resemble the beginning.

But God is not ready to surrender his blessed gift of marital love to the manipulations of Satan. He is ready to forgive and restore. His redemption can accomplish that which no psychiatrist or sex counselor ever dared dream.

## Overcoming Guilt Associations

The two examples of conditioning that I gave (the orange and the chocolate-covered cherries) are minor compared to guilt conditioning. As we discussed, when two things that are not necessarily related happen at the same time, the soul can be conditioned to accept a permanent association. But the guilt that haunts a person in respect to past, sinful, sexual acts is more than mere conditioning, for there is a direct relationship between sinful acts and ongoing guilt. In fact, the guilt is appropriate—even necessary to our happiness.

Knowing that guilt prevents us from functioning normally, you will wonder how I can say that it is beneficial. Think about it. If you did not suffer guilt, you would go on in your sin, unaware that it was leading you in a destructive direction. Guilt is the pain of the soul, the warning that you are endangering your person. In most cases, guilt speaks the truth. Without guilt, we would live like animals, follow our passions, and ignore our brains; but our moral natures will not allow us to live without the voice of conscience.

Guilt doesn't just go away with the years. The soul is not equipped, as is the body, to heal itself from sin. Only God can heal the soul from sin. Even after you have put sin behind you, painful guilt clings to your soul, crying for forgiveness. You cannot forgive yourself. You must go to your Maker whom you have offended. It is his world you live in. It was with one of his creatures that you violated the laws of your nature. It is his air that you breathe, and he holds the keys to eternity. There is a heaven, and there is a hell. Guilt remains to warn you that The Judge of all the earth has not forgotten. Heaven holds your records in anticipation of the day when you will be forced to appear before the judgment and give account of every deed you have ever done. Guilt warns the indifferent soul that "He has not forgotten." Go to your Creator and Savior while there is still time. Receive the forgiveness he so freely offers. Only he can remove your guilt and restore your soul. Then you can enjoy all things, including sex, as God intended.

God didn't make us to feel guilt as a form of punishment. The purpose of guilt is to drive us back to himself. When guilt says, "You are unworthy; you deserve to be punished," it speaks the truth.

## Goodbye, Guilt

But the good news is that God sent his own son, Jesus, into the world to take the place of guilty sinners. Jesus never sinned. He felt no guilt. His conscience was clear before God. Since Adam, there has never been another man like Jesus who did all things pleasing to God. In every way, at all times, without exception, he pleased the Father, whereas we have displeased him.

Yet Jesus did not come just to give us an example. He came to be our substitute—to take the place of us sinners and bear the punishment for all our sin. At the end of his righteous life, he voluntarily died, as if he were the sinner. He took your sin upon himself and died in your place— in the place of all sinners. Forgiveness does not come through the church or through its leaders. Only God can forgive, and he is ready to forgive all who will believe and receive his forgiveness.

**"If we confess our sins, he is faithful and just to forgive us our sins, and to cleanse us from all unrighteousness"** *(1 John 1:9)*.

His forgiveness for you is not measured by your forgiveness of yourself. He forgives even when your conscience is condemning you. It is only after you believe that he has forgiven you that you will be free from guilt. In a short time, as you walk in fellowship with Jesus, the pain and memory of your past sins will fade and you will see a slow change occurring.

Just as quickly as the conscience will condemn immoral behavior, it will approve righteous behavior. You have now read many verses that express God's attitude toward sex. This one summarizes it very well: **"Marriage is honourable in all, and the <u>bed undefiled</u>: but whoremongers and adulterers God will judge"** *(Hebrews 13:4).*

## Practical Advice

You may say, "But it has been many years since I sinned. I confessed it to God, and I know that he forgave me, but I developed this permanent hang-up. How can I make my subconscious mind accept what my conscious mind knows?" I told you of my experience with chocolate-covered cherries. I now know that the candy did not make me sick, and that if I ate it today it would not harm me, but I am conditioned to associate chocolate-covered cherries with regurgitation. If I felt that it was needful for me to overcome my mental block, I would not sit around waiting for my twisted thinking to go away. I would force myself to eat the threatening food until I reprogrammed my mind with pleasant experiences. If I were to eat the candy a few times and enjoy it, the new experiences would become the standard. As it is, every time I refuse chocolate-covered cherries, I confirm the old thought patterns and perpetuate the misconception.

God removes the guilt, something you cannot do. <u>But you must take the steps to reprogram your responses.</u> If you are a woman, you may need to overcome your coldness toward sex. If you are a man, you may need to overcome your lack of sensitivity. Both can be overcome by approaching lovemaking in a pure and holy way. It will take time, but you can reprogram your human responses through several good experiences. And it will be more than worth the effort!

The key is to not wait for some inner signal that everything is all right. Determine to act in a manner that will bless your spouse. Act in a loving way. <u>Do what you ought to do because it is good for the other person.</u> Love is in the doing, not the feelings. <u>If you "do" love, in time you will "feel" love.</u> If you surrender your body to your mate for your mate's pleasure, you will come to enjoy it yourself.

## Romance and Spiritualism

On several occasions when women have explained their coldness toward sex by saying that they want their husbands to be sensitive and spiritual, my wife has responded, "What do you want him to do, sing hallelujah while you are doing it?" The first time I heard her answer a woman that way, I said, "Sometimes I feel like singing hallelujah, but I don't want to disturb the kids."

Women are different from men in that regard. They need romance and emotional bonding. When a husband seeks to be close sexually, but not emotionally and spiritually, a woman will feel that their intimacy is not anything above animal instinct. And, unfortunately, that is often the case. Not that there is anything wrong with the animal drive, but we are created to be more than a body of drives. We are also living souls, created in God's image, and that part of us must find expression as well.

I would counsel the man to meet his wife's needs. Learn to care in more ways than just the physical. Value the soul of your wife, and give her the romance she needs. The doing of it will fulfill a need in you as well.

And I would counsel the wife to recognize that her husband may never be different. Some men are so insensitive that the only affection they ever show is through physical sex. That being the case, if a wife should be resistant to her husband by holding out until he meets her spiritual or social needs, there will never be any resolution. If she were to accept his shortcoming and respond sexually, there is a better chance that through sex he will come to love her in a deeper way. If not, then the woman will still benefit by enjoying sex herself. Why deprive yourself just to prove a point that may never be appreciated?

## Drink Abundantly

When Deb and I first got married, we had occasional fights. She was trying to change me, and I was trying to change her. One day she was complaining to an older woman about my stubbornness. The older woman suggested that Deb just "hold out" on me. "That will bring him around," the woman said. When Deb told me how she responded to the woman, it became my all-time favorite quote. Upon hearing the woman's suggestion, Deb looked shocked and, after a moment of contemplation, said, "But that would hurt me as much as it would him!" I love it! I love her.

We don't fight any more. As the old song says, "It's lovin' in the morning, lovin' in the evening, and lovin' when the sun goes down."

When I called Deb into my office to read the above paragraph, she laughed and said, "Ha! The men will know better. It is "wishin' in the morning, wishin' in the evening, and MAYBE when the sun goes down." I told her, "I meant before we turned fifty. So . . . maybe we skip a day now and then."

On several occasions when I have heard women say "All men think about is sex," I have assured them that this was not the case at all. Sex is not the only thing men think about. Afterward they think about sleeping, and when they wake up, they think about eating. If you can't laugh and enjoy erotic pleasure, you are tied in one knot too many.

You are human and you are flesh—as God intended. If you have not been enjoying the gift God gave to you—your spouse—it is high time you did; it is not too late. I remind you of the exhortation Solomon gave his readers in 5:1, "**O friends; drink, yea, drink abundantly.**" And by now, you know he was not talking about water.

## Multifaceted Being

Sex is the most powerful and wonderful blessing God gave to man. For that reason the mechanics of it can be made to stand alone. It can be wrenched from its intended context and used independently until it becomes the user. Like a hungry bear released from its cage, it can turn and consume you. It can take the place of the Creator who gave it. If allowed to run wild and follow its own course, it can take the place of the personality itself. Like all things God made, it is meant to be managed, harnessed, directed, and disciplined.

We humans are created to be multifaceted beings, a delicate balance of many attributes, especially of the flesh and the spirit. The human personality is inadequate to reach its potential alone. It is because our original ancestor disobeyed God, and separated both himself and all his posterity from fellowship with God, that appetites originally meant to exist in balance now dominate the human race.

Because of the strength of appetite, even the most tranquil and philosophical soul is unable to maintain the balance of his nature. History is a chronicle of that failure. Philosophy and religion are testimony to the confusion and uncertainty of the most noble among us. War, rape, sexual perversions, and divorce are proof that there is a disconnect somewhere. Until the connection is made back to God through Jesus Christ, the greatest blessing will continue to be the greatest curse—producing more heartache and destruction to the human race than all other appetites combined.

Fading remnants of glory remain in all humans. Most people are content to be made captive by their appetites, gaining what enjoyment they can along the way. But the righteous—those who have been born again into the family and fellowship of God, those who walk in subjection to the Holy Spirit and bring their bodies under his discipline—are able to live in the glory others only dream about. As we serve God, our appetites serve us instead of driving us, and both body and soul, now in harmony, experience the fullness of all earthly pleasures—including the erotic. Man was created to be holy in all things. Thank God for holy sex!

## The Summit

If our lives were music, sex would be the crescendo. The musical piece has many gentle and soothing moments, but it builds to a dynamic climax when every instrument joins together to celebrate the entire evening. Applause follows, and the musicians are left drained, but satisfied. Likewise, foreplay and copulation are the satisfactory conclusions to the experiences of two people living daily in harmony. Without the song, the crescendo would mean little, for it would be out of context.

Or, to say it another way, just like the last few steps that bring a mountain climber to the summit, erotic love is best when it is the pinnacle of an extended experience of love. Sex may seem to be the destination, but it is made rich by the trip. It is just the final ascent of intimate love that has been shared during the climb. Without the climb, reaching the summit would be just another road-side stop. In other words, sex is not the whole; it is the ultimate satisfactory conclusion to a great climb, the summit of oneness, when a couple merges into the highest communion known to mortals.

To say it in everyday language, copulation is not the whole party; it is just the fireworks. Fireworks alone may come to be obnoxious, intrusive, and spiritually unsatisfying. The bang is best when it is the celebration of something in the spirit.

I am not trying to make a distinction between foreplay and copulation, unless by foreplay we are referring to every moment between summits and we are including the spirit and soul in the foreplay.

Nor am I suggesting that sex between married couples is wrong unless it is done in a certain spiritual context. The animal passion of sex is to be received with thanksgiving, but we are more than animals; and if we would be all that our Creator intended, there are other areas of our being that must be satisfied. Sex is obviously an act of the body to the gratifying of the flesh. But it is best when it is also an act of the soul and spirit. The merging of bodies satisfies our God-given "itch," but the merging of souls satisfies our God-given spirits.

When love is more than sex, sex is more than you could ever imagine. A man should first love his wife in the same way that he loves his mother, his children, and his dearest friends. There is nothing erotic in that kind of love, but it is deep, unselfish, and pure. You take your infant daughter into your arms, and you inhale her odor; you taste her skin with a light kiss; you hold her tightly, promising to always protect her and be there in time of need. You love till it hurts. You would give your life for that child. Her soul is precious to you.

Men, if you first love the soul of your wife, your love for her body will be well received. Before she feels any sexual passion, your wife will melt under your caring stare. She will long for your massaging touch, and she will willingly yield her body to be tasted and fondled. After having loved someone to distraction—till it hurts—desiring to merge into oneness and stay there forever, the most unimaginable pleasure occurs, and the two rise to the summit to become one.

God made provision for the couple to go beyond the vail, into the holy, intimate place, where none but the two of them can ever go. They return to Eden and perhaps visit a "bit of heaven," and when it is over, their ache for love has been transformed into the purest satisfaction. The two of them are content that they have expressed their love to the fullest. They have become one flesh. God has joined them together. The physical and the spiritual met together and found equilibrium. The two of them can then go out and whip the world together. They are a team. They are one. Forever.

I will be personal for a moment. When I was young and my wife was fresh with the pink, moist passion of youth, the animal ran strong. I loved her, but not as I do today when we are in our golden years. When we were in our twenties, I never considered that erotic pleasure might be anything more than a fun necessity. I knew nothing of the richness that was growing in our spirits. I had no idea that love could ever be anything more than dynamite and lightning. But after more than forty years, my marriage has caught up with my spirituality. I now have a marriage that is proof of the existence of God. I am never so human as in marriage and yet never more close to the divine.

As we age, our passions fade, but our spirits soar. I envision a time—if we live to be old—when the tired animal lies quietly by the hearth while our spirits climb the last few paces to the summit. We may look back and laugh at the vigor we once knew, of passionate fires long since burnt out, but we will not look back in regret, and there will be no sense of loss, for even now the wonderful, glorious flesh has been exceeded by a merging of spirits until the unseen is far more tangible than the seen. As our bodies sag and creak, as the flesh breaks down and leans over to face the cold ground, there has been a life kindled that burns more in the spirit world than in the bedroom. If my wife faded away until nothing was left but her spirit, I would put that dear spirit in a bottle and inhale it until my last breath. Praise God for his wonderful works to children of men.

By the way, I am not that old yet. I feel the fuse burning even now. Lightning will strike before the day is ended.

———————————————

Finally, I will say it one more time. Do you want a better marriage? Fine, so does your spouse. Now go practice Christian love. Give your partner a better marriage and forget about yourself. That is the essence of love— any kind of love.

**Philippians 2:3-8**

3 Let nothing be done through strife or vainglory; but in lowliness of mind let **each esteem other better than themselves.**

4 Look **not every man on his own things,** but every man also on the things of others.

5 Let this mind be in you, which was also in Christ Jesus:

6 Who, being in the form of God, thought it not robbery to be equal with God:

7 **But made himself of no reputation, and took upon him the form of a servant,** and was made in the likeness of men:

8 And being found in fashion as a man, **he humbled himself, and became obedient** unto death, even the death of the cross.

There is no life so rich, no pleasure so thorough, as that of a holy Christian. Humanity reaches its highest expression when in fellowship with Jesus Christ. You know the way. Now go thou and do likewise.

## Created To NEED A Help Meet

Mike's new book can help men understand how to be the husband that God created them to be. Man up!!! *Book.*

- Available in: single volumes and cases of 24 (40% discount)

- Available in audio *1 MP3.*

## Pornography: Road to Hell

Michael addresses the deadly scourge of pornography head-on. He shows how repentance toward God and the power of the gospel of Jesus Christ can break the bondage of this wicked perversion. *12 page booklet.*

## Holy Sex

Michael Pearl takes his readers through a refreshing journey of Biblical texts, centered in the Song of Solomon. This sanctifying look at the most powerful passion God ever created will free the reader from false guilt and inhibition. Michael Pearl says, "It is time for Christian couples to take back this sacred ground and enjoy the holy gift of sexual pleasure." *82 page book.*

## Only Men

Michael Pearl speaks directly and frankly to men about their responsibilities as husbands. Wives should not listen to this message. We don't want you taking advantage of your man. *1 CD.*

## Good and Evil

Award winning graphic novel, 330 pages of dazzling full color art work telling the Bible story chronologically from Genesis to Revelation. Written by Michael Pearl and drawn by Danny Bulanadi, a retired Marvel Comic Book artist. Now in over 30 languages, popular with missionaries and youth workers, this book has tremendous appeal to all ages and cultures–great as Sunday School curriculum. *330 page book.*

## Knife & Tomahawk Throwing For Fun

Michael Pearl demonstrates and teaches knife and tomahawk throwing. *1 DVD.*

## Balanced Patriarch

When do children cease to be under parental authority? *1 DVD.*

## Becoming a Man

This message is for parents concerned about raising their boys up to be men, and it is for fathers who never learned to be real men. *1 CD.*

## Becoming Tempered Steel

Joshua Steele talks to young men about being a man and a minister of the Gospel. Highly recommended by Michael Pearl. *1 DVD.*

## To Train Up a Child

Over 670,000 copies sold in English, translated into many languages. From successful parents, learn how to train your children before the need to discipline arises. *112 page book.*

## Training Children to Be Strong in Spirit

This is not a time for weak spirits. Some call it intestinal fortitude. I call it guts—spiritual guts. The timid and afraid will fall victim to their appetites and not have the moral earnestness to be men and women of character. The greatest gift you can give your children is to train them to be strong in spirit, courageous, unbending in the face of adversity and temptation. *200 page book.*

## Teaching Responsibility

In this seminar, Michael Pearl uses humorous stories and practical examples to illustrate the simple process of training your children to work without complaint. *2 DVD set.*

## Jumping Ship

Learn how to keep your children from jumping ship too early. *106 page book.*

## Alabama Seminar

Two hours of Michael Pearl speaking on child training. These are geared toward the father's role in the family. Tales of Mike and his sons' wild adventures. Boys love it! **1 MP3.**